ROY ACUFF

ROY ACUFF
The Smoky Mountain Boy

by
ELIZABETH SCHLAPPI

cop. a

PELICAN PUBLISHING COMPANY GRETNA 1978

Library of Congress Cataloging in Publication Data

Schlappi, Elizabeth.
   Roy Acuff, the Smoky Mountain Boy.

   Bibliography: p. 266
   Discography: p. 251
   Includes index.
   1. Acuff, Roy. 2. Country musicians—United States—
Biography. I. Title.
ML410.A168S3   784'.092'4 [B]   77-11649
ISBN 0-88289-144-8

Manufactured in the United States of America
Published by Pelican Publishing Company, Inc.
630 Burmaster Street, Gretna, Louisiana 70053
Designed by Oscar Richard

To My Father
John Carl Schlappi, M.D.

Acknowledgments

Initially I did not consider myself a biographer, merely a collector of Acuff memorabilia. My ambition at first was to acquire a complete collection of Acuff recordings. I therefore compiled an Acuff discography (see Appendix B). When Roy was presented with this list of his recordings, he was so impressed that he said, "If you ever come to Nashville, I'll show you a good time." I have taken Roy up on his offer four times—in 1964, 1967, 1970, and 1973—and he and Mildred have made good on the promise. Only after the first two of these trips, during which I gathered a tremendous amount of biographical information, did I gradually begin to consider myself an Acuff biographer. The drafts of this biography have been checked and rechecked by the Acuffs and a great many people in Nashville.

Through the years Roy Acuff has been the subject of many magazine and newspaper articles. Recently his life has been discussed in some books. Album jackets also provide Acuffish information. During my 20 years of collecting Acuff memorabilia, I have corresponded with well over 1,000 people. Many of these letters have yielded biographical data. Naturally I am grateful for all these sources (see Bibliography).

However, the heart of this biography is the information gained during my trips to Tennessee, and I am particularly in debt to the following people:

Mr. and Mrs. Roy Acuff: These two delightful people have provided some of the information directly and have introduced me, sometimes directly and sometimes indirectly, to all of the people listed below.

The Acuff Family: Mr. Roy Neill Acuff
       Mrs. Hartsell D. Phillips (Juanita Acuff)
       Mrs. Robert L. Allen, Jr. (Sue Acuff)
       Mr. Briscoe Acuff
       Mr. Claude Acuff

The Smoky Mountain Boys: All of the boys have been most gracious. The following are the ones I have pestered to the greatest extent:
       Mr. Jimmie Riddle and his wife, Susie
       Mr. Pete Kirby
       Mr. Howdy Forrester

Others: Mr. and Mrs. Powell Stamper
   Mr. Wesley Rose
   Mr. Grant Turner
   Mr. "D" Kilpatrick

Thanks to these people and to all the other fine Tennesseeans who have been considerate to me.

Writing a manuscript is not enough. The next step is publication, and some very wonderful people insured that this was not an insurmountable step. David Butler and Bill Malone of the academic world provided assistance. Richard Wentworth and Judy McCulloh of the University of Illinois Press gave invaluable aid. Mr. Wentworth suggested the manuscript to Pelican. Judy sent reams of information that a neophyte author should have. In San Diego, two experts on books and publishing were generous with their advice: Joe Herweg, a long-time friend, and Ralph De Sola. And, of course, gratitude is due Pelican Publishing Company, especially to editor Herb Luthin, who molded the manuscript into publishable shape, and to Dr. Milburn Calhoun and his brother, James, for having the faith to publish such a comprehensive Roy Acuff biography.

And, finally, I want to thank my mother, who put up with me when I shut myself in my room during four summers for weeks at a time while engrossed in deep concentration and only emerged to obtain her help with some phrasing and a great deal of spelling.

Elizabeth Roe Schlappi

Contents

I. THE EARLY YEARS

3   Consider the Source
4   Maynardville
10   "Rabbit"
13   Goofing Off
17   "Roy, You're Not Gonna Play Baseball"
20   Mocoton Tonic is the Best Medicine
22   An Extra Fifty Cents
25   To the Recording Studio on the Wings of That Great
        Speckled Bird
30   She Didn't Get a Stick Horse After All
32   The Long Road to Nashville
36   Opry Regulars But Still "Fiddling and Starving"
39   A Little Success—But Resignation
40   Roy Acuff and *His* Smoky Mountain Boys

II. THE BIG TIME

44   Coast to Coast
46   "At the Grand Ole Opry Tonight"
50   No Man Is an Island
54   Some Partnerships

III. THE SMOKY MOUNTAIN GANG

71   Great Big Bashful Brother Oswald and His Sister Rachel
82   Jess, Lonnie, Joe, and Curly

85   Boogie-Woogie Man—Jimmie Riddle
91   Fiddlers Charm Creation
96   Smoky Mountain Girls
98   A Few More Smoky Mountain Boys
100   Ode on a Classsical Jug
102   "Roy's Boys" and Roy

        IV. THE ACUFF SOUND

106   What Comes Naturally
114   A Recording Session
119   The Precious Jeweled Cannonball Has Never Wrecked

        V. HIGHWAYS AND BYWAYS

126   On the Road
141   He Did Hear Somebody Pray

        VI. ACUFF-ROSE AND MORE FUN

149   Two Blind Pigs Searching for an Acorn
164   Fun Instead of Profit

        VII. OFF TO HOLLYWOOD

173   "In the Movies There's Nothing to Hold You Up"

        VIII. POLITICKING

182   To Run or Not to Run
188   "I Hope Gordon Browning Will Be the Next Governor of
            Tennessee"
205   He's a Southern Yankee Doodle Boy

        IX. COUNTRY MUSIC KINGDOM

215   King of the Hillbillies
218   Acuff the Man
224   "She's Done a Lot More for Me Than I Can Ever Do
            for Her"
230   He Is Following His Own Drum
235   Sincerity, Showmanship, Success

        APPENDIX A

239   Roy's Overseas Tours

        APPENDIX B

251   Discography

266 BIBLIOGRAPHY

278 INDEX

ROY ACUFF

I

The Early Years

Consider the Source

If one were to ask Roy Acuff to speak of the things of which he is most proud, the subject topping the list would be his ancestry.

In 1066 when William the Conqueror of Normandy invaded England, some of his companions in arms were French soldiers named D'Acre, or Aculf. Theobald Aculf was granted lands from Henry I between 1100 and 1135, and during the 1100s and 1200s Aculf men went on the Crusades to rescue the Biblical lands from the Turks. In so doing they earned the three silver scallop shells that prominently occupy the red shield on the Acuff family coat of arms, which is described in this way:

Acuff—Fitz-Acuff, D'Acre
      Arms: Gules (red), three escallops (scallop shells—badge of pilgrims to the Holy Land), argent (silver)
    Acuff, Dacre of Fitz-Aculf, named from Dacre, Cumberland, descended from Aculf, a companion in arms to the Conqueror, Theobald de Dacre or Aculf granted lands, from Henry I to Carlisle Abbey (Mon: 74). Gilber Aculf, his son made further grant. Adam Aculf was the grand father of William de D'acre with whom Peerage acct comences.

After several hundred years of living in England the Acuffs emigrated to the New World and settled in the mountains of Virginia and the Carolinas. Later they moved to East Tennessee.

Roy Acuff's paternal grandfather, Corum Acuff, who lived and died in Maynardville, was a Union soldier during the Civil War, and also was an attorney and served as a Republican legislator in the Tennessee General Assembly. One of his strongest political credos was that government should be absolutely honest. This belief influenced his children and was to emerge in his grandson's gubernatorial campaign many years later.

A. W. Carr, Roy's maternal grandfather, was a general practitioner of medicine and rode horseback or drove his horse and buggy throughout his native Union County on countless errands of mercy. His practice was first based in Luttrell; then, by the turn of the century, he moved to Maynardville.

Unlike many names, such as Jones or Smith, Acuffs the world over seem to be fairly closely related and whenever one meets another Acuff they usually try to figure out their family tree connections and frequently succeed.

Others usually pronounce the name A-*cuff*, but the Acuffs themselves pronounce it *A*-kf. The Acuff clan of East Tennessee is proud of its heritage and has had many reunions in Knoxville's Fountain City Park. These gatherings, held more or less regularly since the 1930s, draw as many as 500 Acuffs. One is frequently Roy Acuff, to whom probably over half the crowd could be traced as cousins. Sometimes Roy brings his band, on other occasions he comes alone. Once he borrowed a fiddle and then sang a capella. At one reunion Judd Acuff, a Knoxville attorney, read the family history he had compiled.

Other prominent Acuffs include Timothy Acuff, a Methodist minister who, during the last century, established a church that is still standing in East Tennessee; Dr. Herbert Acuff, a widely known surgeon who ran a Knoxville clinic; and Arthur Acuff, a Maynardville banker.

Maynardville

Neill Acuff, son of Corum Acuff, was born in Maynardville on April 16, 1877. As a young man he took a general course at Carson-Newman College back in the days when it was known as Mossy Creek. Around 1898 he married a Maynardville native, Ida Florence Carr, born October 21, 1879, daughter of Dr. A. W. Carr. For the next 21 years the young couple lived in many homes in and around Maynardville. On several occasions they moved as far away as Knoxville. One of their favorite jokes was that after 20 years of marriage, they had moved 20 times.

Ida Carr bore five children, all delivered by their Grandfather Carr. The oldest was Briscoe. Next was Juanita. The family then moved into what was later to be described in one of Roy's songs as "An Old Three Room Shack." Here, on September 15, 1903, was born Roy Claxton Acuff. (Dr. P. P. Claxton was an educator whose efforts for country schools greatly impressed Neill Acuff, and it just so happened that he had given a speech in Maynardville earlier in 1903.) A home or two later saw the addition of Sue, and finally Claude, nicknamed Spot because of his freckles.

Times were hard in Union County and even though Neill Acuff was well educated for a country man, he had a tough time scratching a living for his growing family. As was the custom at that time, he informally read law books, which qualified him to practice law. He was the postmaster for a while, scoring 99.5 percent on the civil service test, and even did a little insurance work. For a year the family tried farming, using the nearby farm of Neill's brother, Frank. Roy was too young to help with the plowing. When Roy was ten or twelve, Neill Acuff decided to become a minister. In due time, he became ordained as a Missionary Baptist minister and preached the fundamentalist faith as pastor of the Maynardville Baptist Church.

Of course, even prior to this time, the family had attended church regularly, partly out of religious fervor and partly, as Briscoe later said, "Out of self-defense. We were desperate for something to do." Spot remembered being dragged along barefooted and crying because he couldn't walk as fast as the others and frequently stubbed his toes. Roy attended church and Sunday school regularly during his young life until his music career forced him to work Sundays.

The children were taught the love of God and to believe fervently in the Ten Commandments and especially in the golden rule. Papa was kind, but a strict disciplinarian and never let the children forget the difference between right and wrong. When father was away, mama was more than capable of administering justice to any of the five who forgot these lessons.

The children occasionally would escape from parental control to roam the countryside and indulge in the usual escapades of youthful rural life. The youngest three were the most active and Roy was the most mischievous of all. Not a day passed but what he didn't get at least two whoppins. The razor strop wasn't so bad, but when papa cut branches off of an old pear tree, blood was drawn. Mama would whop, too, when she could catch Roy.

Roy didn't want to work—it gave him a headache. He wanted to play. He hated to hoe corn; might possibly have liked to plow, but was too small. Papa and Briscoe did that. He would usually play with the older boys, such as Vaughn Moore, and could run and jump as well as any. Just before leaving Maynardville, Roy got a job in a rock quarry where John Huddleston was superintendent. They crushed rock for roads.

One of Roy's escapades involved an elderly neighbor lady's lone goose. There was always a group of politicians hanging around the courthouse, drinking moonshine. One day Roy and Earl "Bill Dirty" Beeler picked up some of this whisky and while "Bill Dirty" held the goose, Roy poured the moonshine down its throat. The goose began to squawk, then pitched back and forth. Finally the drunken creature plunged into a nearby branch flapping its wings wildly—and drowned. The old lady threw a fit and the two boys had to pay the cost.

Most of his other activities were less harmful to property. Roy found that he could balance almost anything on his chin or nose. He would go out into the fields and pick up an item as heavy as a 45-pound plowshare and, using a folded hankerchief for cushioning, walk around with it balanced on his chin. At the other extreme he learned to bounce light objects, such as broom straws, up and down on his nose.

In the summer the kids liked to pitch horseshoes on the courthouse lawn, and sometimes a group of boys would gather rocks, sticks, and dogs and go rabbit hunting. There were no organized sports teams and very little equipment. Town entertainment included the annual Fourth of July celebration on the courthouse lawn, and the square dances on Saturday nights. And there was the County Court Day, which occurred every three months when the Union County magistrates assembled in Maynardville, the county seat. Spot remembered that once Roy and a friend put on a skit, a dialogue between two people. This was probably the first time that Roy Acuff was on stage.

In the winter the children played rook, and enjoyed drinking a hot beverage known as ginger stew. There were no phones or movies. Roy was about 16 before he saw his first movie.

Roy frequently did the family marketing. Mama would send him to the store, sometimes with money and sometimes with trade goods, like chickens or eggs. If what he had was worth more than the items on the shopping list, the storekeeper would give him a "due bill," with the difference written on it.

The family with whom the Acuffs were the most friendly in Maynardville was the Huddlestons. Even today Roy still calls Lilly Huddleston his second mother. John Huddleston was a postman serving with Postmaster Neill Acuff.

The winters get mighty cold in the foothills of the Great Smoky Mountains and one very bad winter the Moores, Ousleys, and Huddlestons helped the Acuffs take wood with a mule down to their home. The snow was up to the mule's stomach. It was so cold that without help the Acuff family might have frozen. Neighbors and family had great importance in Maynardville.

Since other Acuffs, including both Grandfather Carr's and Grandfather Acuff's families, also lived in Maynardville, there were many family gatherings. The rule at home was to always clean your plate before the next course was served. So Grandfather Acuff never failed to serve Roy his dessert first, usually a cobbler or a custard, to make sure Roy would get to eat it.

At Christmas time each of the five children received a stocking containing what to them were rare tropical fruits—a banana and an orange, a nigger toe (Brazil nut), and some smaller nuts. Also, papa somehow managed to scrape together enough money to buy each child a toy. One Christmas Roy received a little wooden monkey that ran up a string, but the toy broke after a few days. Strangely enough, Christmas, not the Fourth of July, was the one time of year when the children were allowed to have fireworks. Once Roy hestitated to throw a five-incher and his hand became burned and very swollen.

Roy had to go to school, but it was the bane of his existence and he hated it. The schoolhouse had two rooms, the Little Room, for grades one through four, and the Big Room, for grades five through eight. Roy definitely graduated from the Little Room, and at least partially completed the Big Room before leaving Maynardville. Two of the many teachers were Professor Patrick and Professor Keller. On Friday of each week students had spelling bees, and debates were held once a month. Roy learned to recite the Presidents in order and could rattle them off years later. He also was especially impressed with the little poetry verses in his speller. His favorite was "Sixty golden minutes, each with sixty golden seconds," and as he commented years later, he thought about how time can never be recaptured once it has passed.

However, as impressed as he was with this verse, Roy spent most of his time in school being, in his own words, "a terror." But he hastened to add "I wasn't really bad, just mischievous." He did much of this mischief behind his huge geography book, which he held upright on his desk. From this concealment he could make faces at the other children, balance pencils on his chin, or throw spitwads at the teacher. Sometimes the teacher would draw a circle on the blackboard and he would have to stand with his nose inside the circle. This punishment was mild compared with the switch—when the business end of it wore out, the teacher used the handle. Perhaps what the young boy considered the most severe punishment of all was when he was ordered to sit next to a girl.

During grammar school Roy received many beatings by the teacher. The most severe of these occurred when he was in the seventh or eighth grade—for stomping the other children's marbles into the playground. His shirt was torn and his back was bloody.

A more pleasant part of Roy Acuff's childhood was the music around him. When he was a very small child, he began playing the Jew's harp, and early in the mornings he would crawl under the kitchen table and entertain mama as she was preparing breakfast. Years later, Roy recalled that he really became so proficient with this instrument that he might have been able to give some real competition to Jimmie Riddle, a member of his band who is well known for his versatility on just about anything musical. Roy also played the harmonica, but with lesser skill.

During the summer the children would often make cornstalk fiddles. The pulp would be cleaned out of a length of stalk and the remaining stringly fibers were "played" with a stick. It was impossible to get any real music out of one of these contraptions, of course, but everybody tried, including Roy. It was something to pass the time during the long summer days.

Family and friends remember that Roy seemed to be always whistling or singing, frequently with accompaniment from an empty tomato can, on which he would get some nice thumps by beating and strumming the sides. During an occasional baseball game, Vaughn Moore and John Huddleston remember, additional entertainment was sometimes provided by Roy with a tune thumped out on his tomato can or a bucket.

As part of their religious upbringing, the children were taught sacred songs. They sang in church, although they were never members of the choir. The influence of these old-time church songs emerged later in Roy's career. Roy also sang in the BYPU (Baptist Young People's Union), and in school.

The most meaningful part of Roy's early musical education was obtained at home. The children were "raised-up" on the traditional music of their forefathers, much of it coming from the British Isles. Some of the songs, of course, were of more recent origin. Roy especially remembers singing the ballad about the sinking of the *Titanic* in 1912.

The Acuffs were well liked and their home was a frequent meeting place where old-time music was played. Roy's father loved to fiddle and was a good country fiddler, and his Uncle Charlie, who also lived in Maynardville, was extremely proficient. Roy's mother played the piano and guitar. Both parents had fine singing voices. Once in a while, Roy would try to play his father's fiddle. Although his papa and Uncle Charlie offered encouragement, at this time Roy learned little except not to touch the horsehair, or where the rosin worked. He usually contented himself by singing lustily.

The musical talent Roy displayed at this time was not extraordinary, and neither family nor friends were particularly impressed. But even though young Roy might not have demonstrated much talent in Maynardville, he feels that his heritage gave him a truly authentic background for his music:

> Many, many times back in Maynardville, when I was just a kid, in the real cold winter nights and the mornings when Papa would get out of bed when the house was warming up after he had build the fires, he would take the old fiddle out from under the bed and play it up there in the hollow, and it would just—it was just so pleasing. Although he wasn't a real talented violinist, he was a good country fiddler. But those tones in the wee hours of the morning just before daylight, before we went out to feed, it was something—it built something in me that I have never forgotten. And I just often think of my father . . . Many times have I at the house where we lived in the little three room cottage—it wasn't a cottage, it was just a little three room shack—in fact I wrote a song on it and recorded it, "The Little Three Room Shack." But anyway, many a night we laid in bed and listened to those dogs up on the hill run a fox, and we didn't have to go to the fields or up on the hill to listen to a fox race. We merely just laid there in the bed or sat on the front porch and listened to them run at night, and it's beautiful. . . . The Smoky Mountains—it has a haze there that the other mountains don't have and it's real beautiful—very, very fine country.*

---

*Stone tape.

After leaving Maynardville, Roy Acuff has made a point of returning often. When he does he just doesn't go past and wave, but spends time talking with the friends and relatives who are still there. And Maynardville hasn't forgotten him. Some time ago the citizens constructed a white wooden marker directing tourists to the "Old Three Room Shack." They put it on the courthouse lawn so it could be easily seen. Sure enough, the tourists mistook the courthouse for an old Acuff mansion and asked if Roy was born there. This marker finally rotted and John Huddleston put up another, but that one fell to "mysterious" causes after a very short time. So a stone monument with a replica of Roy Acuff's Country Music Hall of Fame plaque was erected. When Roy visited on June 15, 1968, he said, "I'm proud of the one in Nashville, but I'm much prouder of this one here in Maynardville."

The courthouse burned to the ground around 1969 and when it was reconstructed the plaque was not included. During the 1960s there were efforts to purchase the "Old Three Room Shack," but the owners refused to sell. The shack subsequently was torn down for construction of a highway.

"Rabbit"

On November 19, 1919, when Roy Acuff was 16, the family piled into Maynardville's only car, owned by John Huddleston, and went to their new home in Fountain City, a Knoxville suburb. Neill Acuff had decided to make this move because of the city's better educational advantages. Spot, who was almost 10, remembered this well, his first automobile ride. John Huddleston had scared him to death with stories about life in the big city and so Spot made a pair of brass knuckles from the handles of an old galvanized wash tub, and carried them on the trip.

(The recollections of Roy and his associates and data obtained from sources such as school annuals and newspapers only provide conflicting evidence of which years Roy went to high school. It has therefore been necessary to fit these conflicting reports together in such a way as to make the most sensible story.)

Upon his arrival in Fountain City, Roy spent at least one year completing whatever pre-high school education had been unfinished in Maynardville. He entered Fountain City's Central High School in the fall of either 1920 or 1921, and 1924 appears to be his official graduation year. However, he played a major role in school activities during the following year and quite possibly was even around as late as the school year of 1925-26. Although his attitude toward the three Rs hadn't improved since Maynardville, his grades were average.

Roy was not a member of the Glee Club, but one day the principal, Miss Hassie Gresham, heard singing outside her office and asked the soloist, Roy, to come in. She proceeded to request that he lead the singing in chapel the next morning. Roy objected, pleading inexperience and fright. She insisted, and under her guidance he soon liked it so much that he sang regularly.

In 1970, Roy said this about Miss Gresham, who retired in 1947: "She has meant more and more to me as the years have passed. I visit her regularly whenever I'm in East Tennessee. She forced me to do things. She knew I could do them, but I was shy." On several occasions Miss Gresham literally pushed Roy onto the stage for class plays.

As with the chapel singing, he soon grew to like performing before an audience and was in most of the school plays. Some were Shakespearean, others were of the minstrel variety. Frequently he played opposite a favorite classmate and school pal, Sarah Peters. She soon married, then died in childbirth. The tragedy so touched Roy that he later wrote and recorded the song, "Sad Memories." Because of the emotions it raised, he rarely sang the song.

He was assistant sports editor of the school paper and worked on the staff of the school annual, *Sequoyah*. Roy also was secretary-treasurer of the "C" Club, to which only varsity athletes could belong.

Roy spent so much time in sports that he really didn't have much time for or interest in dating. He excelled in athletics, earning thirteen letters, four each in football and basketball and five in baseball— not bad, considering he only weighed around 130 pounds.

The colors of Central High were red and black and its teams were called the Bobcats. Sometimes the school was called the Red and Blacks, sometimes the County School. The City School was Knoxville City High School and the blue-and-white Blue Devils were arch rivals of the Bobcats. Eligibility didn't mean much; some "gray-headed old men" were often kept year after year.

Upon his arrival at high school, in 1921, Roy definitely remembers that the first sport he went out for was football. When his classmates inquired if he was going to try out for football, Roy said, "What's that?" In fact, he played in the first football game he ever saw. The team practiced on a rocky unmarked field behind the school. Roy played halfback, mostly as a substitute. The first game the team played on a marked field was when it went to Tennessee Military Institute. By 1922 he started part of the time, sometimes at right half and sometimes at left half. The other backs were Emmett Shawn and Dutch Mathis.

The fall of 1923 saw the arrival of Pinkie Walden, who became a backfield star. Pinkie became well known for his fantastic evasive runs. Emmett Shawn and Roy Acuff became the regular starting ends. Roy was nicknamed Rabbit because of his speed on end-arounds and going downfield on punts and passes.

The team's greatest moment came on Saturday, November 22, 1924, when the Bobcats beat the Blue Devils for the first time in five years, 13-0. The game was played in Shields-Watkins Stadium before the largest crowd in Knoxville ever to view a high school game. After the game Central High was jubilant and Roy scaled a three-story building and painted a large 13-0 on its top. A friend, Nick Charles, climbed up to take a picture, then lost his balance. Nick managed to catch himself but the camera fell to the ground, undamaged, and the picture appeared in the *Sequoyah*. While Roy Acuff was not a star, he was an integral part of Central High football during the 1921-24 seasons. The team's average weight was about 151 pounds.

In basketball the five-foot seven-inch youngster played running guard and sometimes center. On occasion he could leap and touch the hoop. Roy played on the varsity team during the seasons of 1921-25. He was the captain of the Bobcats the last two seasons and they almost won the state championship both of those years. One of their biggest games was a 25-22 loss to Lenoir City on March 7, 1925.

In baseball, his favorite sport, Roy was the team's star pitcher. He had an excellent curve, lots of slow pitches, and fine control. Roy played other positons, usually in the outfield, between pitching assignments. He hit some of the longest homers ever made in the parks at Knoxville, and newspaper reports of some games referred to him as "Home Run Acuff." Roy loved the game and planned on a career in professional baseball, then professional coaching.

The 1925 *Sequoyah* praised Roy's athletic ability, and stated that in his years at Central High School he "has shown one outstanding trait of character—that of loyalty." And loyalty to a teammate caused a fight that Briscoe remembers.

One fall the football Bobcats traveled to Cleveland, Tennessee, for a game. Afterward, a Cleveland player pushed one of Roy's team-mate's face into the drinking fountain, knocking out several teeth. There was no fuss at the time, but the Bobcats knew the culprit. A week or so later, Briscoe and Roy went to a University of Tennessee game. Roy sat on the student side, Briscoe across the way in the visitors' section. Pretty soon Briscoe was amazed to see a fellow come rolling head over heels down the long staircase of the stadium. A policeman, sitting next to Briscoe, casually remarked, "I know what that guy did and I know who hit him." Brisco didn't say a thing.

During Roy's high school years, his father was the pastor of the Fountain City Missionary Baptist Church. Occasionally the congregation would be entertained by a quartet made up of Briscoe, Juanita, Sue, and Roy. About this time, however, a weak stomach, which was to plague him the rest of his life, made his father decide to leave the ministry and enter law. Upon his graduation from law school in Knoxville he was admitted to the Tennessee bar. Although Neill Acuff did a lot of trial work, Roy claims that his father, even as a lawyer, was never well off financially because he was too honest. In fact, he never had enough money to own his own home.

In later years Roy's education became a matter of speculation. Some of the stories credited him to be a law graduate of Harvard; some gave him a master's degree. The truth is that Roy graduated from Central High and has never claimed other scholastic honors.

Goofing Off

After graduating from high school, Roy was offered an athletic tuition at his father's alma mater, Carson-Newman. However, despite his parents' wish for him to continue his education, the thought was abhorrent to Roy and he refused the tuition. So Roy more or less goofed off from the time he left Central High until a fateful July day in 1929.

During these years Roy credits his oldest brother with helping to keep the family together. Briscoe had a state civil engineering job, working on highway construction. As for Roy, well, papa kept urging him to find a good steady job. But the young man, while not actually running from work, really never did make an effort to settle down in a solid occupation.

On two occasions, though, Roy left Knoxville and went north to find work. Although primarily interested in a sports career, he also remembered his pleasant experiences on the Central High stage, and the thought of life in show business had some appeal. Accordingly, Roy went to Chicago to get into the burlesque shows, but the routines were too vulgar and, besides, he didn't have the proper training and so he failed to make the grade. The other time was when Roy, like many East Tennesseans, went to Detroit to get a job on an auto assembly line. He put doors on Fords for exactly two hours. Roy also found that he was uncomfortable in the North. The people there talked too fast for him to understand what was being said.

Back home, he had a few odd jobs. He worked as a levelman with a surveying team of the Coast and Geodetic Survey, which was working on the elevations for Norris Dam. He also helped Charley Duncan, a Negro, shine shoes at Sherman Wallaces's Fountain City Barber Shop. This was strictly for fun, not a paying job. Roy later said, "He would shine one shoe and I did the other one, only I had a better rhythm in my shine rag." After Roy had become famous, Charley hung a diploma in the barber shop that testified to his shoe shining ability, it was signed by Roy. When the shop burned in 1939, Roy flew from Nashville to offer what help he could to Charley.

Having once played on the Louisville & Nashville baseball team led to a job Roy held for two or three years, as a railroad callboy. His duties included rounding up (calling) the crews to their assigned trains and giving orders for turn arounds. On a "turn around" he would direct a train to go from the main terminal to some other place on the line, either another terminal or up a branch track to its end, where the train would be turned around and then go back to Knoxville.* He worked at night and was able to sleep most of the time because his kindly boss would awaken him only when he was needed. This left the days free for ball playing. Roy loved the trains and learned to imitate locomotive whistles by puckering his lips, placing his tongue against his teeth and hollering from deep down in his throat. He put this skill to good use later.

Another favorite loafing place was John Copeland's Fountain City Garage.** It was a place where one thing led to another. Roy was always ready for anything—from a fox hunt to a boxing match. Occasionally, he and some friends would organize some minstrel shows.

---

*Clarification of the terms "callboy" and "turn around" was provided by Scott Irby, a railroad buff.

**A. C. Dubkleberger, *King of Country Music: The Life Story of Roy Acuff* (Nashville: Williams Printing Company, 1971), p. 35.

During these years Neill Acuff practiced law with Hobart F. Atkins and Sam J. Thornburgh. Roy can remember sitting in the courtroom many times and listening to his father plead a murder trial with so much persuasion and sincerity that it would bring tears to the jury's eyes. Like his son, Neill Acuff loved to perform.

Roy also sat in courtrooms for other reasons. He was smaller than most of the other boys and cocky. Although he wasn't a rowdy looking for a fight, his "friends" would start altercations just so they could stand around and watch Roy finish them. He seldom lost. Roy Acuff was unanimously recognized as the best fighter in Knoxville during his younger days.

Bob Wilson, a Knoxville friend, said, "He was murder. I have seen him whip three and four bigger boys. It was not that Roy went around looking for trouble, but it decidedly was that he made no effort to dodge when a fight came his way."

Pinkie Walden, Roy's old football teammate, when recalling this period in their lives, said, "I was a good fighter and I lost very few decisions in my day. But Acuff could hit too fast and too hard for me. He could chill a 200 pounder with a punch that traveled no more than six inches."

Roy was a natural athlete and with the few informal lessons in the high school gym, plus his "postgraduate" experience, he developed into a good fighter and a catch-as-catch-can brawler. Once when Roy was watching a football game, his companion asked for a drink from a jug that Roy had under his seat. As Roy handed it to him, two policemen spotted the goings-on. Even though one pinned Roy's arms, the other was put out of commission by Roy's feet. The law ultimately prevailed, though, and Roy found himself in the jail's "cooling room" until he did just that.

Roy himself has said of this period, "There was nothing I loved as much as a physical fight—an actual physical fight!" Less attractive was seeing the inside of many a courtroom and spending nights in a few jails, although never for protracted periods.

On at least one occasion he was brought to court but avoided jail. A friend of Roy's, knowing of his fighting ability, asked him to go to a certain establishment and help take their drunken buddy home to his family. Roy picked up the 200 pound fellow and started down the stairs. Meanwhile, the lady friend of the inebriated buddy was pounding Roy over the head with the heel of her slipper. After this had gone on almost all the way down the stairs, young Roy finally turned around and broke the lady's glasses with one solid punch. Roy's father acted as his attorney and told the judge, "If you believe my boy guilty then send him to jail; if not, set him free." The judge dismissed the case. As many of Roy's close associates have commented when remembering those years, "God must have been watching over Roy Acuff." And one has to add—God and his father.

This period in Roy's life was turbulent, and his parents would worry especially when he was away from home for two or three days. They kept their feelings to themselves until one night when the rest of the family had finished dinner and Roy and his parents were left alone. Neill Acuff spoke quietly to his son. First he said, "Roy, we are proud of all our children, but of all our children, you are destined to be a leader." Then he pointed out the possible consequences of Roy's drinking and carousing: how his behavior could hurt his family's reputation, how he might possibly get a young girl in trouble, how he might even end up in the penitentiary. Roy was pensive for a moment. Then he looked at his father and said, "Well, papa, I don't know of anything I'd rather go to the penitentiary for than drinking and carousing." At this point his parents got up from the table and left him sitting there. As Roy looked up, he noticed that mama was kind of smiling and papa was, too. Roy is sorry now that he caused his parents so much worry and he also regrets that his father didn't live to see the greater part of his success.

During this time Roy was dating three high school girls. They liked him because he was older. One was Mildred Louise Douglas. Many stories have been told of how Roy first met his future wife. One states it was on a spring day in 1929 and he was driving his first car, a brand-new shiny red Chevy roadster with four cylinders, 60 horsepower, and rumble seat. When he spotted Mildred, who was a Central High freshman of 15 walking along the sidewalk, he braked to a gravel-plowing stop. "Wanna ride?" Roy asked. "If I do, I'll get a stick horse!" snapped Mildred Douglas. Roy was taken aback but he didn't say anything, just shifted gears and drove off.*

The two definitely did meet when Roy came to the high school to play semipro basketball. They also found they lived on the same street—Raleigh Avenue—one block apart. (The Acuff family had moved from the Fountain City suburb to Arlington, a Knoxville suburb, in 1927. Their address was 226 Raleigh Avenue.)

---

*Elmer Hinton, "Along Came This Feller in a Red Roadster. . . ," *Nashville Tennessean Magazine*, April 13, 1958, p. 14.

By this time Roy was five-foot eight and one-half inches tall and weighed 140 pounds. Although the sports in which he participated were called semipro, financial gain was rare or paltry. The basketball team on which he played was called the Kaydets. Roy was one of its organizers and some of his teammates were recruited from Central High's old foe, Lenoir City. They played against good teams, such as the Firestones, Indians, and Celtics. During this period, Roy probably played more basketball than anything else.

However, his major continuing interest was baseball. As late as 1964 he told a reporter, "If I had my choice, I'd still be playing ball." He played city league ball with different clubs, the most prominent being the L&N team. He also played on and managed the Fountain City team. Briscoe occasionally would play, too. Roy never batted less than fourth in the lineup, usually second, third, or clean-up. His positions were shortstop, left field, and center, and when his rotation came up he pitched. Sometimes he received as much as $20 when he had been on the mound. His heroes were, predictably, Babe Ruth and Lou Gehrig—and his father, of course.

Eventually his baseball talents drew the attention of major league scouts. During the spring of 1929 he had a tryout with the Knoxville Smokies, but was unsuccessful. Then, still later that spring, the Yankees sent some scouts through the area and Roy planned to sign with them and go to their training camp the following spring. But fate intervened.

"Roy, You're Not Gonna Play Baseball"

In early summer 1929, Roy went on a fishing trip at the invitation of a fairly well-off friend, Ross Smith. For two weeks they fished at Soldier Key in Florida. Roy, unaware of the dangers of the tropical sun, became so badly blistered that at night he could not lie down but had to sleep sitting up under a canvas shelter.

A short time later, at home, he played in a baseball game for the L&N team at Knoxville's Caswell Park. It was July 7 and Roy was the starting pitcher. The day was extremely hot. He remembers that each time he reached down to get dust on his pitching hand he came up with mud. (The doctor later explained that the palms of his hands were the few places on his body where the skin was sufficiently un-damaged to allow perspiration.) After an inning or two he informed his manager, "My pitches aren't breaking right," but was told, "You're doing all right." After a few more innings, at Roy's request, the manager put him in the outfield. At the end of the next inning, Roy ran in from his outfield position and passed out in the dugout. His arms and legs immediately cramped to such violent extent that three of his teammates were required to pull them straight again. He thought he was dying, right there in the dugout. Briscoe, who was in the stands, rode with his younger brother in the ambulance to the hospital. There, the physician in charge was another member of the Acuff clan, Dr. Herbert Acuff.

Roy later commented on this turning point in his life, "I reckon the good Man up above said, 'Roy, you're not gonna play baseball—you're gonna do something else,' so He knocked me down with a sunstroke."

That evening the 25-year-old Tennessean was released from the hospital and went home and stayed quiet for about a week. But the first time he began to move around, he passed out again. After this second collapse the family doctor, Dr. Carl R. Martin, said, "Roy, if this happens again, you are apt to pass away on us." This upset Roy so much that he stayed in bed for nearly three months.

Then one evening during his recuperation he walked to the corner and happened to witness a fight among some of the boys. Even though he was not involved in any way, he became very nervous and fainted. Again fearing that he was dying, Roy next found himself suffering from a nervous breakdown as well as the remaining effects of the sunstroke. He now realized that a career in sports was out of the question. He felt the world was closing in on him.

But in a short while Roy ventured out once more, this time in what was an effort to prove to himself that he was not seriously ill. A friend and neighbor, Red Jones, was a caddie and a good golfer. Roy started around the course with him one day, but suffered his fourth attack.

As a result Roy spent the year 1930 in bed. His father had some records of great mountain fiddle tunes, played by such early performers as Fiddlin' John Carson and Gid Tanner and the Skillet Lickers, and he collected more. These were put on the Victrola and Roy listened and learned, although it was difficult to tell the key because the record would play at different speeds depending on how tightly the Victrola was cranked. After a few months Roy picked up his father's fiddle and began to pick out some of the tunes by ear.

By the end of the year, Roy's strength was returning and he was beginning to move around more in the house. While becoming more skillful on the fiddle, he also passed the time by teasing his sister, Sue. She was now married and living in a nearby apartment but would often return for voice practice, playing the piano and running the scales, "Ah-ah-ah." Roy liked to sit in the kitchen and copy her—not to learn to sing, but simply to make a nuisance of himself. Sue was proud of her operatic voice and even sang semiprofessionally. On occasion, as Roy remembers, "She'd start bawling, and mama would run me out of the house."

From this teasing he learned to sing from the pit of his stomach, instead of shallowly through his nose and mouth, and his voice developed power if not quality. Later he said of his impish teasing, "That's how I learned to really rear back and sing and come out with a lot of oomph. They used to talk about the nasal voice up until I came along. I used to knock some of the small stations off the air. They were not used to my style. I was one of the first who ever put a real strong voice in country music."

The year 1931 found Roy out of bed, but only around the house or occasionally to a nearby corner. At times he would sit in the shade of the porch and fiddle. He also found himself itching to pitch again; but, of course, this was impossible. For a substitute, he took up Yo-Yoing, which was a new invention and fad. Many of his evenings were spent idly standing at the drugstore corner talking with friends and throwing and catching his Yo-Yo. Some days were spent at John I. Copeland's garage. John I. was an old character who lived in his garage and often slept with his foxhounds in the cars. Roy later said of him, "He would have made a hell of a good hippie." The old man was a fine country fiddler. However, John I. did not play the prominent role in teaching Roy how to fiddle that some have claimed—Roy's father and Uncle Charlie were of primary importance.

"It is hard to express just how dark my life was," Roy has said, "and how I felt about not being able to play baseball and be in sports." However the monotony was frequently relieved by visits from his many girl friends. One of them was Mildred Douglas.

More actually was accomplished during these years than in the previous goofing off period. In looking back, philosophically, at his illness, and also considering the preceding years, Roy later said:

> It was a time in my life when I was very sad. I didn't know what I was gonna do. When I found I was knocked out of a career of baseball and I couldn't play basketball no more, and of course my football days were over, I just couldn't see any light at all—everything was dark. But when I

found the fiddle, I can just say it was a gift to turn me into country music. For if it hadn't come along, I don't know what I would have become.*

Mocoton Tonic is the Best Medicine

As 1932 began, Roy got out of the house more and more. He went to Arlington's Sharp Drug Store No. 2, managed by George Stevens, partly to hang around with the boys and partly to see Mildred Douglas who was a cashier there. She, then a high school senior, had been working at this store since 1930. Roy also spent quite a bit of time fiddling at home.

One evening he was fiddling a mournful tune on the front porch and Doctor Hauer (Howard and Hower are also given as his name) who lived down the street came along. Dr. Hauer had a medicine show and he knew Roy had been recuperating for about two years, and furthermore he liked the sound of Roy's fiddling. He offered Roy a job with his medicine show for that summer saying, "Roy, I think it will do you good." Roy replied that he didn't think he could stand the work because of the heat. When the doctor assured him that they would be working only in the evenings, Roy agreed to try it for that season.

After Roy's parents saw how happy he was, they placed no obstacles in his way, and gave him every assistance they could, even during the lean years that followed. Actually Roy's father once told him, "You are doing what I always wanted to do."

So that summer, the medicine show set out in the Doc's Reo sedan. The back of the car let down to provide a platform for small shows. For big crowds, and the Doc was good at knowing where crowds were, a truck would bring in a stage. They played mountain hamlets throughout East Tennessee and Virginia, staying at a location two weeks before moving on.

The musicians would put on a free show to draw the crowd, which frequently numbered three or four thousand people, and then Doc Hauer would give his pitches—complete with ghastly accounts of little children devoured by worms, who could have been saved by one small bottle of Mocoton Tonic. The label stated "Cures dyspepsia, sick headaches, constipation, indigestion, pain in the side, back and limbs, torpid liver, etc." It contained 10 percent alcohol and sold for one dollar a bottle.

---

*Country Crossroads tape and Trudy Stamper.

Besides the Mocoton, Doc also sold soaps, candies, and corn remedies. The corn concoction was strong. Doc would demonstrate it by pouring it over a mountaineer's heavy shoes, where it would seep right through the leather and completely numb the man's feet, giving the illusion that his corns had indeed been cured.

Jake Tindell was a veteran. He had been with the Doc for years and he showed Roy the ropes, teaching him songs, skits, and jokes, most of which Roy was later to use in his own act. Roy was the fiddler. Jake played the guitar and the two were later joined by another guitar player, Tom (Clarence) Ashley.

Roy especially enjoyed playing the little "after piece plays." They did a different one of these half-hour comedy skits each night for the two weeks they were in a place. Two of Roy's favorites were "Charlie over the River" and "Little Willie Green." Roy sometimes would black-up for a blackface role, at other times he played the parts of an overgrown boy, a young girl, an old man, or old woman.

With no microphones, crooning or normal speech wasn't powerful enough to reach the back rows. "You sang to several thousand people in the open," said Roy, "and you couldn't get to them if you didn't put your lungs to the fullest test. And when you were doing comedy or telling jokes, you had to put out a lot of voice to get out there to them." So Roy continued to develop his voice, which he once described as "a country tenor without training, performing in the 'Old Harp singing style.'" (This is a term that refers to the white Anglo-Saxon tradition. So Roy is not literally correct in its use, since some of his material can be traced to other traditions.)

Roy was paid only a dollar or two a day for working in Doc's medicine show. However, he has this to say about the experience:

> That's the best experience a boy can get—working with a free show like that, even though we'd come in folded forty times and softer than cloth. I didn't make much money at it, but I got a pretty good background in show business. And when I found that I could fiddle and I found out that I could sing a song, or sell a song, and I found out that the people appreciated me, I began to see a new light, and that light has been much brighter for me than the world of sports.*

Roy has never forgotten the grateful appreciation of the medicine show audience—it's what encouraged him to go into show business. Furthermore, the hardships gave him some idea of the "hard dollar days" that were to come.

---

*Country Crossroads tape.

An Extra Fifty Cents

When Roy Acuff returned home from the medicine show in the fall of 1932 he knew what his life's work was going to be, so he started getting acquainted with the musicians around Knoxville. There were lots of them, and all were anxious to pick up an extra fifty cents.

Two of them were a fine little fiddler, Bill Norman, who worked with a guitarist, Lonnie Wilson.* Lonnie and Roy found they could play well together and so they performed at square dances. Red Jones, Roy's golfing neighbor, also was skilled on the bass fiddle, and sometimes joined in. From time to time Roy's brother Spot, who was never seriously interested in the business, would join Roy and Red Jones to form a trio known as The Three Rolling Stones, which performed at various places, like the amateur show in the Tennessee Theater. It was all very disorganized: different musicians were doing different things and playing in various combinations.

By 1933 some organization began to appear. The musicians gathered at George Stevens's corner drugstore, or at Thompson's Garage in the nearby suburb of Lonsdale. One group had Jess Easterday, playing mandolin and guitar, Clell Summey on Dobro guitar, and Bob Wright, mandolin. They called themselves the Tennessee Crackerjacks. There was no leader.

The Crackerjacks played at dances and socials. Sometimes each would take home as much as two dollars for a performance, but usually the amount was close to nothing. It was obvious that these musicians needed a leader, but they were content to go along on dates at someone else's expense.

His summer with the medicine show made Roy one of the few Knoxville musicians who actually had had show experience. He began taking responsibilities and started booking shows. (This became easier once they got on the radio. Roy would simply ask the audience to write in if they would like to hear his band in person.) For transportation, Roy bought Doc Hauer's old sedan and another one for spare parts. He also built a trailer. With the rejuvenated Reo, trailer, and a leader, the Tennessee Crackerjacks began a more extensive range of operation.

To broaden their range even further, they began hanging around

---

*Much of this information about the early Knoxville band was obtained from Lonnie Wilson.

WROL, a Knoxville radio station. In 1934 the band—consisting of Roy, Jess, Clell and Red—finally obtained a program. It was sponsored by "Dr. Hamilton—Dentist."

After a short time Roy heard that Lowell Blanchard, of competing station WNOX, was starting a new show, the "Mid-Day Merry Go Round." Roy and the band switched stations and, with Blanchard as announcer and producer, within months the show became tremendously popular and was moved to the 1,500-seat Market Hall. The program was on every day, except Sunday, from noon to 1:00 P.M., and a nickel admission was charged. The show was sponsored by Scalf's Indian River Tonic, and it was one of the nation's first continually running and very successful local radio country music programs. Other acts performed on the WNOX "Mid-Day Merry Go Round" during and after Roy's tenure. Many performers began their careers on this program. A few of them were Pee Wee King, Bill Carlisle, Archie Campbell, Kitty Wells, and Johnny and Jack.

Roy's band worked on the "Mid-Day Merry Go Round" for almost eight months. One of the many guests was Pete Kirby. Each member of the band received 50 cents a show. Finally, Roy requested higher wages for his boys. He was refused.

In 1935 Roy and his band returned to WROL and started a competing noontime show. It was on this show that the band got a new name. The band was tuning up before the program one day and the engineer suddenly switched to the studio and the show went over the air before it was supposed to. Allen Stout, the announcer, feeling he had to explain to the audience, said, "Listeners, these are just crazy Tennesseans."

The Crazy Tennesseans stayed at WROL for several years. Besides the 30-minute noon show, they had other programs. One was sponsored by the JFG Coffee Company, and a furniture company sponsored two others. At WROL Roy discovered that he had to make an adjustment from his "pull out all the stops" medicine show singing style on these radio shows in order not to "blow the station off the air." So he often crooned the songs.

Roy remembers that on these first shows, as on all subsequent ones, he was allowed to select his own songs. Sometimes the station librarian would make a suggestion, and if Roy liked it he would use the song. But most of the time he made up the program himself. He also remembers that the effects of the breakdown still caused him to be so nervous that he sometimes could hardly hold the fiddle bow.

Between radio commitments during 1935, 1936, and 1937 the Crazy Tennesseans would do their best to make ends meet by driving in their old Reo sedan to schoolhouses in the woods and small theaters in the towns. Cities of any size just didn't exist in their territory. Payment was always on a percentage basis, usually 75-25. For those one-nighters, $25 was big pay. At this time, Roy said, The height of my ambition was to play a date where the box office receipts would total as much as $100." In later years Roy became wistfully reminiscent about those backwoods one-night stands, those times when the band "fiddled and starved."

At the time the Crazy Tennesseans received their name, in 1935, Roy was billed as "Fiddler and Master of Ceremonies." Although musicians came and went, the nucleus of Jess, Clell, and Red, plus a few others, contributed importantly to the band's popularity.

Jess Easterday was born in Knox County, Tennessee, in 1912 and started his musical career in 1930. He said that his professional career started when he entered radio in 1934 with the Crazy Tennesseans. He was billed along with Clell as "Radio's Famous Hawaiian Duo."

James Clell Summey, known as "Tex" because he wore boots, introduced the Dobro to the band. He considered himself to be a mountaineer—born around 1913 in the Smoky Mountains. He moved to Knoxville as a child. His mother and father were musicians, Matty and Jim, and they recorded on cylinders and later on the thick Edison discs. Musicians lived at their house and so as a youngster Jody, as he was frequently called, was taught to play many different instruments. Jody loved the guitar and soon discovered that when the big heavy ring he wore on his third finger hit the strings, a wondrous sound was created. That was the start of his steel guitar. Soon he switched to the Dobro and by 1931 he was playing his own Hawaiian show.

Red Jones was billed as the "Bull Fiddler King and Jug Comedian." Roy has high praise for his skill on the bass fiddle.

Roy's brother Spot joined the group occasionally and formed the Three Rolling Stones along with Roy and Red Jones. By the fall of 1936, Sam "Dynamite" Hatcher was with the band. He played the harmonica and also sang some vocals. Dynamite left the group in 1937.

Jake Tindell, with whom Roy worked on Doc's medicine show, sometimes joined the group as a jug playing blackface comedian. He left this group but later joined Roy's new band in Nashville.

An occasional guest performer was a girl named Alma Cox, who played the Hawaiian National steel guitar. And shortly before the band left Knoxville, Imogene Sarrett, known as Tiny, joined it and was billed as the "Little Girl with the Big Guitar."

Old photographs show faces familiar and forgotten. Among those remembered are such musicians as Bill Norman, fiddle, Kentucky Slim, the "Little Darling," Bob Wright, who played mandolin, and Archie Campbell. Many of these photographs were publicity shots, and do not indicate the groups shown actually played together.

In addition to these part-time players, substitutes were used for short periods. For example, Pete Kirby returned to Knoxville after working in Chicago and took a job in a bakery. One day when Clell wanted the night off, Roy's friend told him about his own younger brother, Pete. As a result Pete played that show, and two or three more, and once went on the road with Roy's band.

During this period of fiddling and starving, some Knoxville musicians turned partly or completely to nonmusic jobs. Did Roy ever think of quitting? The answer is a composite of sources, but Roy agrees to this:

> My goal wasn't wealth, and still isn't. I only wanted to do something I enjoy, to entertain the public. At first I never dreamed of getting anything better. I just loved the country music field so well that I was willing to suffer in order to just earn a living. We were just struggling children at the time, doing what we enjoyed. The lean days never seemed a hardship because I was following a course I believed in. It never occurred to me to change that course because I was positive that some day the field of country music would be good to me—as good as I was determined to be for it.

To the Recording Studio
On the Wings of That Great Speckled Bird

While Roy Acuff was learning his business in Knoxville he met Charlie Swain, who was also performing on WNOX and WROL. Swain and his group, the Black Shirts, performed a song entitled "The Great Speckled Bird," which had an old traditional English melody. It was similar to many tunes, especially to "I'm Thinking Tonight of My Blue Eyes." To this melody the Rev. Guy Smith had written six verses and entitled them "The Great Speckled Bird."*

---

*Figuring out the true and legal ancestry of this song is a very complicated matter. Several individuals claim authorship and several publishing companies have published the song: M. M. Cole Publishing Company—Rev. Guy Smith, 1937, 1964; Leeds Music Corporation—Sarah Dillon and Homer A. Tomlinson, 1941; "Roy Acuff's Folio of Original Songs Featured over WSM Grand Ole Opry"—Roy Acuff, 1941; Southern Music Publishing Company—Roy Carter, 1962.

These verses were based on the ninth verse of the twelfth chapter of Jeremiah: "Mine heritage is unto me as a specked bird, the birds round are against her; come ye, assemble all the beasts of the field, come to devour." To W. J. Cash, author of the *Mind of the South*, the song pictures the church as a group of persecuted individuals who ultimately will gain eternal salvation as a reward for their earthly travail.* Roy Acuff states that "The Great Speckled Bird" is the Bible and the Church. The interpretation of the song's meaning, which probably concerns some fundamentalist allegorical symbol, is certainly up to the individual person and has been the subject of great discussion, especially in the South, for a long, long time.

A few years earlier, Roy had heard bits and pieces of the song and it fascinated him. So in 1935, when he heard Charlie Swain sing the entire song, Roy asked Charlie to make a copy of it and one other song. Charlie obliged, the price was 50 cents. Shortly after this, Swain left Knoxville and Roy started singing "The Great Speckled Bird." It soon became his most popular number.

Down through the years Roy has found that many country musicians couldn't get that little catch, that little extra different something about the tune, and instead played the tune of "Blue Eyes" or "I Didn't Know God Made Honky Tonk Angels." Shot Jackson, who has been with Roy off and on for many years, is one of them. Only a few musicians, including Oswald (Pete Kirby), actually play the true melody of "The Great Speckled Bird."

Of course "The Bird," as the Acuff group has nicknamed the song, became Roy's most requested number and his second biggest record seller. Its name graced his DC-3 airplane. Of the song, Roy says: " 'The Bird' is a musical marvel of the age. Never have I played anywhere that it wasn't requested. We play it and folks frequently get up and dance. Others think of it as a patriotic song." Does it bother Roy when other country artists sing the song? "It doesn't bother me, not one bit, because it only plugs 'The Great Speckled Bird!' They'll always say, 'That's Roy Acuff's "Great Speckled Bird." ' "

Back in 1936 the boys didn't go looking for recording contracts, companies came hunting for them. The American Record Company (which was purchased before November 1938 by CBS and thus became Columbia) was about the only major company that was not

---

*Bill C. Malone, *Country Music U.S.A. a Fifty-Year History* (Austin: University of Texas Press, 1968), p. 203.

hesitant about putting country artists on its labels. Its venturesome field folk music scout was William R. Calaway, the artist and repertory (A&R) man, who had a real feeling for country music. He was particularly interested in tracking down "The Great Speckled Bird" and a man who could sing it. During one of Roy's WROL noon shows in Knoxville, Calaway or one of his associates was in the audience, unknown to Roy. When Calaway found out that Roy knew many songs, especially "The Bird," he signed Roy to a recording contract. Roy later modestly said, "I was quite surprised, I didn't know he was in my audience. He wanted 'The Bird,' he didn't want me."

So in October of 1936, Roy Acuff and his Crazy Tennesseans went to Chicago for their first recording session, staying at the Knickerbocker Hotel. The band comprised Roy, fiddle; Clell, Dobro; Red, bass; Dynamite, harmonica; and Jess, guitar. The session, which began on October 26, was held in a studio and lasted for several days. Twenty songs were recorded, which is the most Roy ever recorded at one session. Recording in those days was much more difficult that it is today. Acetates cannot be spliced like modern-day tapes. Two masters of each song had to be made and both had to be exactly alike. (The extra master was for dubbing in case of breakage.) Roy once said, "By the time you went through the number, timed it out, did the number, and then did another number exactly like it—failed on three or four of them—you were simply wore out and had to go rest. I guess you can tell in a lot of mine. The voice was gone but the spirit was still there." To make matters worse, a big horse pulling a milk wagon bit Clell on the shoulder.

In this first session Roy picked half the songs and Calaway selected half. Roy went along with this arrangement because he knew he was young and inexperienced. After a few years, he selected all the titles to be recorded.

The first song the group did was "Singing My Way to Glory"; Red Jones did the vocal. Roy took the first break on his fiddle, and the rest of the band can be heard clearly urging him on: "Play it Roy—play that thing." During Clell's Dobro break, Roy says, "Play that thing, Clell, come on over here and rap on it, boy. Yes sirree. Lordy, lordy, lordy. Ha. Sing it, Red." After the next verse, it's the harmonica's turn and Roy says, "What about you, Dynamite? Do your stuff. Play that harmonica, boy. Yes sirree. Make it cry like a baby. Uh huh." Then, to Red, after the last verse, "Now slap that thing, Red. Whoo hoo. Slap it, boy. Yeah." Such talk was heard in the background of many of the early recordings.

Red Jones generally preferred popular music and his other solo vocal at this session was "Yes, Sir, That's My Baby." Dynamite Hatcher got into the solo act, too, and did "Steamboat Whistle Blues," "Freight Train Blues," and—most surprising—he, not Roy, sang the "Wabash Cannonball." (Roy was not to record his vocal of this song until January 28, 1947.) However, Roy in the background did do the whistle that he learned as a call boy, and believes that this is what put the song over. A trio, Roy, Red, and Clell, sang "My Mountain Home Sweet Home" and "Gonna Raise a Ruckus To-night."

The Dobro was featured on "You're the Only Star." The harmonica was the lead instrument on "Yes, Sir, That's My Baby."

Naturally, Roy did the vocal on the majority of the numbers, the most important of which was "The Great Speckled Bird." Today three or four verses is considered enough for a recording, but back then the songs were much longer, frequently running over three minutes. Roy knew six verses, but hoped to make two recordings, which required ten verses, five for each record. So Roy, with the help of his father and the Bible, wrote four more verses. He used one of these verses in this first recording. Feeling that the initial verse needed some explanation, he wrote the second verse.

Another that Roy sang was "Charmin' Betsy," of which one line said sweetly, "My gal smells like a billy goat, she's stinking just the same." On "Gonna Raise a Ruckus Tonight," the word nigger* was allowed but not the word hell.

When the session was almost completed, the band still needed two more songs to fill out the 20. In the Knickerbocker, on their final night in Chicago, Roy wrote "When Lulu's Gone" and "Doin' It the Old Fashioned Way." These were recorded the next day. They were based on songs he had known as a youngster but was not allowed to sing around the house, because in those days the songs were considered to be risque. In the catalog and on the label the two songs are credited to the Bang Boys, because Roy would not let them be released under his name. This was the only time Roy used a pseudonym.

---

*In his 1965 recording of "The Wreck of the Old 97," Roy changed the words, "black, greasy fireman" to "Tired, greasy fireman" just to be sure he wouldn't offend anyone.

These 20 songs, as were the songs of all these early sessions, were not released on the parent American Record Company's label but on subsidiary labels. This was due to a nationwide prejudice against hillbilly music. These recordings were considered to be of only regional and rural interest. Sears, Roebuck sold the Conqueror label. Dime store labels containing Acuff songs were Melotone and Perfect. The Vocalion label was soon included and when it ceased to exist in the early 1940s it was replaced by the Okeh label. Around 1945, Roy Acuff songs were available on the familiar red Columbia label. However, ten songs from the first two sessions never reached the Vocalion label and are very rare today. A number of other early songs did reach Vocalion and Okeh, but never got on Columbia.

One more point about these old labels is the description of the music they contained. Typical examples: "Old Time Singing and Playing," "Novelty Playing and Singing," "Singing with Old Time Playing," and "Sacred Duet by Roy Acuff and Red."

An interesting mixup concerning Roy Acuff's first recording session happened 12 years later. On June 21, 1948, he received a gold record from Columbia Records, with an inscription: "To Roy Acuff to commemorate his 18th year as an exclusive Columbia artist." This would have had Roy recording in 1930 when he was flat on his back in bed. The plaque was meant to commemorate 12 years with Columbia and it would seem that when ordering the plaque, 1936 was probably written poorly and the six looked like a zero.

The band returned to Knoxville and five months later, in March 1937, it had another session. This, too, was an American Record Company session and Calaway, again was the A&R man. Portable equipment, run by batteries, was set up in a garage in Birmingham. The band consisted of Roy, Clell, Red, and Jess.

At this session Roy recorded "The Great Speckled Bird No. 2." To the best of Roy's later recollection, the first, third, and fifth verses were the ones he wrote. Also recorded was a song that Roy had written about his birthplace, "An Old Three Room Shack." Red Jones's songs, not surprisingly, were in the popular vein: "Red Lips," "Sailing Along," "Old Fashioned Love," and "My Gal Sal." A few of the vocals were group efforts. Clell, on his Dobro, played one instrumental, "Steel Guitar Chimes."

This old band was to have one more record session, but it would be well over a year and a half before they would do it. Relations between Roy and Calaway and the American Record Company declined rapidly. At this point Roy was beginning to feel that the American Record Company and Calaway were treating him dishonestly, and that the rights to some of his songs—including "An Old Three Room Shack"—had slipped through his hands. As a result, the band quit recording for 20 months.

In this period the American Record Company was dissolved and subsequently purchased by CBS, at which time it became Columbia. Meanwhile, the band moved its base of operations to Nashville, where Roy met Art Satherley. Satherley was an Englishman, with very aristocratic manners in dress and speech. He also had a love for country music and was Columbia's A&R man. Satherley didn't discover Roy, as many have thought, but he was A&R man for all Roy's Columbia sessions. In this capacity he did help Roy develop professionally, although not to the degree for which he is often given credit.

In October of 1938, Satherley came to Roy and asked him to renew his contract with Columbia, promising to personally see that Roy was treated fairly. Roy signed a contract in which the company agreed to record him at least twice a year, or pay the sum of $250 twice during the year if a session wasn't called. Roy was also given the privilege of examining the books to check any royalties due him.

In November of 1938 the band, consisting of Roy, Red, Clell, and Jess went to Columbia, South Carolina, where portable equipment was set up. Roy sang all but three of the 16 titles recorded. Two were instrumentals, and Jones's only vocal solo for this session was "Goodbye Brownie." He and Roy teamed for three duets: "Blue Ridge Sweetheart," "Automobile of Life," and "That Beautiful Picture." These Red Jones-Roy Acuff duets were quite successful, and some people feel that Red Jones made a real contribution to Roy's early success.

Roy Acuff had his first recording session in October 1936 and that alone would have been enough to make it a red-letter date, but another equally exciting event was also in store for Roy Acuff that year.

She Didn't Get a Stick Horse After All

Roy was living with his parents at 226 Raleigh Avenue and also seeing the pretty brunette cashier who now worked at the Lane Drug Company on Gay Street in downtown Knoxville.

Mildred Louise Douglas was born in the little East Tennessee town of Jellico. She has an older sister, Nell, and a younger brother. Her father, Louis, was a butcher; her mother is Nell Sharp Douglas of La Follette.

When she was a baby the family moved to Chattanooga, where they lived until Mildred was in the third grade. Then they moved to Panhandle, Texas, where she graduated from grammar school. In 1928 the family moved back to Tennessee, settling in Knoxville, and she started high school that fall, graduating in 1932.

Roy and Mildred saw a lot of each other at this time.*When he didn't have a show to play he would take her dancing on Saturday nights. It was the mid-thirties, the era of the Big Bands. On their way to a dance Roy would tune the car radio to WSM's "Grand Ole Opry." Mildred didn't particularly like string music, preferring the Big Band sound. In time—and not surprisingly—she learned to appreciate country music.

By December 1936, Roy and Mildred decided that they would get married. The band now had a recording contract, and prospects were brightening for its general success. Another consideration was that Mildred was making $16 a week as cashier at Lane's store. So on Christmas Day of 1936 the two were married by a justice of the peace in Middlesboro, Kentucky, where the waiting period wasn't as long as in Tennessee. Roy's older brother, Briscoe, gave them two dollars for the license. (Roy later said it was "the best investment I ever made.") They wanted to keep the marriage a secret because they feared the news might hurt Roy's career. But they had to tell their parents, and their parents let the cat out of the bag. When the couple returned from Kentucky they lived with Roy's parents for a short time, and then moved into a small house on Raleigh Avenue, right across the street from 226.

One of Mildred's biggest disappointments happened early in their married life. She had always wanted a diamond-studded wristwatch and friends who ran a Knoxville jewelry store offered her one at cost, with weekly terms. Mildred asked Roy if she could have it and then found out that Roy would never buy anything unless he could pay for it. He wouldn't agree, saying, "Mimi, you shall have the watch you want some day." He made good but it took him several years.

---

*These meetings however, were not with Roy during performances. There are many stories that Mildred sang or played with Roy in these early days. The truth is that she never did. Years later she sang once on a home recording; she never made another.

The Long Road to Nashville

When the band was fiddling and starving in Knoxville, Roy was thinking about the "Grand Ole Opry." It was obvious to him that the Opry was the only place where real success could be made. In fact one reason why he continued to struggle in these early years was not just because he loved country music but also because he knew about the Opry—and that if he could ever get on the Opry that maybe he could at least make a partial living out of country music.*

Roy started making trips to Nashville as early as 1934, going at least once a year, sometimes as many as three times. He would drive, ride with others, take the bus, or hitchhike the almost 200 miles from Knoxville to Nashville. He usually talked with Judge Hay, and was always told, "Sorry, boy, but the show is filled and there are many applications in ahead of you."

Between trips, Roy wrote letters. One of them was to Robert Lunn. Lunn had gotten on the Opry in 1935 and by 1936 Robert Lunn and his Talking Blues Boys were acclaimed as the most popular act on the show. Roy signed a letter written by Juanita, his sister and a graduate of Carson-Newman, asking Lunn to help him get on the Opry or get a job in Lunn's band. Lunn, who at that time received hundreds of similar letters, threw it away and never gave it a second thought. Years later, after Roy had become a star and Lunn was a featured act on Roy's show, Lunn told Roy that he guessed he would give him a job.

On one of Roy's many trips to Nashville he was made the spokesman for both his band and Pee Wee King's band. Pee Wee and Roy were friends, having played shows together over Knoxville radio. When Roy, as usual, returned from Nashville with bad news, King left Knoxville and went to Louisville. There he met an agent, Joe L. Frank. Soon after the disastrous Louisville flood of early 1937, Frank got King on the Opry and they both moved to Nashville.

Later in 1937, even though Roy had recorded twice, in October of 1936 and March of 1937, he was still unknown to the Opry and his trips to Nashville continued fruitless. Roy became discouraged and so he called Frank, in Nashville, and asked him about the Indian-

---

*There are many dates given about when Roy Acuff made his first appearance on the Opry. His thirtieth anniversary was celebrated on February 24, 1968, and Roy feels February of 1938 is correct. However his twentieth anniversary was celebrated on October 12, 1957, and Roy has from time to time referred to October of 1937. Friends recollect different dates, but most indicate 1937.

apolis territory. Frank said, "It would be all right once you built it up, but why do that? Have you tried Nashville?" Roy said that he had, but with no luck. Frank then conferred with David Stone, head of WSM's Artists' Service Bureau, who was in the room with him when Roy's call came through. Returning to the phone, Frank asked Roy what he was doing the following Saturday night, and when Roy said "Nothing," an audition was arranged. This was in October 1937.

The invitation was only to fiddle. The group known as the Dixie-liners, which consisted of Arthur Smith, the chief fiddler on the Opry, and Sam and Kirk McGee, was away for some reason and Roy was invited to fiddle during the first 15 minutes of the show.

As the band was riding over from Knoxville they were discussing what Roy should do. He knew he was hired only as a fiddler but he also knew that back in Knoxville he was known as a singer, especially a singer of "The Great Speckled Bird," and he felt that his greatest chance for success lay in his voice. Some band members said he should only fiddle, others agreed that he should sing, but they disagreed on what he should sing. Red Jones, especially, thought he should sing a popular number, possibly one of Bing Crosby's songs. But Roy vetoed that plan.

When he stepped on the stage of the Opry he was extremely nervous. WSM was much more powerful than the Knoxville stations. Roy later said, "I did an awful poor job of fiddlin'. I was scared to death. I played back of the bridge about as much as I played in front of it, and it don't sound too good back of the bridge." The tunes he played were "Old Hen Cackle" and "Turkey Buzzard."

Then Roy began to sing "The Great Speckled Bird." In those days, even back in Knoxville, and especially at that moment on the Opry, he would imitate everybody who was anybody. He delivered a crooning version of "The Great Speckled Bird." In the medicine show Roy had to make a powerful delivery, but when faced with a microphone in these early days he frequently did his level best to croon into it so he wouldn't blow the small Knoxville stations off the air. But WSM was powerful enough to handle the full strength of Roy's voice. It took him a little longer to realize that a Roy Acuff trying to croon is somewhat like a dog trying to meow.

As he sang Roy knew immediately that he was "laying an egg." The band wasn't playing well. Perhaps he had failed to convince them that "The Great Speckled Bird" should be performed. It was all wrong. He knew he had flopped.

He failed to impress the Opry brass and the boys returned to Knoxville. (One result of this experience has been Roy's subsequent compassion for artists who don't make auditions. Since he knows how it feels he has always gone out of his way to help such artists see that their life isn't shattered.) But very early in 1938 he received a letter from David Stone offering him another Opry audition. It was scheduled for February 5, 1938.

In the band that made what became a historic trip to Nashville were Roy Acuff, fiddle; Jess Easterday, guitar; Clell Summey, Dobro; and Red Jones, bass.

At this time the Opry basically featured string bands, such as the Possum Hunters, Herman Crook and the Crook Brothers, the Gully Jumpers, and George Wilkerson and his Fruit Jar Drinkers. There were a few vocalists, such as Uncle Dave Macon, Sarie and Sally, and Sam and Kirk McGee, but most of the performers were more a part of string bands or were comedians than featured vocalists. George D. Hay, the Solemn Old Judge, was master of ceremonies.

The stage on which Roy Acuff made his first big Opry success was that of the Dixie Tabernacle at 410 Fatherland Street across the Cumberland River in East Nashville. It had crude splintery benches and sawdust on the floor and was sometimes called "the old sawdust trail." (The Opry didn't move to the Ryman Auditorium until the early 1940s.)

The night of February 5, 1938, was a cold and rainy Saturday. Before Roy went onstage, Joe L. Frank tried to calm his nerves during David Stone's introduction by asking, "Roy, is Mickey Mouse a dog or a cat?" Roy answered, "Oh, Joe, I don't know nothin' about it. Please don't ask me stupid questions, I'm going on the air."*

As he stepped out onto the stage, Roy tried to think of himself as singing before the medicine show audience, and in this rendition of "The Bird" he put force and feeling into it. Clell played the kick-off on the Dobro (it was the Dobro's first appearance on the Opry) and Roy sang one verse. Then his knees began to shake. Clell had to play a chorus and another verse before Roy could resume singing.

As he sung that one song on that cold rainy night Roy felt that he had put the feeling over to the listeners. But some of the station executives apparently didn't agree, and the band returned to Knoxville.

---

*Stone tape.

On the morning of Monday, February 7, David Stone went to bat for Roy, saying, "Let's bring him back on the Opry." But many at the station kept insisting that he was still just an unknown from East Tennessee.

By mid-afternoon that Monday, sack upon sack of mail began to arrive at WSM. It was the first time the station had ever gotten such a significant amount of mail about an Opry act. This mail proved that Roy was right—the audience had captured the feeling that he had put into "The Bird."

David Stone, guessing what was going to happen, sent Roy a telegram offering him a tentative assignment on the Opry for February 19. However, he could not offer Roy any solid guarantee of pay. Even so, Roy still thinks of it as "the sweetest telegram I have ever received," and immediately wired acceptance.

By Wednesday, February 9, the mail, which was forwarded to Roy, was of huge proportions and it all said "We want Roy Acuff and his 'Great Speckled Bird'!"

On Thursday, February 10, David Stone wrote Roy the following letter:

Feb. 10, 1938

Mr. Roy Acuff
226 Raleigh Ave.
Knoxville, Tennessee
Dear Roy:

I am in receipt of your telegram advising that you will be here for the programs starting the 19th. I will book you for a spot on the Grand Ole Opry and also a series of 7:00 AM programs starting Monday, February 21st.

Since writing to you we have arranged for a commercial spot on the Grand Ole Opry for which there will be a small salary as long as the commercial runs. Of course we reserve the right to change the Opry schedule, but as long as you are on a commercial spot there will be something for you.

I am teaming you up with the Delmore Brothers for several personal appearances. These boys have tremendous popularity in this territory, but they cannot build or manage their own unit so I think it would be a great combination for the two acts. I think I can get some good dates right away and start you out as soon as you get here. This will save a great deal of time in getting your build up with the WSM audience.

We will talk it over in detail when you get here and I feel sure that we can make satisfactory arrangements. If you have any photographs, cuts, or mats, please mail them to me at once so that we can get publicity started.

Very truly yours,

David

David P. Stone

This letter was received on St. Valentine's Day. Roy later said, "It was the greatest thrill I ever had in my life."

On this, his first "one-way" trip to Nashville, Roy had reason to be more confident than ever before. He told his band: "Fellas, if at some time I can have your homes paid for, you can kindly beg or steal something to eat, but no one can kick you out of the house if you own it. I don't think that your taxes will get so far behind that you can't maybe pay them. The one thing that I want you to have is a shelter over you and your family's heads."

So Roy Acuff and his Crazy Tennesseans made their first performance on a regular-playing basis on "the Grand Ole Opry" on February 19, 1938. The next day they played with the Delmore Brothers at Dawson Springs, Kentucky. On Monday, February 21, Roy had a 7:00 to 7:15 A.M. program on WSM, which continued throughout the week.

During this week Harry Stone, brother of David and the manager of WSM, came to Roy and suggested that the name Crazy Tennesseans was a slur to Tennessee and that since WSM was so powerful and reached out into many states that perhaps the name should be changed. Harry Stone further suggested that since Roy came from the Smoky Mountains, he adopt that name. So by their second regular Opry performance on February 26, 1938, the newest Opry act became known as "Roy Acuff and the Smoky Mountain Boys."

By the end of the next week, Roy's morning radio show was moved 15 minutes earlier, to 6:45, and on Saturday, March 5, 1938, he actually headlined two 15-minute Opry segments, one at 8:30 and one at 11:15.

By Friday, March 11, his morning show was moved to 6:30, which meant he opened WSM's daily programming. Even though soon he performed with the band almost nightly within a 200 mile radius, Roy "rose and shown" and opened WSM each weekday morning, without salary, Roy claims, for about the next seven years.

Opry Regulars But Still "Fiddling and Starving"

When Roy Acuff reared back and hit the microphone with a

strong voice during his first successful Opry audition, he was the first performer to bring a clear and distinct style to the Opry. Previously, except for Opry stalwart Uncle Dave, whose strong point was mainly comedy, the Opry vocalists contented themselves with singing such old-time favorites as "Rabbit in the Pea Patch" and "Clementine." However, the music of these performers simply did not transmit clearly over the relatively primitive radio equipment in use at that time. The result was jumbled confusion in the ears of the listeners. "In the din," wrote Jack Hurst, "Acuff's brief and impassioned solo spots stood out like gunshots at midnight."*

As Vito Pellettieri, Opry stage manager, later said, "The string bands were the main thing. What little singing there was, begun with Uncle Dave, and Delmores and Sam and Kirk. But there wasn't a lot of it. We hadn't got to the star business yet, not until the coming of a curly headed fiddler."

Roy knew that his powerful delivery of "The Great Speckled Bird" won him his job, and that it also made him the first featured Opry singer backed by a band who was identified with a particular song. Even so, Roy in this early period as an Opry regular still tried to croon—he was still awed by the power of WSM and the microphone. Furthermore, some band members seemed to feel that crooning was desirable. During these early Opry days the band consisted of the four who originally came from Knoxville, Roy, Clell, Jess, and Red, plus Imogene Sarrett, known as Tiny. She had been a band member during the late Knoxville days and Roy sent for her. Tiny was a regular during this early WSM period.

Their two Opry shows, plus the 6:30 morning show, gave the band exposure and they soon began getting letters requesting personal appearances. Frequently they would get off the Opry at 11:30, and drive to, say, Greensboro, North Carolina, for a 3:00 P.M. Sunday show. The band would then return to Nashville to open the station at 6:30 on Monday morning. The rest of the week the band would play within a 200-mile radius of Nashville and return by 6:30 each morning. On Saturday they'd work all day and be back to the Opry for their 8:30 show, sometimes with not enough time to change clothes. On many occasions Mildred brought fresh clothing down to the Opry. And Roy often went for days without removing his shoes. Roy says of this hectic schedule, "We'd drive all night with

*Jack Hurst, *Nashville's Grand Ole Opry* (New York: Harry N. Abrams, Inc., 1975), p. 109.

the snow or rain hitting against the windshield. Man, you'd think we'd be so sleepy from staying up that everybody but the driver would go to sleep. But we were all so scared, we couldn't sleep."

On these early shows out of WSM, Roy was frequently billed as "Radio's Fastest Fiddler and Master of Ceremonies." (At this time Roy did fiddle fast. He soon slowed down, preferring to hear individual rather than slurred notes.) Also, the audience was urged by the announcer to come and "hear Roy Acuff sing his own song—'The Great Speckled Bird.'" Red Jones cut comedy capers on his bull fiddle. They performed in schoolhouses and movie theaters, sometimes playing second fiddle to the movie, which was considered the main attraction.

Spot had a $35 a week job with a Knoxville newspaper and couldn't leave it. But he used his first vacation after Roy became an Opry regular to visit Nashville and he went with Roy on one of his first WSM tours.

The admission to these first shows was around 10 or 15 cents for children and a quarter or 30 cents for adults. Rarely did the group receive a guarantee of a fixed payment. At the end of the show Roy was handed a percentage of the gate, anywhere from $10 to $30. And if Roy had $20 or $25 left to live on at the end of the week after he paid traveling expenses and the band's salaries, he thought he was doing excellently. His ambition was still, as it had been in Knoxville, to play a date where the box office receipts would total as much as $100. But even after he became an Opry regular, his income wasn't much different from what it had been in Knoxville. They didn't know where their next meal was coming from and a hamburger, when they could get it, tasted good. They were still fiddling and starving during this period of the Depression.

When the band first moved to Nashville in February of 1938 it lived in the Clarkston Hotel. Mildred didn't join Roy but stayed in Knoxville to work at the drugstore, where her earnings at times exceeded Roy's, especially in the Mother's Day candy rush. After Mother's Day, in May of 1938, she joined the band at the Clarkston. That summer, when times continued to be bad for the band, she returned to Knoxville to do relief work at the drugstore. She lived with Roy's parents, and Roy would visit her each Sunday on his way from the Opry to play the territory in North Carolina. That fall she rejoined him at the Clarkston Hotel, and in early 1939 the couple moved into a rented trailer.

About this time, the summer of 1938, Roy Acuff even thought about quitting the Opry. He was sometimes imitating and sometimes crooning, and he had a band that included members who favored pop music and wanted him to sing in that style. Finally he told the band that he wasn't going to imitate or croon any longer—and he didn't. Later he said, "Every person who has been successful has created a style. When I decided to be myself and create my own style, that's when the people listened to me and bought my records. That's when I became successful." In other words, Roy finally realized that his voice was his money and that his voice was powerful. So he threw back his head and sang just as he had done while in the medicine show. And discovered that his strength was not just in singing, but in selling.

So Roy became a seller and not a singer of songs. And when he became his natural self, the results were phenomenal. Fan mail, again, began to pour in.

A Little Success—But Resignation

On September 28, 1938, more than six months after Roy and the Smoky Mountain Boys became Opry regulars, a letter from David Stone revealed that things, in general, were going a little better. Road attendance was up, there were more bookings. One reason was that Roy was now really selling his songs. Another reason was that Joe Frank took a liking to Roy and started working him with Pee Wee King.

By November of 1938, the argument with the recording company had been settled and the band had another session. This one, more than the other two, added to their popularity.

At this time, however, Clell and Red Jones and Tiny became increasingly restless and uneasy because Roy had decided not to croon and play pop music. They disagreed that the future of the band lay in the Opry with old-time hillbilly music. So the three abruptly quit, around New Year's Day of 1939, and returned to Knoxville, where they intended to play pop music.

Even though Jess had tipped off Roy about the intentions of the three,* their action left Roy Acuff in a very tenuous position. Unless

---

*Clell returned to the Opry when Joe Frank brought him back, and he played with Pee Wee King for awhile. Later he developed an act called Cousin Jody, which played both alone and with Lonzo and Oscar. He also performed for a short time, beginning in late 1955, with Oral Rhodes in an act called Odie and Jody. Red Jones went on to become a fair golfer and may have become a golf pro.

he could find talented replacements and find them fast, the success he was beginning to experience would be jeopardized.

Roy Acuff and HIS Smoky Mountain Boys

When Clell, Red, and Tiny returned to Knoxville, Roy set about rebuilding his band with musicians who, in spirit as well as name, would be *his* Smoky Mountain Boys and would exemplify traditional hillbilly music. One source was the old medicine show and Jake Tindell. Jake had also worked with the Crazy Tennesseans in Knoxville. Another source was in Knoxville. Among the first musicians with whom Roy had played in the fall of 1932 was a guitarist, Lonnie Wilson. Roy also had worked in 1933 with Lonnie in the band called the Tennessee Crackerjacks—later known as the Crazy Tennesseans. However, by the time they got on the radio, Lonnie had gone his own way. But Roy recalled how well they played together, and he knew that Lonnie was working as a salesman at Pollack's Shoe Store in Knoxville.

Roy also recalled a Dobro player, Pete Kirby, who had gone to Chicago to try and make it in music but had returned to Knoxville to work in Kern's Bakery. Roy had used him as a substitute for Clell on a few occasions with the Crazy Tennesseans in Knoxville.

The old band quit around January 1, 1939. On January 4, 1939, Roy sent two telegrams to Knoxville. One was to Jake Tindell. The other was to Lonnie Wilson and it said, "Get Pete Kirby at Kern's Bakery and see if you can play together." That night Lonnie went to Pete's house. The two had never met but they found that yes, they certainly could play together. Lonnie wired Roy that Pete was fine.

Lonnie, Pete, and Jake left Knoxville on the morning of January 7 at 10 o'clock and arrived in Nashville the next day at 3:00 A.M. They went to the Clarkston Hotel to join Roy, Mildred, and Jess Easterday.

So now, Roy Acuff and His Smoky Mountain Boys consisted of Roy, fiddle, Pete on Dobro, Lonnie, guitar, Jess on bass, guitar, and mandolin, and Jake (who left the band after about a year) played the blackface comedian role. Roy was not yet satisfied—he was searching for a Smoky Mountain girl. On April 1, 1939, he found Rachel Veach.

The admission prices for performances were billed as "common sense" and ranged from 20 to 50 cents. The "Wabash Cannonball" joined "The Great Speckled Bird" in advertisements.

This new band, with the exception of Rachel and Jake, had its first recording session in July 1939 in Memphis at the Gayoso Hotel. The bedroom was only big enough to accommodate the band, so the portable recording equipment was installed in the bathroom tub, insolated so it wouldn't vibrate, and the engineer sat on the toilet. It was so hot that the men recorded in their underwear. This time there was no argument about recording more pop numbers because all the members of this band were dedicated to old-time music. Roy took the lead on all vocals (as he has done, with only minor exceptions, ever since) although Pete Kirby joined on some of the numbers, notably "Eyes are Watching You." This was the beginning of the Roy Acuff-Pete Kirby harmony that has become so famous.

However even in mid-1939, after Roy had been an Opry regular for a year and a half, and after he had acquired a band that was really with him in spirit, things still weren't going as well as they would have liked. True, they weren't close to starvation, as they had been a year before, but they were thinking of leaving Nashville and trying another part of the country. That $100 gate was still eluding them. However, the mail continued to be good and Mildred offered calm, practical encouragement.

Shortly after the formation of the new band Roy and Mildred moved out of the Clarkston Hotel and rented a trailer in Rosenburg's Trailer Park at 1906 Dickerson Road. Soon they were able to buy a used trailer. Lonnie, Pete, and Jess moved their families to a rooming house on 16th Street; after a few months, Pete and Lonnie moved to a house at the trailer park. Then they lived in a succession of trailers, which they swapped frequently. One of Pete's trailers burned and the group used it as a rumpus room. Other Opry performers, including Pee Wee King and the Golden West Cowboys, also lived in the trailer park.

Life at Rosenburg's was an adventure for everyone. For example, Mildred didn't know much about cooking. Once a friend gave her a recipe for pork chops and sauerkraut, and when she opened the can of sauerkraut she threw it away thinking it was spoiled. Cooking and doing laundry were difficult because the water froze every night during the winter. In these early days Mildred frequently went on the road with the group to sell tickets and settle with the sponsoring agency or theater at the end of each show. She also kept the books and was responsible for the band's salaries, duties she continued to maintain. The payroll was modest, in keeping with the troupe's general financial situation. For example, Pete Kirby started with a salary of $22 a week. To bolster their finances, Mildred would occasionally go back to Knoxville to fill in for vacationing employees at the drugstore. During this time, by careful saving, the Acuffs accumulated a bank account of around $100.

Then a dream came true. Toward the end of 1939, Roy Acuff and His Smoky Mountain Boys played their first $100 house. It was at the McFaddin School in Murfreesboro, Tennessee. The one-room school was jammed—people were standing and sitting everywhere, including the windowsills. Other such dates followed and by early 1940, about two years after Roy became an Opry regular, Roy and Mildred had enough money to buy the first home they could really be proud of: a brand new trailer. The dealer's price was $600, but the Acuffs only had $500 and so that was accepted.

Beside her domestic and bookkeeping duties, Mildred had the added responsibility of tending a zoo. On one of his tours, Roy had bought a little squirrel monkey and, down in Florida on another tour, two boys gave him a pair of pet raccoons, which had to be bottle-fed. A squirrel was soon added. The two coons and the squirrel were kept in a single cage. One day Roy and Mildred came home to find that someone had opened the cage door and the animals had escaped. The mischievous little coons had pulled all the hairs out of the squirrel's tail and someone had shot it thinking it was a rat. The coons finally came home after that escapade, but they were half wild and never did settle down. One day they escaped and were never seen again.*

In April of 1940 the band went to Dallas to record and in May they went to Hollywood to film the movie, *Grand Ole Opry*. Also during 1940, Roy and Mildred compiled a songbook that had many of Roy's most successful compositions; it also contained a few pictures. It was entitled *Roy Acuff's Folio of Original Songs Featured over WSM Grand Ole Opry*. At this time the copyrighting of songs was difficult. Roy had copyrighted some songs by writing them on postcards and mailing the postcards to himself in the hope that the postmark would be proof of legal ownership. This method was of debatable value and so, to put the ownership of his songs on firmer

---

*Much of the information about life at Rosenburg's trailer camp was obtained from Dixie Dean, in "The Woman Behind the Man," *Music City News*, December, 1965, pp. 17-18.

legal ground, Roy hit upon the idea of a songbook and Mildred had the plates made.

Each of the postcard-type fold-out songbooks cost a nickel to print and sold for a quarter. It was put on sale in 1941. One announcement on the Opry brought 5,000 orders the first week. Mildred, plus six girls hired from the National Life Insurance Company, worked for six months to address them. Juanita and Dixie, who was Lonnie Wilson's wife, and Mildred worked another year and a half doing the same thing. On February 28, 1942, the "Roy Acuff Songbook Show" debuted on the Opry. Each day during this period the quarters from the orders were collected from under the beds and other furniture and hauled to the bank.

Eventually almost a million copies of the songbook were sold, and it provided a large part of the revenue for the founding of Acuff-Rose and the purchase of the Acuff's first real home. (Even though prosperity was beginning to come their way, they continued to live in the trailer camp until 1943, when they finally had enough money to buy their own home. At this time, Lonnie and Pete also brought homes in suburban Nashville.)

By 1942, a decade of fiddling and starving was ending for them. Even though they were by no means rich and famous, it was beginning to be "all downhill and shady" for Roy Acuff and His Smoky Mountain Boys.

II

The Big Time

Coast to Coast

When Roy Acuff became an Opry regular in February 1938, the "Grand Ole Opry" was one of the most important country music shows in existence. However, the Opry was still only a regional show, but it was broadcast by station WSM, which had the maximum allowable power of 50,000 watts.

About this time the R. J. Reynolds Tobacco Company, through its advertising agency, William Esty and Company, recognized the sales potential of both the Opry and Roy Acuff. On January 7, 1939, Reynolds bought a half-hour portion of the show. On October 14, 1939, that segment of the Opry was placed on the NBC Red Network of 26 stations; five more stations were added by transcriptions within a few weeks. Roy was the first act to be heard on this partial hookup, and he was designated as permanent star and host. As far as Roy knows, he was the only one ever approached for the top spot on the show. There is very good reason to believe that were it not for Roy's great popularity there never would have been a network Opry. On that first show, though, the band didn't have its timing quite right and was yanked off the air; but it was corrected by the next Sunday night.

At first this partial network included only the southeastern part of the country, but early in 1940 the Red Network reached to Arizona and by July 20, 1940, of the total of 40 stations, 25 carried the Opry to the West Coast. During this time they operated on a "split network," which was two half-hour shows, each exactly alike.

44

By October 1943, time was cleared for a single half-hour show and contracts were signed creating a full NBC coast-to-coast network of more than 125 stations. By 1953 the number had grown to 176.

This meant that Roy Acuff and His Smoky Mountain Boys—as stars of the "Prince Albert Show"—were heard nationally every Saturday night. Many people were asked to write a theme; Roy's composition, "At the Grand Ole Opry Tonight," was ultimately selected as the program introduction.

Being the star of the coast-to-coast portion of the Opry gave Roy nationwide exposure. Additionally, it generated more demands for personal appearances, which, at that time, were his main source of income.

This development, though, was a two-edged sword. Saturday night is the best night for attendance at shows on the road, but Roy always had to break his schedule, whether from a regular personal appearance or an "Opry Tent Show," and rush back to Nashville every Saturday night so he could make his network Opry appearance. In publicity these Opry shows were worth their weight in gold, but Roy actually got very little for them.

Occasionally, he was too far away to return. This happened when he was in Hollywood making films. During the filming of *Night Train to Memphis*, in the latter part of 1945, he did the Opry from Californai by remote telephone wire. However, even though the network portion kept him from making extended personal appearance tours, he continued to fit the Opry into his schedule until April 1946, when he left the Opry completely, after six and a half years on the network "Prince Albert Show."

When Roy left, the network portion was taken over by Red Foley, a newcomer to the Opry, and he hosted the program until the mid-1950s, at which time it was decided that the stars should take turns and Roy, long since returned to the Opry, made 18 appearances as host on the network portion. These appearances began on February 4, 1956, and were spaced about every three months, with the last one May 7, 1960. At this point, due to the growing popularity of television, the network Opry gradually faded away and soon it was, once again, only heard over WSM.

While Roy's two and a half years as exclusive host of the coast-to coast full network Opry was his first and most continuous simultaneous national exposure, he's had similar wide public exposure at various times throughout his long career. Writers for many national magazines have written about him in general articles about the Opry or country music. One such article was in the August 11, 1952, issue of *Newsweek*, where he was on the cover. Also, articles exclusively about Roy have appeared. Examples are: *Colliers*, March 5, 1949, "Caruso of Mountain Music"; *American Magazine*, May 1944, "Backwoods Sinatra"; and *Coronet,* September 1948, "King of Mountain Music."

Roy Acuff has also appeared on such national TV variety shows as the "Kate Smith Show," "Dinah Shore Show," "Jackie Gleason Show," "Jimmy Dean Show," "Johnny Cash Show," and "Kraft Music Hall." He has also been featured on television news documentaries: "This Proud Land—The South," and "Music from the Land." Naturally, when 60-minute "Grand Ole Opry" televison shows were presented over a national hookup in 1955 and 1956, Roy performed, appearing on three. And Roy has been a guest on such currently popular TV talk programs as the "Mike Douglas Show" and Tom Snyder's "Tomorrow Show."

"At the Grand Ole Opry Tonight"

Roy Acuff's Opry performances have varied down through the years, of course—times change, as do audiences and the responses of the performers to them. Roy has always displayed warmth and sincerity, and his shows have been thoroughly professional, a capital reason for Roy being named "The King of Country Music."

The network Opry show was about the only part of the approximately four and a half hour show that was in any way rehearsed, because timing was more critical on the national segment. (And perhaps it was slightly more "formal" than other segments, if such a word can be used in connection with the "Grand Ole Opry.")

Roy frequently read poetry over the air, especially in the early days on the network Opry. He collected poems he liked and now they occupy a considerable number of binders. Some poems were cut from magazines and pasted on blank pages, others were copied by Mildred in her distinctive, beautiful handwriting. Most of the poems had a homespun quality. Some were recent compositions (although Roy never wrote any of them); others were old, such as "Twenty Years Ago," which is said to have been a favorite of Abraham Lincoln.

Some of the poems that were read over the air to background

accompaniment by the band were: "When the Preacher Came to Dinner," "Etiquette," "Working on the Farm," "Just Plain Ole Timie," "Galvanized Washing Tub" (Roy's favorite), "Home," "My First Shave," and "Complaints About Napkins." The latter poem is one very typical of the type that appealed to Roy:

Complaints About Napkins
By Cottonseed Clark

Now I ain't much of a man to complain
But I got a complaint to make.
And the complaint I got is about napkins
What some folks put on my plate.

Now when I sit down to fried chicken,
Or maybe corn on the cob;
I don't want to have to wipe my hands
On some dinky little ole thing-of-a-bob.

I want some cloth to play with;
Big enough for my hands and face.
And I don't want no little ole doily
Trimmed up with some crocheted lace.

Why, the napkins that some folks furnish
Barely cleans your upper lip.
And while you're busy cleaning the upper 'un,
The lower 'un will drip.

Of course I don't want to be unreasonable,
But I've got a right to howl;
Cause when I eat food with my fingers
I want a turkish towel.

Naturally the book of etiquette
Has got to make its own defense.
But what's the book of etiquette
Got to do with common sense?

And while I'm on the subject;
I've got myself another little peeve.
It's about them little cups of water;
Called finger bowls, I believe.

Why, the very idea;
Expecting a man to wash himself in that!
Why them things ain't big enough
To give a humming bird a bath.

I got my rights and I'll tell you now
I ain't asking any more
Than to live a peaceful happy life
Until my days are o'er.

But I'll never live it with finger bowls
And some napkins that I've seen.
But I'll live to be a ripe old age,
And what's more I'll live it clean!*

Soon Roy's recitations became so popular that other artists started doing their own readings. So when others imitated him and the number of Opry commercials began to increase, Roy finally discontinued poetry readings altogether.

In the early days at the Opry there were many spirited original Opry acts, but as time went on more of the featured vocalists simply stood up, introduced their latest record, and tried to imitate it as best they could.

Roy and his group have concentrated on keeping their act, both on the Opry and on the road, lively and entertaining. Of course an Opry "set" is somewhat more formal than a personal appearance because of exact timing, which is important for the demands of radio. Also, each word has to be watched closely and "slips" avoided because it is a live radio show directed toward a family audience. The Opry House audience is kept fully entertained even during the radio commercials. One question that puzzles listeners who have seen the Opry is, "Why does the audience laugh so much during the commercials?" Partially it is due to the comedic actions of the performers—to the medicine show antics, the leaping and dancing and the cutting up that used to occur during the entire Opry—but it is primarily noticeable during the Acuff segments. Perhaps the enjoyment is due to Roy's Yo-Yo, which is frequently chased by Oswald's feet. Or back in the days of the "Royal Crown Cola Show" (which Roy hosted from 1947 until its demise in early 1956) it might have been caused by Os Kirby getting his weekly Saturday night bath in the R. C. Cola cooler. Oswald was one of the greatest scene stealers on the Opry and frequently weeps loudly and unabashedly into the mike during a guest's (rarely one of Roy's) sad song.

The "Royal Crown Cola Show" was probably Roy's most famous Opry segment, next to the Prince Albert network show. Another well-known Acuff show was sponsored by American Ace Coffee; he also had his own "Roy Acuff Songbook Show" on the Opry. Although Roy has never really used a special theme song for these shows, through the years "Down in Union County," "Carry Me Back to the Mountains," and "Wabash Cannonball" have served as themes.

Roy introduces his guests graciously—usually mentioning the company for which they record—because he knows that most artists, as he himself did in his earlier days (and still does to some extent), like to plug their latest record. As they perform their song Roy usually steps back quietly, but once in a while his Yo-Yo manages to do some tricks, to the delight of the audience, if not always the guest.

Guests on his show usually have a generous amount of time to perform because Roy, unlike many segment hosts, will kindly cut his songs short, or dispense with them altogether, to give a guest, especially a newcomer, a chance to become popular.

As for Roy's Opry singing, he always picks his own songs and sometimes tends to get in a rut; singing one particular song every week for several weeks at a time. He is aware of this habit and tries to control it. However, the weekly requests for his famous songs, such as "The Bird" and the "Cannonball," made by people who have traveled hundreds of miles for a once-in-a-lifetime visit to the Opry, practically force him to sing those songs at least every week. Because of these requests and because of the limited time, he rarely gets to sing his older songs on the Opry.

Before each Opry segment the band gathers in the dressing room. During most of the years at the Ryman, it was the tiny first room just off stage to the audience's left. In 1965, working conditions at the Opry became much more pleasant for the Acuff band when Roy brought his museum from Gatlinburg to Nashville and they used the back of the Exhibit complex as a dressing room. It was spacious and pleasant, and served as a much more comfortable waiting room for the hours between Opry segments. In March of 1974, when the Opry moved to Opryland, the Acuff group was assigned Dressing Room no. 1. As Roy said, "It beats changing clothes in the back of a car." The gang does not consider that it rehearses as such. It simply gathers to make sure that all the instruments are in tune, that everyone is agreed on the key of each song, to warm up Roy's voice, and to get the tempo straight for each song, and to figure out who is going to "kick it off" and when and what "breaks" will be taken.

Despite these rehearsals, Roy's Opry performance of a song today is frequently much more informal than a road rendition. Roy will sometimes announce the key, and occasionally he will say something like, "I am going to throw you boys a curve. I don't know who takes it off, or the key." Once he gets into the song the performance is frequently reminiscent of an early recording session. Between the verses, breaks are announced, such as "Fiddle one, Howard" . . . "Let's go, Shot" . . . "Come in there, Jimmie, yea" . . . "Come in here with that Dobro, Os" . . . "Play it, yea." Or when there is a little confusion, Roy will say, "Who's got it, boys?" During the song, if the microphone level slips, Roy has been known to complain, audibly, in a nice way, right over the air. If the "clock on the wall" is running out on them, the song, especially if it's a train song, will sometimes end by Roy saying, "Blow us out of here!"

Roy usually tries to end most Opry segments with a hymn, which he frequently likes to perform with his band grouped around him. He calls this a "family group style of singing," and no attempt is made at close harmony. Roy frequently starts a song with one of his favorite expressions, "Gather 'round me, children." On these hymns the mountain frivolity stops, Oswald removes his hat, and the whole group lets go in a style that convinces some listeners that they are singing to heavenly accompaniment.

No Man Is an Island

Opry appearances, even for the biggest stars, have never provided enough income for any act. Of necessity, the performers have had to go out on the road. When Roy first came to the Opry, he continued to play at schoolhouses and auditoriums, much as he had done in Knoxville.

In 1941 the idea came to use a tent show to reach the people during summertime. The first Opry tent show was performed in a big 85 by 180-foot tent owned by Ollie Hamilton and managed by Jamup and Honey. Uncle Dave and Roy were also part of the act.

The following summer the tent bore Roy's name, although he did not actually own it. By the summer of 1943 Roy purchased a tent and equipment and, with Ollie Hamilton and Ford Rush* as his managers, headlined a tent show that made very successful tours of the South, and even ventured north during the summers of 1943, 1944, and 1945. The tent had five posts and could seat 2,200 people. When overflow crowds would clamor, the sides were lifted and

---

*Ford Rush had performed as a solo act, known as the High Sheriff, on the Opry and then took over management of the Artists' Service Bureau when the post was vacated by David Stone. He then left to become manager of Roy's tent show.

another 400 people could see the show. Besides Roy, acts included Uncle Dave, Sam and Kirk McGee, and Robert Lunn. Other Opry performers, such as Bill Monroe, took out their own tent shows. However, it was generally felt that any tent show troupe having Roy had "all the Grand Ole Opry that really counted."

Of course, the big headache of the Acuff troupe at this time was that every Saturday night they had to return to Nashville for the network Opry. Also, the tents were expensive and cumbersome to carry, and needed a large crew of canvasmen to erect and dismantle them. But these "Grand Ole Opry" tent shows were an excellent way of meeting the people and Roy continued to work with them through the summer of 1945.

As a "Grand Ole Opry" performer, Roy Acuff's popularity grew and was at its peak during the latter war years. It is not an exaggeration to state that Roy alone transformed the Opry from just one of the many regional barn dances into a national institution. But during this period Roy was becoming increasingly dissatisfied with the network "Prince Albert Show." Many reliable sources staunchly maintain that the sponsor, in response to Madison Avenue marketing ideas, wanted him to get away from the more traditional styles and modernize his performances. Roy maintains that no such pressure was applied, that the trouble lay elsewhere.

At this time, during the height of his career, Roy's road business was tremendous and he was receiving lucrative movie offers, but he began to feel that returning to Nashville every Saturday night was not only a headache but a financial disaster. It was generally understood on the Opry that all the stars were paid equally, at regular union scale. This arrangement though, was not fair to Roy, who was the heart and soul of the "Prince Albert Show" and the Opry's biggest star. He felt that others were receiving more money than he, while he was carrying the burdens of the show. When Roy requested what he considered was fair remuneration, considering the circumstances, he was refused. April 6, 1946, was his final Opry appearance. (In a letter written by Mildred and signed by Roy to Jimmie Riddle offering him his job back, this date is given as the final date Roy was to be on the Opry. The newspapers, however, listed him through April 27, 1946.)

In the one year that Roy Acuff was away from the Opry, his affiliation, or lack of it, was a matter of semantics. Some maintain he "quit the Opry cold," others say he was given an "extended leave of absence." Roy says, "I had connection with the Opry at all times—through Harry Stone." During his absence his act was frequently billed as "Roy Acuff and His Grand Ole Opry Gang."

With Roy's immense popularity on the Grand Ole Opry tent shows of the previous summers in mind, Ollie Hamilton sold Roy on the idea of spending the summer of 1946 performing in his own tent show. Roy spent thousands of dollars for the equipment to get the Roy Acuff Tent Theatre on the road. Hamilton handled advance bookings. Ford Rush acted as master of ceremonies, and Spot, out of the navy, went along and handled the money. In effect the show had three co-managers.

From Nashville they went through the Virginias and Carolinas and then to Pennsylvania. In Ohio, during early July, they were joined by Jimmie Riddle, also fresh from military service. From there the show proceeded through Texas and then snaked through the deep South, and by November it was in Florida. About once a month Mildred would drive the wives to see the boys.

Persons connected with the troupe remember that, except for one small area in Pennsylvania, the attendance was very good. Spot especially remembered Austin, Texas. Torrential rains had placed a foot of water on the ground, so the huge crowd sat on the backs of their chairs, with their feet on the seats.

Even though the attendance was satisfactory, for various reasons the Roy Acuff Tent Theatre gradually came apart at the seams. Hamilton dropped out somewhere, leaving Spot and Rush as co-managers. There was trouble with the roustabouts, and the managing and handling of the tents became unbearable. After so many summers under hot and confining tents, Roy was getting extremely tired. He further believed that he could do better with regular appearances, even though the show was making money, and the idea of a West Coast tour became increasingly attractive. Ford Rush begged him to stay with the tent show and Roy accommodated him for awhile, but finally, in Florida, Roy decided he'd had enough tenting and returned to Nashville. Rush phoned and asked what should be done with the equipment. Roy said to sell it, and it was sold at a considerable loss.

Roy was not home long when word came that Foreman Phillips and Marty Landau, prominent West Coast bookers and promoters, wanted to sponsor a West Coast tour. This tour lasted the first three months of 1947. The troupe, including Spot, went up U.S. Highway

99 and came down U.S. Highway 101. In January, in Hollywood, they recorded one of their Columbia sessions. It was an extremely worthwhile tour and Roy had the satisfaction of earning nightly the amount the Opry had refused him.

Upon his return to Nashville, Roy was hospitalized for a minor ailment. There he had two visitors, Harry Stone and Ernest Tubb. Harry said, "Roy, the Opry is losing many of its people, and it looks like maybe we're going under if you don't come back and be with us. Please come and help us out." Roy was surprised that he meant that much to the "Grand Ole Opry." "Roy, you mean everything," Harry assured him. "We wish that you would change your mind and come back." Roy responded, saying, "Harry, if I mean that much to WSM and the 'Grand Ole Opry,' I will come back and I will do everything I can to help the Opry at all times."

Why was it apparently so easy to get Roy to return to WSM? Roy says simply that Stone's and Tubb's pleadings turned the trick. Also a return to WSM entitled him to the station's Artists' Service Bureau's booking and management privileges. And, of course, before actually returning, Roy found that he would be paid more than union scale. (From this point on Roy has continued to receive more than union scale for his Opry appearances. This is no secret—all the big stars receive extra money. However, the extra wages are not equal to what they could make on a Saturday night personal appearance elsewhere, but the prestige of being on the Opry is more than enough compensation.)

So on April 26, 1947, Roy Acuff returned to the Opry, as host of the "Royal Crown Cola Show." The fans welcomed him by regularly giving Roy's show more applause than Red Foley's network "Prince Albert Show."

There are accounts that Roy wanted to be reinstated as the host of the network P. A. show, but Roy maintains that was not the case. Without the network pressure to be in Nashville every single Saturday night, Roy's schedule had more flexibility.

Roy Acuff's year away from the "Grand Ole Opry" was not entirely a happy one. Roy had started off elated that he didn't have to sacrifice every Saturday night's road revenue to the Opry "Prince Albert Show." Optimism was extremely high: Roy Acuff and His Smoky Mountain Boys had been the rage of the "Grand Ole Opry," and they had every reason to believe that on their own they would be extremely successful. But events dampened their expectations.

In retrospect, it appears that the apex of Roy's career was reached just before he left the Opry, and that while the West Coast tour was successful and his return to the Opry was satisfying, he never totally regained his pre-1946 popularity. Perhaps, to be fully successful away from the Opry, Roy had needed a topnotch personal agent. Perhaps the times and changing trends in music would have diminished Roy's popularity even if he had remained as host of the network "Prince Albert Show." In any case, Roy was still very popular and, as of April 1947, the name of Roy Acuff was again linked with that of WSM's "Grand Ole Opry."

Some Partnerships

Even before Roy first appeared on the "Grand Ole Opry," he was awe-struck by it. When he became a regular, and his popularity grew, he had even more reason to be grateful for the opportunity the Opry gave him to make good in the country music business. In his first songbook, Roy stated that next to his family he owed his success to WSM. Certainly the events of the summer of 1946 only increased his admiration of and respect for the power of the Opry and its value both to his performances and to country music.

Roy believes that most important to the rise of the country music industry was the founding of station WSM by the National Life and Accident Insurance Company and the employment of George Hay as station director. It was Hay who started the country music program that later became known as the "Grand Ole Opry." The Opry, in turn, brought country music to the nation and kept it in the limelight.

"Without the Opry we wouldn't be here today," is one of Roy's typical comments. In his speech for the thirtieth Opry anniversary, he spoke of how much the National Life's WSM and the Opry meant to him and his family, and how he would always be very grateful and would endeavor to be faithful to the Opry's traditions.

Despite Harry Stone's statement in 1947 when he visited Roy in the hospital, Roy has his own feeling toward the Opry. "I never thought the Opry needed me," says Roy. "I need the Opry. I still get a little shaky every time I go out on that stage." It is not surprising, therefore, that few people guard the Opry's traditions more closely than Roy Acuff. His attitude toward the old-time string bands is one example of this.

I owe much to the boys that started the "Grand Ole Opry" and I shall always be grateful to them. Such people as Sam and Kirk McGee, the Possum Hunters, the Crook Brothers, the Gully Jumpers, the Fruit Jar Drinkers, and many, many others. They made it possible for me to come to Nashville and to be among people who live country music.

When Roy first came to the Opry, these musical groups had a big part in the shows, but through the years, despite their many contributions to country music, they have been all but obscured by the featured vocalists who have, beginning with Roy, increasingly dominated the Opry. The old-time groups have been relegated to fill-ins, playing for the square dancers and for the "bridges" between programs. They're rarely formally introduced and are scarcely noticed by the audience. In fact, during the early 1960s, they were informed that there were too many old-time band groupings for the spots allowed for them on the show, and so they were forced to consolidate into only two. The names retained were the Crook Brothers and the Fruit Jar Drinkers.

"D" Kilpatrick, Opry manager at the time, instituted this consolidation and defended it, saying the measure was needed for the economics of time-selling, because the groups often played three or four minutes instead of the two they were supposed to play. Also, he said, the groups weren't really the old-time bands anyway, since about half of each group consisted of younger replacements for members who had died.

It's unfortunate that these wonderful old-time musicians are neglected by the very institution to which they gave life. This is true of every Opry segment, save one—Roy Acuff's. Even if they just have a fill-in part at the end of his show, they can usually count on a lavish introduction, which includes each member's name and the history of his original group. This history frequently alludes rather pointedly to the fact that a number of bands were pared down to two. In these introductions Roy usually says "We need them bad," or "We don't ever want to lose them." or "They held down the fort before I came and now I am holding it down." And more often than not, Roy's introduction is followed by a performance, not just fill-in accompaniment. The time for it was often obtained by Roy giving up one of his own songs.

Roy's concern for the preservation of a musical tradition has been marked by his resistance to the trend leading away from traditional instrumentation on the Opry. (Around 1939, Sam McGee tried to play an electric guitar on the Opry, but due to Judge Hay, it was only played briefly.) In 1940 when Pee Wee King introduced the first electric instrument, a steel guitar, Roy was clearly upset—"This will ruin everything!" A few years later Bob Willis was a guest on Roy's network "Prince Albert Show" and refused to perform without his drums. A compromise was reached and the drums were placed behind a curtain. In the early 1950s, when other barn dances were failing and the Opry officials felt that change was needed to survive, drums and electric instruments began to appear regularly. Roy objected very emotionally but eventually he, too, went along.

For many years many country music artists who have never been on the Opry, or who have long since left it, have billed their performances as "Grand Ole Opry Shows," or as being "Direct from Nashville." Many of these presentations were inferior and the audience would blame the Opry. Roy has always been keenly aware of the importance of Opry billings, and of assaults on its identity, and such misrepresentations disturb him greatly.

Roy's concern is that the Opry continue to thrive. One worry of his is the lack of showmanship on the program; he believes that a large percentage of the huge crowds the Opry continues to draw go away disappointed. But his part of the Opry remains lively, with plenty of clowning, such as the actions of Bert Hutcherson, an original Gully Jumper who was relocated to the Crook Brothers.

In one routine Bert snuck up behind Roy and reached in his coat pocket. Then we learn that Roy had accidentally lost his coat in an outhouse, and had to fish it out with a stick. Bert told him that the coat was ruined and so why did Roy bother? To which Roy replied, "Oh, I know, but my lunch is in the pocket!" Such old jokes figure prominently on the Acuff Opry segments, and are one reason why Roy says his years on the Opry have been "fun and a pleasure."

This camaraderie between an old-time band member and the biggest star demonstrates the spirit of the Opry that used to be a predominant feature, both on and off the stage. The cast of the show had no caste lines. Roy would bob up periodically with gift boxes containing freshly killed pheasants and all the condiments to go with them. Other stars would do the same. However, like many other things in this modern world, the family unity and fellowship of Opry personnel has been lacking somewhat in the past few years. However, the love of what they do can still be seen—as when musicians do some jamming between their segments, and when Roy Acuff and Bill

Monroe—the "Father of Bluegrass"—sing their hearts out together in a dressing room to practically no audience.

Roy has tried to maintain Opry camaraderie and spirit by countless good deeds. So many, in fact, that he is known backstage as "Helping Hand Number 1." He is always loaning money to someone. An example was Judge Hay, who seemed to frequently be in debt. Roy even bought the country music newspaper *Pickin' and Singin' News* and let Hay run it to help him out. The introduction of guest dignitaries or new acts is usually given to Roy because of his prestige. Roy has become a father figure to Opry personnel and is the patriach of the program.

Roy Acuff is constantly on the lookout for talented artists who deserve the same chance to develop as he had on the Opry. In 1940, the Wilburn Family—consisting of five children and the parents—were on their way to Birmingham, Alabama, to perform in a talent contest. On the way a tire blew out and they were too late to enter. Roy and Bill Monroe were also in Birmingham. So Pop Wilburn lined the kids up by the Acuff car and when Roy came out the family was singing the hymn "Farther Along." The selection of this particular hymn was providential because it was a song that Roy had heard and wanted to learn. They taught it to him and that night Roy put the Wilburns on stage, even though they weren't eligible for prizes, and the audience responded enthusiastically. When Roy returned to Nashville he asked David Stone to bring them to the Opry and Stone complied. Stories similar to this are numerous.

Roy discovered Little Jimmie Dickens in Michigan and arranged for his Opry audition. Then Roy loaned him the Smoky Mountain Boys for his first Columbia session, in which one of the numbers was "Take an Old Cold Tater and Wait." When Patsy Cline first came to Nashville, she slept on park benches because of lack of funds for a hotel room. Roy was one of the first to give Patsy a chance, says Dorothy Gable, formerly of the Hall of Fame, when he featured her at Dunbar Cave and on his "Centennial Park Show."

Uncle Dave Macon was the Opry's biggest star at the time Roy arrived. The two took a liking to each other and Uncle Dave coined the name "Roy Boy." Roy and Minnie Pearl headed a committee that carried out a project to erect the Uncle Dave Macon Monument on U.S. Highway 70 near Woodbury, Tennessee. With typical modesty, Roy later explained, "Frank [Governor Clement] saw that the monument was put up." The truth is that the governor did, indeed, arrange for the land, but Roy contributed heavily to the monument fund.

He always makes it a point to visit ailing Opry artists. When George Wilkerson, the great fiddler and leader of the Fruit Jar Drinkers, lay near death with a radio by his side, Roy sang "Thy Burdens Are Greater than Mine" on the Opry and dedicated it to Grandpappy George Wilkerson. Roy also joined Grandpa Jones and Minnie Pearl in visiting Pop Stoneman just days before his death on June 14, 1968.

When WSM Vice President Bob Cooper proposed the creation of an Opry trust fund to provide for needy people connected with the Opry and country music, Roy was on the first beneficiary committee. Through the years he has been very concerned about artists who have found themselves in financial trouble. "The evil of it all is money," says Roy. "Some of them just seem like they can't take success. Maybe they're just not ready for it or something, I don't know."

One of the most obvious examples of Roy Acuff's loyalty to the Opry is his determination that no matter what happens the show must go on. For example, one Saturday night the lights went out, and Roy sang appropriately, "Wait for the Light to Shine." However the most memorable incident along this line occurred on April 6, 1968.

Martin Luther King, Jr., was killed on Thursday, April 4, 1968, and on Saturday a 7:00 P.M. curfew was ordered in Nashville because Negro rioting was feared. This meant that for the first time in its long history the "Grand Ole Opry" would not be presented live; a taped version was played on the air.

On Saturday morning hundreds of people began to line up as usual outside the Opry House to get tickets. Some didn't know about the curfew. Many of them had heard about it while driving to Nashville but they couldn't believe the Opry would be cancelled; after all, the "Grand Ole Opry" had never missed a live Saturday night show in its entire 43-year history.

About this same time, 10:00 A.M., the Music City Playhouse was having its grand opening around the corner from the Opry House. Its premier attraction was a 39-minute film showing some of the Opry performers, with interviews of others. Roy and many celebrities were in the audience.

At the conclusion of the film the lights went on and the audience of celebrities and tourists prepared to leave. Just then Roy Acuff stood up in the middle of the theater and said:

> Friends, can I have your attention a minute? There's something I'd like to say. We all know there's a curfew on in Nashville. It starts at 7:00 o'clock and there's not going to be any Opry tonight. It seems a shame that so many people have come in from out of town and won't be able to see it. Let's see if we can find a place and give them a show!

Roy then went to see Eddie Cummings, manager of Mr. Ed's, a square dance hall, which was located above Roy's Exhibit, an attration for tourists where Roy had his famous collections. The arrangement to use the hall in the building was easily reached—the space was rented from Roy.(The empty Ryman Auditorium couldn't be used because it would have required police and firemen, and they were all deployed at trouble spots.) The word spread to the milling crowd outside and by 2:00 P.M. the place was jammed.

This substitute Opry was presented by Sam and Kirk McGee, some guest stars, and, of course, Roy Acuff and His Smoky Mountain Boys, along with Harold Weakley. During the show there was a rumor of a march uptown and so Oswald's crocodile tears had to compete with siren screams. Some nearby buildings were closed by uniformed men with rifles. But upstairs there was laughter and applause, for the audience was doing what it had come to Nashville to do—attend the "Grand Ole Opry."

When Roy joined the Opry, he marked the transition from a country music band featuring a singer, as in the old string bands, to a singer who was backed by a band. Shortly after his arrival, the Opry entered into agreements with R. J. Reynolds and Republic Pictures that resulted in bringing national recognition to the Opry. What occurred was, Roy Acuff's immense popularity transformed the "Grand Ole Opry" from a local barn dance into a national program that featured star talent. During World War II, the names of Roy Acuff and the "Grand Ole Opry" became synonymous. While it is hard to pin the success of the Opry on any one person, many, including Judge Hay, feel that Roy Acuff was without question the biggest drawing card the Opry has ever had. Sponsors, especially during the 1940s, clamored for Roy because he boosted their sales so tremendously.

Other stars have joined Roy in the Opry limelight. But it is still true, to quote Wesley Rose, "Going to the Opry and not finding Roy

Acuff is like going to Yankee Stadium in 1927 and not getting to see Ruth or Gehrig."

The Opry is aware of its debt to Roy. Anniversary ceremonies usually aren't a part of Opry programs, but several of Roy's Opry anniversaries have been celebrated. Before his thirtieth anniversary show he told a reporter during an interview that he doubted there would be any ceremony. "It'll just be another day to me." Roy said. "They don't pay any attention to how long you've been here." But on his segment he was duly honored.

Today, the most important aspect of Roy's partnership with the Opry is with Opryland. It was assumed by many of Roy's closest friends that the "Grand Ole Man of the Grand Ole Opry" would so resist change that he would not approve of the new Opryland. The assumption was far from the truth, as shown by this incident. On June 30, 1970, at the new Opryland ground-breaking ceremonies, Roy was introduced as "a senior statesman of country music." Roy responded, saying, "This is a beautiful day in my life," and he blew on the steamboat whistle box given him by Judge Hay, the one used by Hay during his long tenure on the Opry. The whistle was the signal for Oswald to break the ground with a plow pulled by two mules. As the ground broke Roy said, quoting Hay's famous Opry line, "Let 'er go, boys!"

Opryland opened in May 1972, but it was a body without a heart. While crowds flocked to the new park, they still had to go to the old Ryman to see the Opry. Opryland received its heart with the gala opening of the new Opry House on March 16, 1974.

Late in 1972 Roy said, "I've made a request that if I'm still here when the Opry House opens, that they let me be the first one to go on the stage. I just want to open the curtain and sing two songs. Then they can have it." At the time Roy could not know what an oversimplification this was.

In 1973 National Life conceived the idea of inviting the President to attend the opening of the new Opry House. In so doing they used Roy's name. The invitation was repeated by Wesley Rose and Tex Ritter when, on December 14, 1973, they presented President Richard Nixon with a recording that thanked him for having country music at the White House.

In January 1974, a six-foot circle of the Ryman's oak stage was inserted into the front center of the new Opry House's large maple stage and Roy was the first to walk across it. Thus the first part of his request was honored. By early March, word came that the second part of his request, to be the first performer on that stage, would be accomplished at an event attended by the President.

When the great day came, Roy had trouble getting to the Opry House. He was carrying a multitude of materials needed for the big night and he was stopped by Secret Service men as he entered Opryland. Roy tried to tell the Secret Service men who he was, but they didn't believe him. Finally another agent approached and said, "He's telling you the truth, because I have seen him on television."

The President and Mrs. Nixon landed in separate planes at the Nashville airport about six o'clock that evening and were met by Governor Winfield Dunn and Senators William Brock and Howard Baker. While they were on their way to the Opry House, the first performance of the "Grand Ole Opry" began at its new Opry House.

It was 6:30; everyone knew Roy Acuff would be the first performer*and that he would sing the "Wabash Cannonball." However, no one expected what appeared—the startled audience saw on a huge screen a 36-year-old Roy Acuff singing the "Wabash Cannonball" in the 1940 movie *Grand Ole Opry*. About half-way through the song, the house lights came on and revealed a 70-year-old Roy Acuff and his group onstage below the screen. They blended into the singing of the song without missing a note. The effect was awesome. Many people later told Roy that the performance was fantastic. Following a few introductory remarks, Roy then led the entire cast, which was assembled onstage, in singing "You Are My Sunshine." After calling a square dance, he then introduced Bill Anderson and retired to his dressing room.

A few minutes past seven o'clock the Nixons arrived and sat in the balcony where they could be seen by almost everyone. The politicians wanted to introduce them on the stage, but Nixon was adamant, saying, "Roy Acuff will do it." The Nixons were accompanied to the stage by Mrs. Tex Ritter and William Weaver, chairman of the board of National Life. Weaver gave the President a yellow Yo-Yo saying, "Mr. President, if you want to bring the house down, pull this out of your pocket when you get onstage."

When the presidential party arrived, Roy was called from his dressing room and ended his short introduction with these words:

---

*The stars appeared in alphabetical order. In this way Roy's request was honored, and without animosity.

> Tonight we're honored by the very first President to visit with us at
> the Grand Ole Opry—and you can know that we boys and girls, we're just
> delighted that this has happened while *we* are here at the Grand Ole Opry.
> I just couldn't say the words that would *really* let you people know
> how delighted I am that I can be here and take the microphone and ask
> the President and Mrs. Nixon, with their troupe, if they would mind
> honoring us and coming down and be on the stage here this evening. We
> would be delighted to have you.

At this point the Opry House band played "Hail to the Chief"
and the presidential party walked down to the stage. It was one of
the warmest welcomes the President had ever received. The atmosphere was relaxed and friendly. After the great applause died down,
Mrs. Ritter presented a dulcimer to Mrs. Nixon.

Roy then suggested that everyone should sing "Happy Birthday"
to Mrs. Nixon, and added that he hoped it wouldn't be imposing if
he asked the President to play the piano. Nixon replied, "Well, in this
very professional company, I'm a little embarrassed to try and play
that thing there. I haven't even learned to play with this thing." At
that moment he pulled out the Yo-Yo and it promptly fell to the end
of its string. Roy was completely surprised, having known nothing of
Weaver's idea.

After the President played "Happy Birthday," he played "My
Wild Irish Rose" as an encore. Roy then said, "He's a real trouper."
At this point the dedicatory plaque that now rests in front of the
Opry House was unveiled. When Roy returned to the microphone,
Nixon quipped, "Must be time for the commercial." Roy, in an aside
to announcer Grant Turner, remarked, "He's got me stunned."

Roy then formally introduced the President:

> Ladies and gentlemen, about a year ago I was invited to the White
> House, along with many others, to entertain the prisoners of war. After I
> sung my song, Mr. Bob Hope, who was the master of ceremonies, asked me
> back to the stage, and I remarked that it was the highlight of my career.
> But you know, I never *dreamed* that a night like this would ever come to
> Roy Acuff. So I'd like to say to the world that is listening in from our new
> home here in Opryland USA—Ladies and gentlemen, the President of the
> United States—Richard Nixon.

Nixon responded by telling of Roy's appearance before the
POWs. Then he proceeded to heap praise on country music, and
ended by stating that country music makes America a better country.

At this point the President again tried to "play the Yo-Yo," with very little success. Roy showed him how to put the string on his finger and advised, "Now turn your hand over and let it go out. Now, jerk it back!" When these presidential Yo-Yo lessons obviously didn't work, Nixon said humorously, "I'll stay here and try to learn how to use the Yo-Yo, you go and be President, Roy."

Roy then asked everyone to sing "Stay A Little Longer." Nixon, who had told Roy that he was thoroughly enjoying himself, thus putting Roy more at ease, complied with obvious zest. Roy asked, "Mr. President, do you belong to the musicians' union? You'll get some talk on this if you don't. Come on over here, I want you to play the piano again." The President replied that he was an honorary member of the musicians union in New York City, and everyone stood and sang "God Bless America" with presidential piano accompaniment. After this, the Nixons left the stage.

Offstage Roy had a special gift for the President. It was his idea, his project. He presented Nixon with a replica, specially made, of the steamboat whistle horn Judge Hay had used to open the Opry. On the side of the horn was engraved the names of the entire Opry cast. The presidential party left the Opry House shortly after eight o'clock.

Many people said that with the President's Watergate troubles, the Opry did him more good than he did the Opry. Roy vehemently disagrees. Roy was practically ecstatic that evening and it was as he said, the highlight of his career. "Something like this wouldn't happen again in 100 years, or even one million years," said Roy. "Everything just worked out! The President's visit was the greatest thing that's ever happened to the Opry and country music."

His partnership with the Opry is really a part of another partnership: with country music as a whole. One of the primary ways in which this partnership manifests itself is in the obligation Roy feels to other, less fortunate, members of the industry. Archie Campbell stated it well: "Roy Acuff's a compassionate man. He cares about everyone in country music." Many a hotel bill has been paid for a country music performer and only the cashier knew from whom the payment came. One time Roy spent $500 on advance promotion for a show in Georgia before learning that a small, unpublicized outfit had been previously booked. Without a word he took the loss and withdrew his engagement. The small group earned $300; Roy would have netted $2,500. Another time, Roy had promised to make a

guest appearance on Wally Fowler's "All Night Sing" one New Year's
Eve, then learned his agent had booked him for an out-of-town party
that night at a $2,000 fee. January 2 found no increase recorded in
Roy's bank account.*

Not only performers benefit from Roy Acuff's fatherly attitude
toward the industry. According to Bob Cooper, one day Roy was
looking through WSM's music library and he overheard two secretaries talking about a lady who needed $500 for an operation. When
he came out of the library he said, "Give me that lady's name and
address." The secretaries, guessing what he had on his mind, said that
they were sorry he had overheard and that he really shouldn't give
away his money like that. Roy replied, "I make my money the way I
want and I'll spend it the way I want."

Where did country music get its name? It used to be called hillbilly music. On the "Johnny Cash TV Show" Roy said, "I didn't
resent being called a hillbilly because we—we are hillbillies. In fact I
thought it was quite an honor—a hillbilly fiddler." During his March
1974 appearance on Tom Snyder's "Tomorrow Show," when asked
if he resented the word hillbilly, Roy said:

> Not at all. I was raised back in the hills, back in the mountains. The
> word hillbilly was a real good word. Back in Maynardville, Union County,
> where I'm from, we were considered hillbillies. We didn't resent it; we
> took it proudly, because there is nothing wrong with a hillbilly. I love
> people from the rural sections. I like people in the city too; it takes us all
> to make the world go. But we should never forget that the hillbilly, the
> guy that's out in the early morning on the farm milking the cow, followin'
> the plow through the day, and feeding the stock at night is making the liv-
> ing for you and I.

Country musicians don't necessarily dislike being called hillbillies. But they have become convinced that many people react ad-
versely to the term, so country music is now usually substituted.

Who plays real country music? The answer is folk musicians, but
the term folk is rarely used to apply to Roy and similar artists, although Roy has played at various "folk" festivals, including the one
at Newport. Roy Acuff has seldom called himself a folk artist, although he is one in a truer sense than the urban performers, such as
Pete Seeger and Joan Baez, who apply the term to themselves. The

---

*Dickson Hartwell, "Caruso of Mountain Music," *Colliers*, March 5, 1949, p. 42.

true folk don't think of themselves as folk; therefore, the term is used by those outside the rural culture.*

In Roy Acuff's opinion country music is the backbone of American music because it has a good moral foundation. It's real and it's emotional and it always reappears when the fad of the moment falters. Country music is full of Christianity and sympathy and understanding. It helps to make people better. There will always be a demand for it. Roy also believes that "If you aren't a country boy, you can't write or sing real country music." An exception to this statement was Fred Rose.

The songs have a simplicity and heartfelt feeling that can be put on paper or performed only by someone who is raised in the culture. As for the instrumentation, Roy believes that "the fiddle and banjo have made country music—every bit of it." But he concedes that the guitar and other instruments have their place. Generally speaking, Roy has gradually gone along with the newer instrumentations. The Nashville Sound he believes to be simply a term that was invented in the Nashville recording studios and immediately performed in studios in New York and Hollywood. The difference is due more to the engineers with their new echo chambers, reverb units, and the like than to the sound of the performers.

As for bluegrass music, Roy believes it is a type of country music that is presented a little differently. He always goes out of his way to point out that Bill Monroe was the "Father of Bluegrass."

Rock and roll hurt country music record sales, although not personal appearances, during its tenure in the 1950s. Roy feels that it had its place, which he knew was just a passing phase, but he thinks that it did not mix well with country music. Roy says:

> When rock and roll came alone, my son was a teen-ager and we bought every record that came out. I used to sit and listen with him. They made a lot of noise, but they were pretty good.
>
> I've worked with rock and roll performers, but I don't approve of them going down on the floor wriggling around. As far as listening to them sing on a record, I don't mind at all. But I don't like to watch them.
>
> Elvis Presley was a country boy to start with, and he just kindly put a swivel on his hip and did country music. I like to swing out, but I swing it from the heart. Presley swings it from the hip.

Roy believes that the singers who put the greatest feeling into

_____

*Bill C. Malone, *Country Music U.S.A. a Fifty-Year History* (Austin: University of Texas Press, 1968), p. x.

their songs will be the most successful, and this characteristic applies to popular music as well. "In my book, Ray Charles puts more feeling into a song than any singer alive." says Roy. He has a great understanding of lyrics. You can tell in his voice that the songs he sings go to his heart, and he passes them on to you the same way that he understands it himself. I think every great artist does that."

What about the Beatles? "The Beatles, animals, bears, and bugs— they're all right. Must be, since millions think so. They sing country-type music in a different style. I believe their hairdos put them over but I have to give them credit for being smart." It takes a showman to know one!

Basically, Roy feels that long hair, beards, and dirty clothes are hard to accept in our society, let alone in country music. "Country music reflects our good American way of life. It is down to earth, for the home—not to get all hepped up and smoke a lot of marijuana and go wild about." Even so, Roy cut an album with the Nitty Gritty Dirt Band in 1971.

In his personal taste, Roy says, "I like symphonic, especially the string section, opera, and semiclassical music. I like anything sweet. When I am relaxing I don't want to listen to country music, and I hope the other fellows feel the same about my music when they are at home." Once Roy and Howdy Forrester sat in the third row of one of the violinist Nathan Milstein's Nashville concerts and were the biggest attraction there.

Roy Acuff has seen country music change, and has even changed his presentations, but in general he is a living example of the old saying, "You can take the boy out of the country but you can't take the country out of the boy." Furthermore, he has spent his career defending country music from a formidable quartet: exploitation, infiltration, desecration, and despoilment. Once when the city fathers of Nashville were vacillating about a country music project, Roy went before the chamber of commerce and told the members in very strong terms just what country music meant to Nashville.

In the late 1950s a bill was before Congress which, if passed, would have been detrimental to country music by killing Broadcast Music, Inc. (BMI), which is the performing rights licensing agency that gives country artists a chance to earn a living from their creativity. In his testimony—presented to the subcommittee by Governor Frank Clement—Roy reiterated his feeling that country music has more human understanding and feeling than any other kind of music:

> I see it when I stand in front of my audiences. I've seen them cry and I've seen them with all the joys that are possible with country music. Why shouldn't they? The music is respected in every way. I have spent my life in country music and I want to object violently to the idea that country music is cheap or inferior or that it is being forced on the public.

The audiences comprise another partnership of Roy's. There's a core to this relationship. "I just try to be a friend to people," says Roy. "I have never felt that I was above my public. Whatever I accomplish depends on them."

Roy takes pleasure in walking around Nashville and meeting people. "I don't hide. I walk around downtown and sign autographs, but I don't stop too much. I keep moving. It's fun to hear people say when I go by, 'Isn't that Roy Acuff?' I'm glad when someone can recognize me."

When tour buses began making a curcuit of various stars' homes in Nashville, Roy had the buses come in the driveway so he could walk out and meet the people. After awhile, though, there were so many tours that he curtailed this practice. But a tour guide still reports, "Roy Acuff is one of the few stars who doesn't run inside his house when the tour bus stops."

Mainly out of concern for his fans is why Roy supports Opryland so enthusiastically. "I have seen people sitting on the curb in front of the Ryman with their feet in the gutter crying because they could not get Opry tickets. At Opryland they are at least able to sit on a bench under a nice green tree to do their crying. Opryland provides a better environment—it's a place where lasting friendships can be made."

On his final Ryman show, Roy told the audience:

> Certainly there are certain memories of this old house that will go with us forever. Not all of them are good. Not all of them. Many of them are. But some of them are *punishment*. Punishment in a way that we ask you to come to visit with us and then we sit you out in this audience here and in the hot summer we sell you a fan for a dollar. You do your own air-conditioning. And some of you, we sell you a cushion to sit on because the seats are not just the most comfortable as they can be. But out in Opryland, when you come to see us, we'll furnish the air-conditioner. We'll furnish the cushion seats.
>
> You just don't know how much we do appreciate you people. It's *you*

who have made the Grand Ole Opry so successful. Will you not forget us
when we move into our new building? You'll love us for being out there
and we'll love you for coming to see us. Thank you. God bless you all—
good night.

The most outstanding characteristic of a country music fan is his
loyalty. An Acuff fan it seems, is an Acuff fan for eternity. Frequently Roy's contacts with fans are touching. An example is the
woman who asked Roy for his autograph and then told him that she
was going to have an operation. "Nothing serious I hope?" said Roy.
The woman replied that she was going to have a hysterectomy and
asked if she could kiss him. Roy, long adept at handling emergencies,
acceded to the request, commenting, "Maybe that'll help you get
well sooner."

At the height of his career, Roy received about 2,000 letters a
week, some of which contained proposals of marriage or adoption.
He's also received advice in letters, some of it well over ten pages
long, on everything from how to grow spiritually and live longer, to
exactly how and where to escape from Mildred so he can be free
once more for a new life of wedded bliss with the passionate fan who
cannot live without him. Through the years Roy has had three or
four fan clubs. One was started by Mrs. Gussie Glasscock in 1949.
The last one was formed by Willis Glenn in 1954. During the course
of this club Roy bought it a mimeograph machine and entertained
the Glenns at his home.

Stories of famous personalities visiting grievously ill fans are told
about many stars. Roy is no exception. One concerns Charles Brown
Edwards of Houston, who suffered a stroke on the very day he had
retired from a 30-year career with the post office. Day after day his
wife sat by his bed, but there was no recognition. One day Roy was
in town for a police benefit and she called him because her husband
loved his music. "You just hang up and relax," said Roy. "I'll be out
in 15 minutes." When Roy arrived she introduced him to her husband but there was still no recognition. Mrs. Edwards then hummed
accompaniment for Roy's soft singing of "The Precious Jewel." The
paralyzed face seemed to smile and tears filled the stricken man's
eyes. They filled Roy's eyes, too. "I kind of believe he knew me."

Another sad story concerns the death of a soldier in World War
II. Among his personal belongings that were returned to his mother
in Fort Worth was an Acuff songbook turned to the page of "Lay My
Old Guitar Away." Although requests coming into the Opry by mail

for special numbers usually are too many to honor, Roy threw everything he had into the song that night.*

There are times, however, when Roy can't accede to the requests of fans. Because he is part owner of Acuff-Rose Publishing Company, fans frequently bring him songs they claim to have written and want him to publish them. One such case occurred in Knoxville in the summer of 1964. A rather distinquished-looking elderly gentleman approached with a briefcase containing songs that his son had written and asked if Roy would play the music. Roy replied, "I hate to say no to a man of your obvious caliber, but this sort of thing can only mean lawsuits and I try to stay away from it." The gentleman said that he had sent the music to Roy's company but had gotten no results. Roy then had to explain that he didn't have much to do with the company, and that he didn't even have an office there, and stated again, how sorry he was. Later when speaking of the incident, Roy said, "Things like that bring tears to your eyes but there is nothing you can do about them."

His fans will frequently go to great lengths to see him. One old Kentuckian walked 21 miles from his isolated mountain home to catch a train and rode to a city he had never seen before just "to see this man Acuff in person." And all Roy Acuff's fans don't live 21 miles up in the mountains. When a sophisticated New Yorker was chided for openly admiring him, she responded saying, "I know it's silly, but he makes me cry, anyhow."

The reactions of Roy's fans who haven't seen him for a long time are interesting. At a political rally in Spencer, Tennessee, in the summer of 1964, one lady commented, " Last time I saw Roy was 20 years ago and he hasn't aged a bit." Another said, "That Roy Acuff sure has aged. Why, he looks twenty-five years older than than when I last saw him." When asked how long that was, she said, "Twenty-five years."

Of course, there are certain tricks that Roy's fans play on him. When signing autographs he usually makes it a point to use his own pen (and when a ball-point pen ceases to work it usually gets thrown across the room in great disgust). But fans frequently claim the pen is theirs, apparently not only wanting Roy Acuff's autograph but a souvenir as well. In return, Roy has a few tricks of his own. When he wants to get through a crowd without signing autographs he some-

---

*Ross L. Holman, "King of Mountain Music," *Coronet*, September, 1948, p. 45.

times will fiddle through, or occasionally will carry a cup and yell, "Coffee, hot coffee." If it's imperative that he get to the next appearance and fans are surrounding him, he'll escape by saying, "I'll be back." But usually, at a time when most performers are relaxing backstage, Roy makes it a point to go out and mix with his fans.

There's a reason why Roy's popularity with audiences hasn't dimmed one bit through the years. It's mostly due to his attention to them and his undeniable affection for them. Who wouldn't be affected by these incidents: The extremely old man who walked a long distance to the Spencer, Tennessee, courthouse lawn on the afternoon of July 16, 1964, just to see and talk with Roy so he could "take a mental picture" home to his bedridden wife. And the scrawled note handed to Roy by an elderly couple while he was on stage at the Opry on July 11, 1964, saying, "Dear Roy: We have waited twenty-five years to see you. Please sing 'The Great Speckled Bird.' " These appreciations mean much more to him, Roy says, than thousands of record playings and sales.

III

The Smoky Mountain Gang

Great Big Bashful Brother Oswald and His Sister Rachel

Roy has continually kept his end of the bargain in his partnership with the Opry, country music, and his fans. To him it has been a matter of both integrity and professionalism. But one of Roy Acuff's most important partnerships has yet to be discussed.

On a more personal plane is the association of Roy Acuff and His Smoky Mountain Boys and Girls. It is impossible to overemphasize their contribution to his success. What they have added as individuals, as well as their contributions as a group have been immeasurable. The collaboration has been a continuing success story.

Leading these highly talented musicians are Pete Kirby, "Bashful Brother Oswald," and Rachel Veach, known as Oswald's "Sister Rachel."

Beecher Ray Kirby was born in the heart of the Great Smoky Mountains of Tennessee, Sevier County, on December 26, 1911. He had eight brothers and two sisters. They all played musical instruments, but not professionally. As a youngster he decided that he disliked the name Beecher, and so he adopted the name Pete because it was short and he liked the sound.

His father was a farmer who also ran a barbershop in Sevierville. Os remembers his only early "toys" were a pair of high-top boots and a double-edged ax. When just a kid he rose at two in the morning and chopped firewood, then hauled it to town so his father could heat water for his shop. Before returning, he would go to the store and purchase hay and haul it back to the farm.

Os left school in the third grade. There he had the frustration of having his left hand—he was a natural lefty—tied behind him to teach him to write with his right hand. The effort by the teacher was unsuccessful. (When Os first joined Roy's band, Roy thought Os could read—but he was only looking at the pictures. For a time it was necessary to draw pictures of such things as trains and whistles so Os could learn the words to songs. Soon though, with Roy's help, Os learned to read and write.)

His father played the fiddle, guitar, and five-string banjo, and also taught "the Old Harp singing style." Os became quite proficient on the guitar and banjo long before he learned to do anything else. Playing music is the only thing Os does righthanded.

When he became older, he played baseball. Sometimes his baseball shoes were his only pair, so when he walked the mountain trails to the games he carried them. As a young man he worked in a sawmill in nearby Knoxville, and would supplement his meager earnings by playing at parties and passing the hat for nickles and pennies.

When Oswald was about ten, his father was very close to losing the farm. So Mr. Kirby went to the sheriff and explained that to save the farm he had to be allowed to make corn whisky. The sheriff gave him one of the confiscated stills stored at the jail, and Mr. Kirby set it up near his house. The sheriff would make a raid every now and then, but he always seemed to select the wrong hollow.

In any batch of corn whisky, the first distillation is the better or "drinkin' " whisky, and the last is the "sellin' " whisky. Os was the family's distributing agent and he'd fill his guitar case with the sellin' variety, carrying his guitar in the other hand as he made his rounds. The town's unknowing wondered why he carried two guitars. Os helped his family in this way for about seven years.

When he was 17, in 1929, Os decided the time had come to leave home and so he rode a big white mule to the highway, dismounted, and, with his straight Spanish guitar, hitchhiked to Flint, Michigan, where one of his uncles was an executive in the Buick factory. But his hopes for a job vanished as the Depression appeared. However, Os stayed in Flint for about two years, playing at station WFDF, and during that time he learned Hawaiian music. The manager indicated that the station needed Hawaiian music and Os, to keep his job, bought an all-metal Dobro, called a National, and learned to play it. At this time he heard a very proficient Dobro player, Rudy Waikuiki. Os liked his style and so, with Rudy's help, he soon became very skilled.

Then Os returned to Knoxville because his mother had died (his father lived to be well over 90). He stayed there about a week, and left for Chicago to work at the Century of Progress exposition, which began in 1933.

During the days he was a fry cook at the fair, sometimes serving such personalities as Frank Buck and Sally Rand, but at night he played his National in beer joints around the city. Once, he got a job playing on a lake touring boat. Time after time the captain couldn't figure out what made the boat go astray. Finally he concluded that the all-metal Dobro was affecting the compass. Oswald's subsequent performances were away from the bridge and toward the stern.

After the fair was over he returned to Knoxville and obtained a job at Kern's Bakery. During this time he played with various groups and, at times, with Roy Acuff and his Crazy Tennesseans. In Knoxville, he and Dynamite Hatcher occasionally played at a certain restaurant. Once, while on his way to substitute in Roy's band, he met the sister of the owner and took a shine to her. Lola and Os were married April 4, 1936. When Roy called Os, Lonnie, and Jake to join his band in Nashville in early 1939, Os brought along Lola and their three-week-old son, Billy. Linda was born in 1941.

Soon after Roy hired Os, Lonnie, and Jake for his band, he also found Rachel Veach. How it came about was that after Tiny Sarrett quit, Roy started searching for another girl band member, because he believed that a girl was needed in his act—men in the audience like to see a girl on stage.

Roy was particularly searching for a girl who could play a five-string banjo. David Stone was helping. Soon Sam McGee came to Roy and said a girl, 18, who was kin to him might fill the bill. Sam brought Rachel Veach to Nashville.

Rachel was born on a farm near Peytonville, Tennessee, and had five sisters and three brothers. The family made its living by sharecropping. Rachel attended school through the seventh or eighth grade, and for her own entertainment would pick her five-string banjo.

Even though she lived relatively close to Nashville, Rachel had never been away from home, had never seen such things as showers, locks, or elevators. Sam took Rachel in a studio and worked with her, trying to keep her busy playing. Roy and David were listening in an adjacent room. Rachel was scared to death and not really doing much of anything. David turned to Roy and said, "That will ruin your act. You don't want anything like that, do you?"

Roy replied, "If 'that' can pick up her banjo and listen to me, she's what I want. She's country!" This was on April 1, 1939, and Rachel later said she was the biggest April Fool that Roy ever had.

At first she was billed as "Rachel, Queen of the Hills." Lonnie and Pete were known as "Pap and Oswald, Rachel's Two Country Comedian Boy Friends."

But then Roy began to get letters from people who found it difficult to understand how a girl could travel with the group and still maintain her status as a lady. These letters worried Roy and Mildred greatly. The boys accepted Rachel and had no trouble even when they traveled at night and would sleep on each other's shoulders. But the public, not being show business oriented, was skeptical.

One day in late 1939 the band was traveling to play schools in North Carolina. Roy tells it this way:

> Os would always sit in the car and give that big horse laugh, that 'Haaaaaa' thing that he always did and I'd get so tickled. We'd go through some little town, he'd see something funny and he'd laugh like that. It was a put-on laugh, of course, but it was funny to us. Well, it sounded like a backward, bashful laugh. So I said, 'Let me make you Rachel's brother and bring you two together as Rachel and her Great Big Bashful Brother Oswald'. So I teamed them together and it was a tremendous success right off, and my mail stopped immediately because they thought it was great to have a boy and his sister. So I fooled the public to protect the name of Rachel. I don't think that was wrong. I had to have a girl in my act. Your audience will guide you.*

In the early days the Acuff band, including Roy, usually dressed in blue jeans, plaid or checked shirts of different designs, and black hats. Rachel wore a typical country dress. The first night of their new act was in Robbins, North Carolina, and they decided that each should black out one tooth. Os wore a black wig, checked visored cap, and big britches with suspenders. Rachel made sure her bloomers could be seen beneath her dress, and put on white stockings and high button shoes. When the time for their entrance approached, they both suddenly became embarrassed and so scared that Roy had

---

*Cherry tape.

to push them onstage. They didn't sing at all—they simply stood and gawked at each other because the audience was laughing so hard.

This act became a highlight of any Acuff performance. Os's famous laugh, which he learned from his next-door neighbor Bill Christian in 1927, convulsed thousands of people. Rachel's laugh was almost as funny. The two would tell jokes, sing duets, and, when Os would laugh, Rachel would follow right away with her laugh. Audiences during the first half of the 1940s were treated to the finest performances ever given by the Acuff troupe. In June of 1942 Rachel and Oswald recorded two songs, "Roll on Buddy" and "Weary Lonesome Blues," during one of Roy's regular Columbia recordings sessions. This is the only regular session that Rachel attended. Unfortunately, these numbers were never released. Later the band made one Decca recording together, "She's My Curley Headed Baby" and "Fireball Mail." At the same session Rachel also did the vocal on another Decca record for Jimmie Riddle, "I Want My Mama."

Rachel remembers one particularly embarrassing experience during her years as a "Smoky Mountain Girl." One evening, before an Opry Tent Show, she was starting down ladderlike steps to the stage and the back of her dress caught on a nail. Kirk McGee held her around her knees and lifted, but she lost the entire back of her skirt. Rachel played the rest of the show carefully, but with modesty intact because of her long white pantaloons.

Around 1943 Rachel married Bill Watson, a farmer, who subsequently went into the armed forces. By 1946, after he returned, Rachel virtually stopped appearing with the Smoky Mountain Boys, thus closing what could be called their Golden Era. She and Bill raised four daughters.

The group never really learned why Rachel quit. A probable major cause was her family of four girls—she'd get lonesome for them on the road. Also, at this time, the group was beginning to travel by air and Rachel did not enjoy flying.

Once in a great while Rachel will join the troupe. One time was a December 1956 benefit at Franklin, Tennessee, to fill Christmas stockings for the needy. And during the late 1960s she appeared with Oswald on three television shows—"Porter Wagoner," "Wilburn Brothers," and "Flatt and Scruggs." Her most recent appearance was with Os in June 1975, at Nashville's Fan Fair.

Os particularly misses Rachel, and is outspoken in his belief that the band was never the same. He says that Rachel's unsophisticated hillbilly girl act contributed the needed flair of showmanship to put the act over to the public. And he believes that the sophisticated Smoky Mountain Girls, who have been a part of the act since then, have not contributed to the success of the show. Jimmie Riddle agrees.

After Rachel left, Velma Williams for a time was given a vaguely similar billing, but in general Os had lost his "sister" when Rachel quit. He, though, has kept the nickname of "Bashful Brother Oswald," and is very proud of it. The other band members usually call him Pete offstage, but Roy nearly always calls him Os. In 1963, when Lee Harvey Oswald assassinated President Kennedy, the group received a great amount of mail and Roy became worried. He went to Os and asked him if he should stop using the name Oswald. Os simply said, "No, I made that name famous long before he did."

With the years Os has acquired more nicknames. Judge Hay made up the "Casanova of the Cumberlands." Sometimes he's billed as "Famous Oswald." And once in awhile, when he went off the deep end during a show, Roy said, "In his old age he's getting so wild I'm afraid we ought to call him 'Brazen Brother Oswald'." The reason here was that now and then Os imbibed a little too much "Tennessee Corn Liquor" that was delivered weekly to him backstage at the Opry in a gallon fruit jar. This white lightnin' was as clear as glass, but the smell was more powerful than ammonia and waves could be seen flexing above it, much like the rippling heat waves from a radiator. But Os was an expert: he tested each shipment to make sure it burned with a clean blue flame—"If it don't, it'll kill you"—and he carefully measured his regular sips, with only infrequent miscalculations.

One day in Chattanooga a lady told him to please hold his pose for a photograph a little longer because, she said, "It might take two shots." Os replied, "Oh, that's okay, m'am. I've had two myself." Another time, one dark night, Jimmie was driving too fast and Roy, who was following, gave him a blast on the siren in the car. When Jim stopped, Os was sent by Roy to act as a police officer. Jim, knowing what was going on, got out and started walking menacingly toward them. Os immediately raced back and jumped into Roy's car yelling, "He don't know me, Roy! He don't know me!" One time the troupe was touring with a rodeo and Bozo the Clown asked Os to ride the bull with him. Os, full of "undiluted" courage, agreed and climbed on the bull in front of Bozo. As the chute opened, Bozo simply lifted himself off the bull, leaving Os to ride alone. The result was a broken wrist and two broken ribs—Os's.

Os is a man who is kind and considerate at all times. Anyone who appreciates his music is treated to all the pickin' they could ask for. On the road he points out sights of interest, such as a little old lady putting snuff under her lip, that a newcomer might otherwise miss.

Bashful Brother Oswald (or Brazen Brother Oswald) was summed up perfectly by a lady who owns a restaurant near the Ryman to which the performers, including Os in costume, often went. One evening as he was leaving, she looked at him in beaming admiration and then turned to the other customers and said, "Ain't he a mess, I love him!"

In December 1969 Os entered a hospital, and tests showed that he only had about 10 percent use of his liver. The doctor, Perry Harris, was amazed that Os was still alive, but informed Lola that that condition would only persist from six months to two years—unless Oswald stopped drinking immediately. From then on, Os has never touched a drop. Of this new state, he comments, "I never craved it. I drank because I liked the taste. I don't crave it now, but I do miss it. I feel better, although I don't think I have as much fun."

Os's "whisky" gets into the act on stage. He has an explosion device, dubbed the Smudge Pot, that he carries in a typewriter case. During the act Os will pull out a half-pint whisky bottle full of water and Roy will complain about drinking on stage, then Os will spit out the water in a long arc at the Smudge Pot. The device is loaded with smoke bombs, black gunpowder, and firecrackers, which Jimmie, stationed just off stage, sets off electrically for a dramatic blowup.

Os's most famous costume came about in 1943 when Roy started raising Tennessee walking horses. Roy boarded them with Oswald's next-door neighbor while Roy was having a barn constructed on his own property. One day Os was plowing with some mules in his yard, and he was wearing a pair of blue bib overalls. A man from a magazine came to take a picture of Roy's stallion, Pearl Harbor. To assist the photographer, Os jumped aboard and the nearly uncontrollable animal stood perfectly still. When Roy saw the picture he was so impressed that he decided then and there that Oswald's new stage costume would be blue bib overalls. An oversized chain leads from one bib pocket to the other, which contains a watch of equal proportions. Os has several of these big gold watches and they all work, after a fashion.

The costume also features large shoes and an old beat-up hat, which is frequently removed when a fan takes a picture during a show. Os occasionally slips these big shoes into an even larger pair, a specially built size 44. These had been made by a German shoe company for a window display, and when the company was through with them they were given to Os.

Sometimes Os will go into the crowd and dance with willing ladies, or sit on their laps. When Roy "walks the dog" with his Yo-Yo, Os will slap at it with his feet as if trying to kill a bug.

In the past few years many of the Acuff troupe have discarded their outlandish hillbilly costumes, but Os, who is in full agreement with Roy about showmanship being needed on the Opry, hasn't given up his costume. Occasionally he will do an informal short show without it, but he really feels unnatural that way. There's an unwritten rule that Os will never have to give up his blue bib overalls, nor all the paraphernalia and shenanigans that go with them.

As important as they are, Os's comic antics are only a part of his contribution to the act. From the time he joined the band he has added his voice to many of Roy's songs. Roy said of Os's voice, "It is called a high tenor, but it varies from alto to tenor to bass. Sometimes he hits above me, sometimes below. He hits any kind of harmony that a country boy can find." Whatever it is, his voice is outstanding and provides one of the highest and most easily recognized harmonies in country music. Occasionally his comedy mixes with his harmonizing, like the time on the Opry when Roy missed his cue in the middle of "Just a Friend." Os said loudly right over the air, "Why don't you sing when you're s'posed to!"

Os, like most country musicians, can play many instruments. One, the five-string banjo, was popular on the early Opry and then fell to disuse, but was kept alive during the 1940s basically by Os and Uncle Dave who willed one of his banjos to Os when he died in 1952. Os used this Macon banjo until the mid-1960s, when he traded it to Roy's Exhibit for an equally fine but not as historical an instrument.

Rachel picked her five-string; Os tends more to flail his. But his style, like everything he does, is distinctive and all his own. He will use his banjo to accompany Roy on such numbers as "Baldknob Arkansas," "Coming From the Ball," and "When I Lay My Burden Down." However, Os usually puts it to use for his own solo numbers, such as "Surely Is a Train," "The Girl I Love," "Roll on Buddy," "Weary Lonesome Blues," "Columbus Stockade Blues," "Nobody's

Business," "Southern Moon," "Rabbit in the Log," and the one into which he puts more than his usual gusto, "Mountain Dew."

Before he starts to sing he rarely, unless pressed by Roy, mentions the true name of the song. Instead, he'll say, "This beautiful little number is called: He was tall in the saddle till his blister busted" . . . or "Lay over and give me half the bed or I'll rip up the sheet" . . . or "You've worked all your life for us, Mother, now get out and do something for yourself." Frequently he'll say something like, "This number has never been played on any radio station anywhere in the world—brand new—and that's the truth if I ever told it" . . . or "I might as well sing, 'cause when I get through here I got to go somewhere else" . . . or "Now, don't go away; it can't get any worse, I'll promise you that." And as he finally lurches into the song, he might say, "Hang on, children, here we go!"

Offstage, Os is shy with strangers, but once he gets to know a person he is very communicative and, in fact, will become extremely outspoken. His opinions concerning country music are especially valuable because he is, even more than Roy, absolutely dedicated to the old-time traditional hillbilly music. He has little patience with modern country music, even when presented on the Opry.

Naturally, Os believes that Roy Acuff performs the finest country music. However, Os thinks that the band should be striving to recapture its old sound of the early and mid-1940s when Rachel was in the act. He does not approve of the electric guitar or the drums, and is critical of the group's recordings that feature these instruments or choral voices.

Os and Roy have a mutual respect and feeling for each other that is able to withstand strong, differing opinions. Roy, for example, felt that the group had to adopt some of the modern country sounds to keep alive professionally. Os disagreed and still does. But it's a disagreement between two men who have the welfare of the band as their primary concern.

This love of really old-time country music and tradition is exemplified by Os's primary contribution as a Smoky Mountain Boy, which is his playing of the Dobro. This instrument more than any other, even the fiddle, has had more to do with creating the distinctive Acuff Sound, and has played as great a part as Roy's powerful voice in making Roy Acuff and His Smoky Mountain Boys known almost everywhere.

The history of the Dobro is complex and old. During the 1500s, in the Age of Exploration, Spanish sailors took the Spanish guitar around the world, including the islands of the Pacific. Later, with the discovery of the Hawaiian Islands, this guitar made its appearance. The islanders quickly learned to play it, and included it in their music, which up to that time had been limited to percussion instruments and reed flutes and whistles. In time, the gut strings were replaced by metal ones, but the guitar was still played in the conventional manner.

In 1879 a small guitar was brought to the islands from Portugal. The Hawaiians named this tiny guitar ukelele from *uke*, meaning "to strike on wood," and *lele*, meaning "to strum" or "to jump." In time the word *uku*, meaning "flea," became *uke*.

In 1893 Joseph Kekuku, who was a student at the Kamehameha Boy's School, accidentally dropped a pocketknife on the strings of his uke. From then on, the new sliding style swept the islands and by the early 20th century, in an effort to achieve more volume, the islanders were raising the strings on the regular Spanish guitars with a piece of bone and using a flat piece of steel instead of a knife. In a few years the Spanish guitar—played sideways—became the most popular instrument in Hawaii, and when tours from the United States came into vogue, the instrument was brought to this country via San Francisco. By the end of World War I the instrument was known as the Hawaiian steel guitar. It was extremely popular.

In the early 1900s the United States received another import: the Dopyera family of Czechoslovakia came to the land of the "Lady of Liberty" in 1908. (Some members of the family omit the "y," but John Dopyera, from whom most of this information was obtained, isn't one of them.) John, the oldest son, had learned and loved his father's trade as a violin maker. When he first arrived in this country he and his four younger brothers—Rudy, Louis, Bob, and Ed—worked as laborers, but spent all their spare time trying to develop innovations on various fretted instruments.

A demand for greater amplification grew during the early 1920s. In 1925 John amplified the banjo because he especially loved this instrument. He did it by adding concave and convex metal discs, resembling hub caps, which delivered the greatest amplification of sound of any instrument then known. He then adapted the same resonator system for the guitar. In 1926 in Los Angeles, John, Rudy, and Ed formed the National Company to manufacture guitars, which at first were mostly of wood and later of metal. They soon sold this company. Then in 1929 John invented a similar but improved guitar. While the brothers were trying to name it they first thought of *dobro,* which means "good" in their native Czechoslovakian language. They settled definitely on that name for the new guitar when they discovered it also meant **DO**pyera **BRO**thers. The word also has five letters—for the five brothers.

The Dobro Guitar Company (and many other companies) continued to make various metal and wooden guitars, and such other instruments as banjos and mandolins with metal resonators until 1939 when a wartime shortage of metal stopped them. The company was always located in Los Angeles but a major outlet was in Chicago.

Besides its use by Hawaiian bands the Dobro guitar was played by many early country music groups, such as those of Jimmie Rodgers and of Cliff Carlisle, but it was not until first Clell and the Os in Roy Acuff's band started using it that the instrument became noticed. This popularity quite likely was influenced by Roy's records, which sold many millions of copies, and his songs came to be identified with Os's matchless style of playing the Dobro.

When Oswald joined the Smoky Mountain Boys in Nashville he had the National he had purchased in Michigan. But earlier he had heard and preferred the sound of Clell's Dobro. So when Os arrived in Nashville he ordered a Dobro at a music store which, in turn, ordered it from Chicago. The Dobro had a white top made of spruce, and it and its case cost $60. It was his all-time favorite, and Os continued to play this Dobro until around 1943 or 1944 when it was stolen out of the car as the band was playing in St. Augustine, Florida. Os bought another spruce-top Dobro but sold it to Ray "Duck" Adkins, who played with Johnny and Jack. Later realizing his mistake, Os tried to buy it back but Adkins wouldn't sell. Through the years Os has played various types but, with few exceptions, they've been old Dobros.

One exception to the rule of using only an old Dobro was the electrified Dobro that is evident in the movie *Night Train to Memphis*, filmed in Hollywood in late 1945. Os played it off and on (mostly off), and, when the troupe went on a West Coast tour early in 1947, Roy insisted that Os take it along because Roy thought its sound would be better for the dances they would be playing. After the tour Roy admitted, "The thing screeched so much!" Upon his return to Nashville, Os, gave the hated electrifying guitar to one person and the amplifier to another, hoping that its sound would never be heard again.

In the movie *Sing Neighbor Sing* Os played an old Dobro. It was an "f" hole type, which the studio loaned him.

At present, Os occasionally plays fancy modern Dobros given him by musical instrument companies.

Predictably, Os plays the Dobro in a style all his own. It is more brilliant because he uses the "high bass A tuning" of A - $C^\#$- E - A - $C^\#$ - E instead of the conventional lower G -B - D -G - B - D. Os uses three wound and three plain heavy-gauge strings, and the round metal bar with which he frets is unusually heavy. He also frequently frets with the little finger of his left hand. The strings usually are picked in pairs. Os produces distinctive harmonics and sweet, gentle tones.

The other exception to Os always playing the Dobro occurred during the late 1950s and early 1960s, a period when even the Acuff group went overboard for the modern sound. At that time Os stuck to the straight guitar, rarely taking his Dobro out of its case even for instrumentals. The fact remains, though, that Os has been largely responsible for keeping this superb musical instrument alive on the Opry during a period when electric insturments were overwhelming country music. And with the Dobro is produced the Acuff Sound.

Although Os—Pete Kirby—was not with the band when it originally came to Nashville (for obvious reasons, Roy usually will say during a performance that Os came with him to Nashville) next to Roy himself Os has been its main stalwart. As himself, and as a thoroughly professional musician and entertainer, Os has contributed greatly to the success of Roy Acuff and His Smoky Mountain Boys.

A respected and astute member of the Grand Ole Opry family is Trudy Stamper. She came to WSM around 1941 and served as sort of a mother hen to the Opry cast until her retirement in 1965. Trudy said, with obvious affection, "Oswald is one of those truly rare human beings who come along only once every hundred years!"

Jess, Lonnie, Joe, and Curly

These four Smoky Mountain Boys were with the band for substantial periods, and each played his own distinctive role.

Jess Easterday. Jess was the only one of the original Crazy Tennesseans to stay when the others quit, and Roy, of course, was greatly appreciative. Roy says Jess was an honest and good person whose showmanship added greatly to the success of the band.

Jess occasionally sang vocal choruses and acted as master of ceremonies. In the act the audience especially remembered him for his 20-foot-long shirt, which made him appear fat because it was rolled up around his waist. At the end of each show Pap would grab it and Jess would run off the stage, unraveling the shirt. Jess played the bass and occasionally the guitar. His mandolin, which was the only one the troupe really ever had, provided a wonderful harmony with the Dobro. He played deadpan and never smiled on stage. Offstage he was much the same, sitting silently, smoking his pipe, with his hat on.

Jess was married and had a daughter named Wilma Jean, born about 1939. In 1946 he became extremely upset over an impending divorce and quit the band for a year. Roy finally persuaded him to return, but Jess stayed only a month. During a West Coast tour, about 1948, he left the band and took the bus back to Nashville. Jess died recently.

Lonnie Wilson. Lonnie was born and raised in the Great Smoky Mountains. He studied engineering for about a year at the University of Tennessee. Lonnie played in the band in the very early days in Knoxville and then joined Roy in Nashville in 1939. He is married and has a daughter, Gail, who was born in the late 1930s.

Soon after joining Roy's Nashville band, Lonnie became known as "Pap" and, around 1940, perfected this character in the trailer camp's burned-out rumpus room. The character was adopted from his real-life uncle who as Pap says, was "truly a character"* with a sparkling wit. People in the community didn't quite know what to make of Lonnie's uncle but they loved him anyway.

Lonnie's character of Pap wore chin whiskers and exaggerated hillbilly dress, and developed into a hilarious rube comedian. As Pap, Lonnie played guitar, and occasionally bass. He worked hard on the stage and was considered a better showman than musician. Lonnie sang baritone in duets with some of the other band members.

---

*Robert Shelton and Burt Goldblatt, *Country Music Story* (New York; The Bobbs-Merrill Company, Inc., 1966), p. 120.

His was jovial slapstick comedy, even to the extent of balancing the bass fiddle on his nose in imitation of Roy.

Onstage Pap might launch into something like this: "Oh, it's hot!" and he starts to strip off his clothes.

Roy: "We're not putting on that kind of a show, 'Pap.' Not tonight!"

Pap: "No, but brother I'm willin'!"

Roy, laughing: "I guess you are, but we'd have to go down to the swimmin' hole when we put on a show like that."

Lonnie was in the navy in World War II and served as a radar technician with the U.S. Marines on numerous invasions in the South Pacific. His time in the service was from April 1, 1943, to December 15, 1945.

From 1939 until 1961 there were periods when Lonnie wasn't with the band. He appeared in all the movies, except when he was in the navy, but he didn't go on many of the overseas tours, especially in the early 1950s, and sometimes he wasn't in stateside performances. Perhaps the reason for this on-again, off-again is in what Lonnie once said: "Roy and I can go along together just so long and then we drift apart." Occasionally Lonnie tried to supersede Roy. In any case his tenure as a Smoky Mountain Boy ended permanently in June 1961.

Joe Zinkan. When Lonnie went into the navy in April 1943 his place was taken by Joe Zinkan, who joined the band late in the year. He was a Smoky Mountain Boy continuously until 1958. When Lonnie wasn't with the band, Joe played the Pap character and was known as Joe "Pap" Zinkan, playing the guitar. When Lonnie returned from the navy and was with the band, Joe usually kept his outlandish costume but took off the chin whiskers and switched to bass. At these times he played another rube character known as "Smilin' Joseph" because he never smiled. During the periods when Lonnie wasn't with the band, Joe would go back to guitar and play the Pap character. Os considers Joe to be the best showman with a bass that he has ever seen.

Joe had a dry humor and was silent, but was very reliable. He resigned from the band to become a studio session musician in Nashville.

Oral (Curly) Odie Rhodes. Rhodes joined the band during the last half of 1940 and stayed until early 1942, when he went into the army for four years. During this time with Roy he played the bass and was the rube comedian, Odie. The billing was "Pap and Odie," sometimes "Pap and His Son Odie." He also played the guitar. After his discharge, Rhodes was with the band off and on from 1946 until 1955. Although he didn't appear in any of the movies, he went on many of the foreign tours, especially during the early 1950s, and occasionally in stateside performances. During Lonnie Wilson's sporadic absences, Joe Zinkan moved up to the Pap character and Oral Rhodes took Joe's place on bass as Odie.

Boogie-Woogie Man—Jimmie Riddle

If one makes the analogy that Roy is the president of the Smoky Mountain Boys and Os is the vice president, then Jimmie Riddle must be the secretary-treasurer, for Jimmie, like Oswald, is a band stalwart. It has been his duty over the years to take care of correspondence and protocol—in general, to be the band's brain truster.

Jimmie was born in Dyersburg, Tennessee, on September 3, 1918. When he was one month old the family moved to Memphis, but he was frequently taken back to Dyersburg to visit Granddaddy Boone. One day, when Jimmie was almost four, his granddaddy handed him a harmonica and the youngster played a tune. Jim listened to his granddaddy play some country breakdowns, which he quickly added to his repertoire. His favorite tune was "Run, Nigger, Run." Jim's first performance came when the teacher discovered that he could play the harmonica. Knees shaking, the first grader gave a rendition of "That's My Weakness Now."

At the age of nine Jim picked up the harmonica, which he had been playing right-handed, and turned it around and it sounded better. Ever since, he has played it backwards. On a chromatic harmonica he pushes the plunger with his left hand.

"I was just born with it," he later said of his harmonica playing. "I really think we are all instruments of God, and He plays through us, and this is the way He chose to play through me."

When Jim was ten Mrs. John Clark, a lady who lived next door, gave him his only formal music lessons—she taught him some chords on a guitar. His father worked as a telephone company supervisor and in the company warehouse was a dance hall with a piano on its second floor. When he was 12, Jimmie picked out chords on the piano and taught himself to play it. The following year his mother bought him an accordion.

Jim's childhood wasn't entirely occupied with music. "I did really mean things when I was a kid, much worse than Roy. We loved to go up on an overpass bridge and throw buckets of water at hayriders. We even threw filth at passing motorists." Despite these dubious activities, Jim received straight A's during his years in the St. Paul Elementary School at Memphis.

In 1930, he entered Bellevue Junior High School and his grades gradually declined as he became more interested in music. This trend continued and Jim dropped out of Technical High School in the spring of 1936 before receiving a diploma. By that time he was fully involved with music.

Jimmie's career was launched around 1934 when he began playing the harmonica with two much older musicians. The trio toured the beer joints and passed the hat. Sixteen-year-old Jim was paid off more in beer than in nickels and dimes. After awhile he began to ride the bus to station WMC, where he performed with Uncle Rube Turnipseed and the Pea Ridge Ramblers. They toured in a 100-mile radius of Memphis.

Shortly before quitting high school Jim obtained a job with the Swift Jewel Cowboys. Jim would fill in for members on their vacations. At this point he added a new instrument to those he had mastered, the bull fiddle. In late 1939, shortly after Roy's new band had its first session there, the Swift Jewel Cowboys had a Columbia session at the Gayoso Hotel. Art Satherley was the A&R man. Jimmie played boogie-woogie style on the harmonica for such instrumentals as "Dill Pickle Rag," "Raggin' the Rails," "Kansas City Blues," and "Fan It." He played the piano for "My Untrue Cowgirl." During this period, 1935-39, Jimmie played with many other groups in Memphis.

In 1939 he went to Houston, Texas, and played with the Crustine Ranch Boys, who called themselves the Texans. From Houston the Texans were based at various times in Greenville and Jackson, Mississippi, and in Victoria and Austin, Texas. In 1941 the Texans returned to Houston.

Jim's daytime job was in the Brown shipyard. When tired after playing all night, he pretended to be dumb on the job. Every two or three days his fellow workers would send him for a left-handed monkey wrench, a sky hook, or a certain length of shore line. He would simply go into the hull of a ship and sleep. At the end of the day he would awaken when the workers stopped chipping and return with the explanation, "I've been to every one of the 15 tool sheds and I can't find it!"

In March 1943, the Texans were second billing on an Acuff show in Houston. Backstage, Jimmie jammed with the group, especially Lonnie. Roy liked the sound of his harmonica, and offered Jim a job because he needed a replacement for Oral Rhodes, who had been drafted. Jim did not jump at the chance right away because he knew that if he left the shipyard, which was doing vital defense work, he probably would be drafted. By September, however, he was so sick of the shipyard that he called Roy, who was in Lake Charles, Louisiana. Roy said, "Catch the next train." Jim did. He was hired for his harmonica, but occasionally would play the accordion.

On April 24, 1944, he received a preinduction physical notice from the army but was deferred because the group was in Hollywood making *Sing Neighbor Sing*. Jim was inducted in September 1944 and remained in the service until June 1946. During this time he took a test and earned his high school diploma. He won a marksmanship metal despite the fact that he deliberately tried to miss the target. He did this, Jim said, because he knew he could serve his country better as an entertainer. However, he was stationed at Camp Blanding in Florida, guarding German POWs. Finally the army came around to Jim's point of view and he was assigned to special services at Fort McPherson at Atlanta. During Jim's absence from the Acuff troupe, his accordion playing duties were taken over by Sonny Day, but the group was without a harmonica.

Just before his release from the army, Jimmie got a letter written by Mildred and signed by Roy telling him that his job with the band was still open. Talented musicians are hard to find, and conscientious, and intelligent ones are even rarer. Roy knew that Jim was such a person. Jimmie joined the Roy Acuff Tent Theatre in Ohio early in July 1946.

Jim has about 100 harmonicas in all keys. They range from the one-inch Little Lady to the one that is two feet long and has 48 chords, and in price from 75 cents to $150. He performs only with Hohner harmonicas and has visited the factory while on tour in Germany. Years ago Jimmie preferred the Hohner Old Standbys to the Marine Band type, but has since reversed himself.

The most famous of Jim's solo numbers is "Fox Chase." In his early days with the band he recorded two sides for Decca, "Three

Trees" and "I Want My Mama." In all performances he has demonstrated that his billing for movies and tours was indeed correct—the "Harmonica Wizard."

In the late 1940s Roy had been getting many letters from fans indicating the accordion was not popular. Roy realized the piano would be much better, and so the accordion was phased out. From that time, when not playing the harmonica, Jim has played the piano. He prefers one tuned to A-440. In 1967 the band purchased a small electric piano to carry with them for Jim's use if a larger one is not available. When harmonicaist Onie Wheeler joins the band for brief periods, Jim is more often at the piano.

Asked if he minds being more in the background, Jim said, "Roy needs the piano to hold the rhythm, and when we don't have one it makes a difference. I've had 25 years up front so I don't mind. Besides, I get a chance to sit down during the shows and that helps the 'ole' boy a lot."

Jim is ingenious about producing odd and unusual noises with his mouth and hands, such as in "Fox Chase" and other numbers. He can also tap out the "William Tell Overture" on his throat. However, by far his greatest talent is exhibited in Eeephin', which Jim learned at the age of six from his Uncle Ralph, who called it "Hoodlin." Jim's description of it is: "E, pheitt, gasp-hiccup, I, pheitt, gasp-hiccup." Such "foolishness," as he puts it, earned him a job on television's "Hee Haw Show," which was first shown in 1969 and soon became a network show and is still being produced for syndication. Jim's affiliation with "Hee Haw" has meant that he has to meet TV taping schedules, and since September 1, 1970, he has been absent from some of Roy's shows. (During the last three months of 1973, all affiliation was severed, but early in 1974 Jimmie rejoined Roy.) Although still a Smoky Mountain Boy, he is now better known and so plays occasional shows as his own act. As a single, he made a Decca 45 rpm, "Wildwood Eeeph"/"Yakety Eeeph."

Vocal talents serve Jim well in his role as a jokester—one always has to be on the lookout when around him. Once Jimmie came up behind Roy while he was loading the car trunk, and said in a quavery little old lady voice, "I certainly did enjoy your show, Mr. Acuff." Roy turned and politely said, "Oh, thank you," only to find Jim. During the next few weeks this happened four more times. On the fifth time Roy said, "Oh, go to hell!" and turned around only to be confronted by a real, and indignant, little old lady. Then there was the hot summer day when the troupe stopped at a gas station. Jimmie picked up the water hose, hooked it under his belt and inside his pants, and made a hissing sound like forced air. "Oh boy, does that feel good!" Another member of the troupe said, "Let me try that, Jim." So Jimmie handed him the "air" hose—with very wet results.

By a previous marriage Jim has a daughter, Susan, who was born on February 7, 1942. On April 17, 1947, he married Susie Gusler, who is very intelligent, sweet, considerate, and understanding. Their son, Steve, was born on January 22, 1952. Steve has considerable musical talent and is following in his father's footsteps, as "Drum Wizard."

Jim does not care for team sports, but he does like hunting and, especially, fishing. He and Susie, who likes to fish even more than he does, will wake up at three or four in the morning and drive halfway to Memphis to a secluded lake rather than fish the well-stocked lakes near Nashville. On the way they stop to get every variety of worm or grub that could possibly lure a fish. At around 7:00 they arrive at the lake and plan to fish until about noon, but usually end up sitting there until dark, even if the fish aren't biting well. They frequently fish in the old Southern rural style, with long, heavy bamboo poles without reels. Jimmie also likes to wade through creeks with a light at night gigging frogs. Susie is an expert cook of frogs' legs and catfish.

Whenever the troupe arrives at a state capital, Jim goes to the archives and searches for records of his ancestry. He has traced his family back six generations to the first Riddle in this country. The name itself means someone who harvest crops in a dell. He has also researched similar data in libraries in small towns. In the course of this study he found that one of his cousins married Almeda Riddle, the folk singer.

Jim owns and uses a telescope, and is familiar with astronomy and related subjects. The boys like to forget about teasing him, and writing silly poems, and calling him crazy in the 1940s when he would discourse at length on road trips about men walking on the moon. Furthermore, Jimmie enjoys philosophizing and has studied the classical Greek philosophers, reincarnation, and the macro-micro cosmic theory, which reportedly states that our universe might simply be a flea on the back of a dog.

Between road trips, philosophizing, hobbies, and fishing and hunting excursions Jim, like most of the other Smoky Mountain Boys, does a great amount of freelancing. During the past 14 years he, like Os, has recorded albums of his own. These contain lively jazz, country, and boogie-woogie songs that reflect his real taste in music. That he prefers this type of instrumental music to the slow, sad country ballads is not surprising in light of his Memphis (Beale Street) upbringing. Roy, when referring to the fact that Jim is the only member of the act who is not a country boy, says, "Jimmie is an extraordinary fellow. He will beat a mean hillbilly tune on stage and then go home, rig up his hi-fi outfit with two hours of jazz, classical, and semiclassical music, and enjoy every minute of it." So there's truth in saying that Jimmie is within his heart a boogie-woogie man. Further, while Jim has worked in recording sessions with such artists as Johnny Horton, Red Foley, Bill Anderson, Rex Allen, Johnny Bond, Jim Reeves, and Jimmy Dean, he is also in great demand with noncountry artists, such as Joni James, Johnny Ray, Anita Bryant, Connie Francis, and the Four Guys.

When he is onstage as a loyal member of the Smoky Mountain Boys, he provides the finest of country harmonica and piano playing, in the true Acuff tradition. But behind the scenes, Roy takes full advantage of Jim's other talents. "Jimmie is the brains of this outfit," Roy readily admits. If the group is on a military tour, Jim's duties in protocol include making introductions and writing thank-you letters to generals. And it's his responsibility, both on and off the road, to entertain the many official and semiofficial visitors that the band receives.

If newspaper coverage is required and a professional reporter is unavailable, Jimmie is called into service. During the 1953 Korea tour, his press releases were datelined "With the Troops in Korea." Jim has kept a record of the group's overseas tours which contains the exact dates for each tour and the countries visited. He takes full advantage of travel by sightseeing, frequently on his own, at every opportunity. A record of these adventures has been kept by Jim on film, and the "home" movies at the Riddle household are just as likely to be of Saigon and other exotic places as of Susie and Steve.

For the tour contracts, Jim is usually the chief witness and is sometimes designated as "manager." Roy signs below as an "employee" with the rest of the Smoky Mountain Boys. On one occasion, in 1969, the musicians union called Jim and asked him to gather six performers for a show at the Tennessee State Prison. Jim was designated the leader and Roy was listed along with the others as one of Jim's performers. So Jimmie is the only Smoky Mountain Boy to ever be in the unique position of hiring a sideman named Roy Acuff.

Dobro, banjo, guitar, harmonica, and piano: traditional instruments, every one. It can be argued that sidemen and their leader are instruments of music. They give real charm to country music. Basic to this charm is the next subject, the most traditional hillbilly instrument of all—the fiddle, and the men who play it.

Fiddlers Charm Creation

In the Southern mountains a call to fiddling ranks in dignity with a call to preaching. There is a gradation in status among rural musicians and the fiddler is clearly at the summit. Among old-time musicians, if an act consists of a guitar and fiddle the guitarist is considered to be strictly as backup for the fiddler, because the fiddler is tops in the pecking order of rural musicians.*

When Roy first took up the fiddle, it was in this tradition. He was fascinated by its tone, which is, in his opinion, much like the human voice. As his show business career unfolded, Roy came to believe strongly that the fiddle and banjo were the two instruments primarily responsible for the development of country music. In fact, Roy is slightly annoyed that the Dobro, a relative newcomer, has played such an important part in the development of his style of country music, the Acuff Sound. He wishes that the traditional fiddle could have this distinction.

Roy has had four fiddles that have meant a great deal to him, and he has used them extensively. His first fiddle was his father's. It was made by Andrew Lafayette (also known as A. L. or Fate) Cassady, Roy's great-great-uncle, who lived in Maynardville and was the town's blacksmith. He forged his own tools for his fiddle-making and soon became the finest fiddle-maker in that part of the country. Neill Acuff bought Cassady's seventh fiddle in 1907. Roy learned to play music on this fiddle and began his Knoxville career with it.

His next fiddle was purchased in a pawnshop at Gallipolis, Ohio, for $12.50. It then had only two strings. Roy used this fiddle on all his early recordings.

---

*John Greenway, "Country-Western: the Music of America," *American West,* November 1968, p. 35.

The third fiddle, until recently, was Roy's finest. It is worth over $1,000, although Roy did not pay that much. It was purchased in 1942 from Mrs. Edith Gordon McMillan in Bristol, Tennessee. The instrument was made by a student of Amati about 250 years ago.

The fourth fiddle is the one Roy uses today. It has a tone personally most pleasing to him, and it has the most interesting history. When John E. Johnson of Hickman, Kentucky, first heard Roy's recordings of "The Great Speckled Bird," he was so infatuated that he learned to play the guitar and sing Roy's songs. During World War II he made Roy Acuff fans out of his buddies. In the latter stages of the war, he—along with Lonnie Smith, Richard Shreeve, and Wayne N. Yarborough—was assigned to the Special Amphibious Troops of the 348th Engineers that landed on the Fox Green section of Omaha Beach on D-Day. This group of buddies was in five major battles. When they got to Frankfurt, Germany, they found a fiddle in an old bombed-out music store. Johnson and the others thought of Roy and sent the fiddle to him. Roy loves the tone and has used it ever since.

Roy, of course, has used other fiddles. A. L. Cassady gave his fiddle construction tools to his great-great-nephew, Evart Acuff. Evart was Uncle Charlie's son and Roy's first cousin and he became a skilled fiddle-maker. Evart's nineteenth fiddle was made from an apple tree from Uncle Charlie's yard, and Roy purchased it when he came through East Tennessee in 1945. Roy has used this fiddle on occasion.

For a long time Roy had yearned for a truly superb fiddle that would be alive with brilliance, one with great age and value, and a pedigree to prove it. During the summer of 1973 he pressed his search in earnest, and bought such a fiddle from Salvatore Picardini, a retired concert violinist living in Ripley, New York. The instrument was made in 1720 by a member of the Guarnerius family. However, Roy has never used this fiddle on stage, but he has turned it over to Howard Forrester, who plays it regularly on the Opry. If Roy ever does perform with this fiddle, the question is: will he balance it?

When Roy Acuff first came to the Opry he came as a fiddler, and although he didn't regard himself to be of championship caliber, he had full confidence in his ability and wasn't worried about any fiddler on the show, not even its chief fiddler at that time, Arthur Smith. But in October 1943, when the "Prince Albert Show" went on a full network status, he began to have doubts. "I began to realize that I couldn't read continuity, sing, introduce people, and fiddle all at the same time." Because of these realizations, and also knowing that his singing was his main contribution to the troupe's success, Roy stopped playing the fiddle and starting balancing it on his nose to keep it in the act.

Late in 1943 Roy hired a fiddler, Tommy Magness, who had previously played with Bill Monroe. Tom was so proficient that on March 16, 1948, Roy asked him to record his repertoire of fiddle tunes on a home disc recorder. Magness, backed by Os on the straight guitar, thus recorded a great many fiddle tunes for Roy, announcing each tune's key, and usually the title, before playing it. Magness also did the fiddling, at the recording session of January 1949, of eight fiddle tunes that were released as one of Roy's Columbia albums, "Old Time Barn Dance."

However, the band lost Magness's services at just about this time. One story why Tommy left was that during an extended tour, he received word his wife had purchased a new Chevy, which was too much for the easygoing fiddler. He simply couldn't wait to get home to drive it. A more likely reason is that Tommy, like Rachel Veach, had an aversion to flying.

Through the late 1940s and into the last part of 1951 there was a succession of fiddlers, including Tommy Jackson, Hal Smith, Arthur Smith, Floyd Ethridge, and Benny Martin. Then in late 1951 Roy Acuff acquired Howard Forrester, known as "Big Howdy," or just "Howdy."

Howdy was born in Hickman County on March 31, 1922, the youngest of four boys, Clyde, Clayton, Joe, and Howdy. Their father, a talented fiddler, was killed in 1927 when a car in which he was a passenger was struck at an unmarked crossing by a train.

Despite this tragedy, the family remained on their Tennessee farm. Various uncles would visit occasionally to help out. One was Uncle Bob, a champion old-time fiddler. Howdy started to pick the banjo. Then, when he was 11, he contracted rheumatic fever and, although it was not an extreme case, the youngster had to convalesce quietly for almost eight months. There was no record player available, but his mother would hum tunes to Howdy and help him pick them out on his dad's old fiddle. A grandfather had traded for it and it had gone through the Civil War. The boy's talent was further developed with help from Uncle Bob.

Howdy and his brothers soon formed a band and worked square dances. Clayton danced while Clyde played the guitar and Joe the bass. Howdy would sit and fiddle; he was so small that his feet barely touched the ground. The family moved to Nashville in 1935.

In Nashville Howard got his first professional music job on a small station. Soon he was on the Opry playing fiddle for an ex-member of the Vagabonds, an old-time act that had split into singles. Then he joined Harold Goodman's Tennessee Valley Boys, another Opry act. It was Goodman who tagged him Howdy.

He left the Opry and migrated west playing with western dance bands in Oklahoma and Texas. There, in 1940, he met and married Billie, known professionally as "Sally Ann," who is adept with fiddle, piano, accordion, bass fiddle, and guitar. She's also a fine singer. Howdy and Billie returned to Nashville and worked with Bill Monroe, then Billie continued with Monroe while Howdy served a three-year navy hitch, which ended in 1946. Upon his return, both continued with Bill Monroe for awhile. In 1947 their only child, Bobby, was born. Besides being a good musician, Bob is a teacher of higher mathematics.

In the late 1940s Howdy and his family returned to Texas and he again worked with Western swing bands. He played on KRLD in Dallas and obtained a job with a well-known fiddler, Georgia Slim. With Georgia Slim and the Texas Roundup, he did a session on the Mercury label. Slim played two fiddle tunes and Howdy two. In 1950, Howdy was back at the Opry working with Cowboy Copas, and in the latter part of 1951 he became a Smoky Mountain Boy.

Howdy does not appear to be an old-time country fiddler: he doesn't have chin whiskers running down to the fiddle, he doesn't hold it on his chest, and he doesn't slouch when he plays. Howdy tucks his fiddle under his clean-shaven chin and stands straight, with feet placed in the manner of a concert violinist. Furthermore, he insists on using a tuning fork. But looks are deceiving. When the music pours out it is powerfully evident that Howdy Forrester is, indeed, one of the finest of all the traditional country fiddlers, and certainly the finest fiddler Roy ever had. In fact, Howdy is the finest fiddler he has ever known.

When asked where he learned the fiddle Howdy says, "I studied down in Hickman County, where a large percentage of people try the fiddle but not very many of them actually learn it." Of his music he gives an answer that many talented musicians subscribe to, "The ability to play the fiddle is just born in you and you've got to get it out of you."

Howdy provided talented fiddling for Roy Acuff for over ten years. More important, he was a stalwart of the band during this period. By January 1964 he tired of traveling and Roy, knowing this, remarked that they were all getting a little older and asked Howdy if he would like to take a crack at something different. In this way Howdy was brought into the Acuff-Rose establishment, under the late Jim McConnell, to learn the booking business. By 1965 he became the manager of the Acuff-Rose Artists' Corporation. From January of 1964 until mid-1967, he rarely traveled with the Acuff troupe. (When asked if he went on a Vietnam tour, he answered, "Oh, no, they shoot agents there!") But he appeared regularly with them on the Opry. In the late summer of 1967 he resolved not to play professionally again, but this only lasted about three months. Howdy now performs with Roy on the Opry.

A number of fiddlers filled in during Howdy's absences. Benny Martin sometimes joined, especially for foreign tours. Jackie Phelps occasionally traded his guitar for the fiddle. Jimmy Lunsford did some fiddling in 1966 and 1967, and Joe Green fiddled in 1969. Currently Charlie Collins puts down his guitar and does a little fiddling.

However, on rare occasions, the Smoky Mountain Boys have been treated by the return of a long-lost fiddler, Roy himself.

In the mid-1960s, partially due to the automobile accident and partly from a general slowdown in activities, Roy Acuff found that with more free evenings at home he was becoming restless. He began to wander off to his room by himself in the evenings for an hour or so of practice on the fiddle, instead of sitting with Mildred and watching "Green Acres" or "Sanford and Son" on television. As his practicing continued—it had been 20 years since he seriously played the fiddle—he gradually regained his ability and could play a few tunes with reasonable skill.

He got out the Magness home disc recordings and began to enjoy them again. Then Roy began playing the fiddle in the dressing room with the boys. Gradually he realized something important: "I really lost something, and I didn't know it. Hiring someone to fiddle for me was something I should *never* have done because fiddling is something I dearly love."

Although Roy feels that the fiddle will always be used in country music, he is concerned that its use in old-time breakdowns is decreasing. "We don't have as many young boys as we used to learning the fiddle, and even some of the older boys are forgetting the old fiddle tunes. We don't want to ever let these tunes get away from us and lose their parts on the 'Grand Ole Opry.' "

Even though confident he could play a fairly good country fiddle, Roy was still reluctant to play it in front of an audience. Many urged him to do so, knowing that his playing would give old time fiddling a boost. Os suggested that Roy sit alone on the Opry stage to present some tunes, but Roy hesitated a long time before he played his fiddle publicly. The first occurrence was on the Opry in early 1966. It was toward the end of the program and they had a little extra time. Roy played a rollicking rendition in the key of A of "Sugar in the Gourd," which was accompanied by Os's antics and followed by great applause. Afterwards Roy said that this applause scared him so much that "I was as nervous, honestly, as the first time that I tried to fiddle on stage."

Another incident occurred on the "Wilburn Brothers" TV show a couple of years later. Roy had reminisced about the difficulties he'd had getting on the Opry, and then he tried to get by simply "playing" his Yo-Yo. But he was prevailed upon to fiddle "Turkey Buzzard," which was one of the tunes he had mentioned earlier on the show.

In the early 1970s Roy occasionally fiddled on the Opry and even played at the Renfro Valley Hoedown in June, 1971, and at Nashville's Fan Fair. Jim Riddle commented, "Roy has improved greatly and can fiddle the heck out of a great many tunes."[*] But Roy usually maintains that he is not good enough, and in his nervousness he gets thrown off and switches from one tune to another.

So today Howdy does most of the fiddling. But now that Roy has even more free time, he will, no doubt, continue his practicing and, perhaps, play the fiddle to a greater extent during his Opry performances.

Smoky Mountain Girls

Rachel was the most famous Smoky Mountain Girl, but there were others.

Velma Williams. Velma and her sister, Mildred, joined in 1942 when Odie went into the service. They were billed as the "Williams Sisters" during the tent show that summer. Mildred soon left. Velma

---

[*]Charlie Collins has done much to encourage Roy, and about 1970 or 1971 Roy asked Charlie to back him on the guitar while Roy recorded some fiddle tunes. The two went to Acuff-Rose where they, along with an engineer, recorded 20 tunes. So material for an Acuff fiddle album exists, waiting to be released.

played the bass and sang. Upon Rachel's departure, Velma was billed with Oswald as "Oswald and his Big Sister," but the act never caught on as well as that of Rachel and Oswald. Velma left permanently around 1948, and married Hal Smith who was doing the fiddling for Roy about this time. Her departure marked the end of the exaggerated hillbilly girls in the Acuff act. From this point on the Smoky Mountain Girls became sophisticated and non-hillbilly.

La Croy Sisters. Helen, Inez, and Ann joined the band around 1949. They recorded "Waltz of the Winds" and "Waltz of Broken Vows" with the Smoky Mountain Boys at the regular Acuff recording session of January 16, 1951. The sisters also worked on a series of 52 15-minute transcriptions for the Royal Crown Cola Company. They left the act around 1952.

Jerry Johnson. Jerry Johnson is a member of the Leary Family of entertainers. Her sister is Wilma Lee (Cooper). She appeared with her husband Johnny and formed the team of Jerry and Johnny, which appeared on the "Louisiana Hayride" and "Wheeling Jamboree" shows. Jerry played bass, and had a big voice and was billed as the "Smoky Mountain Sweetheart." She was with the troupe as a regular from August 29, 1953, until May 7, 1955. Late in 1960 she went on an Acuff overseas tour.

June Webb. June joined the band around 1957 and appeared continuously until mid-1960.

Melba Montgomery. Melba played with the band as early as 1958, and continued off and on until mid-1962.

Margie Bowes. Margie performed with the troupe around 1959 and 1960.

June Stearns. June came from a prominent musical family in Franklin, Indiana. Not expecting to really get a job with Roy, she wrote him a letter when she was 22 and enclosed a picture. Her husband later said, "Roy has never gotten over that picture." The photo showed her sister and herself and under it she wrote, "I'm the one with the guitar." Her first appearance with the band was on September 30, 1960. Her ankle was broken in Roy's automobile wreck of July, 1965. When Roy made his first appearance on the Opry after the wreck, the much more seriously injured Shot was with him, but June was "still recuperating." She did not appear again. While she was with the band, the boys teased her because she took every opportunity to sleep and rest.

After the departure of June Stearns in 1965, the troupe has not had any more female performers who could be considered regular Smoky Mountain Girls.

These girls, then, are the ones who have played with the band, at least for a short period, regularly in the United States. Other girls have been Smoky Mountain Girls for short periods during overseas tours to entertain servicemen, but they have not been included.

A Few More Smoky Mountain Boys

Quite a number of musicians have been Smoky Mountain Boys for short periods. Listed here are those who have made substantial contributions in their brief time with Roy Acuff's troupe.

Sonny Day. Francis Jacob Tamburin—"Sonny Day"—came to the band in September 1944 as Jim Riddle's replacement when Jim went into the army. When Jimmie returned in July 1946, Roy kindheartly kept Sonny Day on and he continued to play the accordion, sometimes with Jim playing a twin accordion, with the troupe until he was drafted around 1949.

Shot Jackson. Harold B. Jackson was raised on a farm in southern Georgia, and he used to walk two miles to his aunt's to hear the Opry every Saturday night. For years he thought that Roy played the Dobro; later he discovered that Roy was singing and Os was picking. The instrument fascinated him. He was a member of the Bailes Brothers troupe on the Opry both before and after his navy service during the war. Around 1948 he went with that troupe to Shreveport, Louisiana, and played on the "Hayride" show. In 1952 he returned to Nashville with Johnny and Jack.

During 1955 and 1956 when Johnny and Jack and Kitty Wells were playing closely with the Acuff troupe, Shot could almost be considered a Smoky Mountain Boy. After this tour Roy heard that Shot was out of a job and phoned him and said, "I have told Mildred to put you on the payroll." Shot, playing the electric steel guitar, was with the band steadily from 1957, except for a brief period in 1962 and 1963, until the wreck of July 1965. Since then Shot has made occasional appearances in Roy's band.

Having personally built houseboats for lakes at Dunbar Cave and at Roy's Hendersonville house, in the early 1960s he and Buddy Emmons teamed to create the Sho-Bud Company, which manufactures various types of guitars. At first it was in a garage on the outskirts of Nashville. Right from the start business was good, and the company now is located around the corner from the Ryman in downtown Nashville.

Jackie Phelps. Jackie joined the band on August 5, 1961, at Atlamont, Illinois. He was the first Smoky Mountain Boy to play an electric Spanish guitar. Jackie was hired to replace Lonnie Wilson, and he occasionally appeared in costume for the antics during the Classical Routine. For a time he dressed like Os and took part in a Big Os—Little Os act, but this fizzled. After being hired in 1961, he stayed with the band until the latter part of 1963. Jackie joined up again in 1967. In 1969 he began appearing with Jimmie Riddle on "Hee Haw" and on September 1, 1970, he resigned from the Acuff troupe in order to devote more time to television and related activities. Even so, he has appeared as a Smoky Mountain Boy at various times.

Jimmy Fox. James A. Headrick was with the band for a short time from late 1964 to early 1966. His instrument was the electric take-off guitar.

Gene Martin. Gene is the brother of Benny Martin. He played the rhythm guitar with the group on a regular basis starting early in 1962, and stayed until the end of 1965. He now appears with the group occasionally.

Onie Wheeler. Onie joined the band late in 1964 and stayed as a regular until July 1967. He has returned to the group periodically. When he is with the band he plays the harmonica, and even docs the whistle for the "Cannonball." When Onie is there, Jimmie plays the piano.

Nelson Brothers. Doyle Nelson played the flat-top rhythm guitar with the troupe in 1966 and 1967. Jay, who played the electric Spanish guitar, joined the band in 1965. They both quit in July 1967 to work in Shot's Sho-Bud shop. Jay performs with the band from time to time, and when he does he usually plays the flat-top rhythm guitar.

Larry McNeely. He joined in July 1967 with his banjo, and was a refreshing young addition to the band during his short tenure. He resigned in the late spring of 1969 to appear on the "Glen Campbell Show."

Charlie Collins. Charlie joined Roy's troupe along with his good friend Larry McNeely in July 1967, and resigned with Larry in the spring of 1969. However, Charlie soon returned. The older members agree that Charlie is the finest rhythm guitar player they have ever heard, who does a beautiful job of keeping Os on time and Roy on key. Charlie also plays the fiddle and mandolin. He has a wife and three children. Charlie was born in 1933 and only wishes he had become a Smoky Mountain Boy about 15 years earlier.

Ode on a Classical Jug

All of the Smoky Mountain Boys and Girls, many of them dressed in outlandish costumes, have taken greater individual parts in the show than do members of most country bands. Each is talented and amusing. In fact, Roy has always prided himself in having a group that can perform individually and collectively. Down through the years, the band has developed two sub-acts of particular note, the Jug Band and the Classical Routine.

The Jug Band is an act that features two special instruments. Os puts down his Dobro and plays a jug by blowing across its top. In the 1940s the jug was sometimes played by a small 13-year-old Negro boy named Bobby Hebb, who also played the spoons and danced and sang. He was a regular Smoky Mountain Child for about a year. The other instrument in the Acuff Jug Band is a washboard with horns and gadgets attached. This was played by Jess Easterday, who originally was the leader of the band. Upon Easterday's departure, Odie would manipulate this contraption. Sometimes Robert Lunn was a featured Smoky Mountain Boy, and he would play the washboard. Lunn was one of the originators of the jug and washboard band idea. During Jug Band performances, the rest of the group usually stands by, watching, although some members might join and frolic with a few noisemakers.

During the 1940s and 1950s the Jug Band put on regular performances. Jimmie Riddle and Joe Zinkan did duets on "Shot Gun Boogie," "Thirty Days," and "Chiquita Banana," and Riddle soloed on "I'm Walkin' " and "Yes Sir." The whole band would play "Uncle Noah's Ark" and "Uncle Eeep's Got the Coon," and the Jug Band backed Roy on "Sixteen Chickens and a Tambourine," which was recorded for Capitol in the early 1950s. The record was labelled "Roy Acuff and His Jug Band."

The Jug Band has never officially broken up. Every now and then—time permitting—it will huff and puff a tune or two. When it does, Jimmie usually sings "Yes Sir," and Os once in a great while will do "They Cut Down the Old Pine Tree."

The act that's come to be called the "Classical Routine" took much more time than the Jug Band's one or two tunes. It was put on mainly during road performances, because the economics of broadcast time precludes long acts on the Opry. Since the troupe no longer travels much, the Classical Routine is performed only rarely these days.

It was Roy's idea and it evolved in the mid-1940s. Many of the jokes and the shenanigans were learned in the medicine show. Sonny Day, with a fiddle, was originally in charge; his cohorts were Lonnie and Joe Zinkan. After Sonny's departure, Jimmie and his harmonica led the routine and he has been responsible for teaching it to new members, such as to Jackie Phelps.

The Classical Routine, like the Jug Band, had its heyday in the 1940s and 1950s. Here is what a typical performance was like.

Roy started by quieting the audience, then began a very formal introduction:

> You know, friends, when we walk on the stage wherever it may be we realize that everyone in the audience might not enjoy the informal way in which we put on a program. So we are going to switch now from the country field of music and entertain those of you who would like maybe a little different style. These boys are versatile, they can switch around. They can play pop music or rock and roll—but we are going to pass up those fields and do what some folks call "eatin' high on the hog." We're going to eat there right now and play what actually is our second choice in music, classical.

At this moment Jimmie, Pap Wilson, and Smiling Joe Zinkan (or if Lonnie Wilson was not with the group, Joe would be Pap and a substitute bass player, such as Oral Rhodes or Junior Huskey would be called) made their appearances dressed in formal although woefully unpressed black tails and various types of corresponding hats. The audience, naturally, began to laugh. Roy continued his introductory remarks:

> Now I don't want you to let these little suits bother you. When we do classical music we dress a little bit on the formal side. If you should sit at a symphony, you'd see people dressed in frocks like this. I'll admit they'd probably be a little better pressed, but we've been on a tour and haven't had proper valet service.
>
> But Jimmie Riddle and the boys are perfectly capable of playing classical music, and you'll enjoy the style in which they go at it. Listen to them. The first number—I should say rendition—when speaking of classical music, will be "Hot Canary."

Os and the others thereupon lurched into the "Luke Warm Jay

Bird." During this number, Howdy, not dressed formally, windmilled his arm while fiddling and Jim played quantities of harmonica. As the tune ran its course there was much whistling, with Os doing a lot of crazy yelling.

Then Jim acknowledged the applause by announcing, "Thank you, all you lovers of classical music. Now that we have found out what you sure enough do appreciate, we would like to do another number for you."

And Os said in a very loud voice while rolling his eyeballs, "By all means!"

Jim, again trying—futilely—to enforce the propriety of the performance, pleaded, "Now, let's be serious."

Os responded, "You be serious and I'll be Roebuck."

Jim, believing Os would conform, said, with satisfaction, "Our next number will be, 'Czardas.' "

Confidently and serenely, Jim started it off with the harmonica, followed by a heavy guitar strumming, which was in the Spanish classical style reminiscent of the tune's Gypsy origin. Then there was uproar—a wild bass fiddle break, general merriment and pranking, and a loud clatter and yells and a gunshot, followed by Indian drums and war whoops and a lively rendition, mostly harmonica, of the "William Tell Overture." Finally, Os yelled, "Hiyo Silver!"

Today, on the rare occasions when the Classical Routine is performed, Jimmie still leads. Os, attired in a black frock coat, is the second man. The third member of the act varies, but still does a lot of leaping and dancing in this old, familiar, but very popular riotous act.

"Roy's Boys" and Roy

Country musicians tend to be transient, to wander from band to band. Roy Acuff has been fortunate that the nucleus of his band has remained with him longer than have the members of any other Opry act. No sideman has been with any star longer than Os or even Jim. Furthermore, many of Roy's other regulars, such as Lonnie, Joe, Howdy, and Charlie, have had remarkably long periods of employment. There are a number of reasons.

The way the Smoky Mountain Boys—Roy's Boys—are allowed to dress has been an influence. The leaders of most country music acts wear flashy Western outfits, and the members of their bands, while dressed in less flashy garb, have a uniform exactly like that of the sideman next to him. This tends to stifle individualism, which is necessary to the creativity of a musician.

First things first—the Smoky Mountain Boys are not cowboys, nor do they sing cowboy music. They are hill-country people and play hillbilly music and so they dress like country boys.

The realization that the band should dress individually came early in Roy's career. The dress of his early band featured differing plaids and checks, and these outlandish hillbilly costumes, worn by most of the band, were in vogue for over 20 years. Today only Os wears a real costume, but the casual dress of the Smoky Mountain Boys remains individualistic, and each can be more easily identified on stage because of this. About the only way Roy differs from the rest is that he usually is the only one wearing a jacket. In very recent years the band has appeared rather regularly in shirts of the same color or pattern. Of course, Os continues to wear his overalls even if his shirt matches those of the other Smoky Mountain Boys.

Between Opry segments or road show performances most members of Roy's band usually return to the dressing room for a jam session. These often include musicians from other acts, and from time to time Roy participates.

Unlike most acts, the Smoky Mountain Boys do many nonmusical things together. When Roy owned Dunbar Cave the band frequently was there on its free time to build improvements and barbecue grills and make water bikes. It was hard work, but even June Webb got in the act. Not very good with hammer and nails, she was designated the official painter. During this period, in the mid-1950s, Shot Jackson supervised the construction of two houseboats. The *Shot Jackson Ferry* was built for the lake at Dunbar Cave and Roy became so fond of it that Shot built another, the *Blind Barthimaeus*, for Roy's home on Old Hickory Lake. Both boats were used extensively by Roy and his boys for pleasure, and the cost of outfitting one of them for a party was about $250.

Camaraderie is wonderful but it doesn't feed hungry mouths, which leads to a big reason why many of Roy's Boys have remained with the band so long. Most stars pay their sidemen a salary only during road trips (and with some stars the musicians were lucky if they could even collect that), and pay them only for specific shows when the group is in Nashville. That has not been the way for Roy's Boys.

As soon as a musician had been with the band a reasonable time he was paid weekly not only when on the road but he also qualified for a weekly home salary, which was slightly less than his road salary. He received this home salary even though his only work during the week was to play on the Opry. Roy did this because, he said, "They've got to live like everyone else. They've got families to raise, obligations to meet and I think it's only right to see to it that they can depend on a regular income." Payment came on Friday, usually with checks written by Mildred.* But by check or cash, Roy Acuff never missed a payday, and such scrupulous honesty is most unusual in the country music business. Recently more stars are paying their bands regular salaries. Hank Williams was one of the first to follow Roy's example.

Roy generally looks after his band like a father would. He has kept band members he didn't need because he knew they needed him. An example of this occurred during World War II when the draft depleted the band and he had to hire new boys. After the war he took the regulars back, and also kept the substitutes for varying periods. Musicians have been hired simply because Roy felt he could help them develop as individuals; some have been fired for short periods for the same reason. Roy generally considers it his duty to obtain medication and professional care, if needed, for the boys.

For the musicians who have been the nucleus of the Smoky Mountain Boys for so many years, Roy has also contributed greatly to their financial welfare. Howdy was placed in Acuff-Rose, but what of Jimmy and Os? Most country musicians, even if they've worked many years for a particular star, are out in the cold when the act ceases to exist. Jimmie and Os, though, don't have to worry about either their immediate or distant futures.

When Opryland opened in 1972 and Roy curtailed his road activity, he immediately obtained employment for Os—and for Charlie—in the park. They work daily as strolling musicians. Jimmie, of course, has "Hee Haw" and other commitments. Besides these provisions, Roy, in keeping with his steady concern, no doubt is thinking about the long-range welfare of these boys.

In the early days Roy was pushed around, and he knows how it feels. It is not surprising, therefore, that he stands up for his boys at all times. Furthermore, he has always been able to joke and kid around with his troupe and be one of them. He feels this has been a

---

*As of very recently, because Roy has cut down almost entirely on touring, he no longer pays his band directly. They are paid by WSM and Opryland.

big factor in the cohesiveness of the group. Roy attributes a great measure of the success he has attained to his band, and calls them the greatest team of country music performers in the world. But more than that, he treasures their loyalty and friendship. The feeling is mutual.

IV

The Acuff Sound

What Comes Naturally

The Acuff Sound needs very little rehearsal. For the Opry, there are some gatherings, though not really formal rehearsals, in the dressing room. On the road, the troupe usually has its performances pretty well fixed in its mind before leaving, and the boys never have what most people would term a rehearsal.

Occasionally this policy is a source of consternation, particularly to a stage manager. One example was a November 1971 appearance in California at the John Wayne Theater in Knott's Berry Farm. It is a beautiful theater, with a water curtain and much equipment. The man asked for a rehearsal. Ray ran through the first two numbers quickly so the technicians could get a sound check, and then quit. The stage manager gulped, and said quietly that he had never seen such a rehearsal. Roy was nonplused at the man's surprise. Later Roy put at ease a drummer and electric guitarist, who were going to back him up for that one show, by saying, "Don't worry. If you get in a few extra beats, I'll congratulate you."

About the only time the Acuff gang goes through anything even remotely resembling a rehearsal would be for a big Las Vegas show, especially if other acts are involved. Of course, if a new Smoky Mountain Boy joins the group, there usually is an informal musical get-together to indoctrinate him to the Acuff Sound.

None of "Roy's Boys" ever had formal music lessons and none can read music really well. Howdy and Jim can, but slowly. So during performances the boys pretty much "just do what comes natu-

106

rally." Once in a great, great while this naturalness turns out to be ragged, with confused vocals, breaks, and kickoffs, but it's rare.

One would think' that a lack of rehearsal would have to be made up for on the stage, but such is not the case. Kickoffs and breaks are frequently announced vocally, and because this oral direction is part of an informal country presentation, the audience readily understands it. However, a country music audience is extremely unforgiving about any gestures relating to the tempo, length, or cessation of a song. Such signals have to be very surreptitious hand movements, always done with the hand that is away from the audience's view. Probably the tempo, which is supposed to be set by the rhythm guitar, or the piano when it is in use, gives the troupe its most concern. Of this Roy says, "I usually take the cue from the boys. They usually start the number. Sometimes they start the correct time, sometimes they don't. But whatever it is, I go along with it." This is about all he can do, because changing the tempo would take too much visible directing.

The Acuff Sound is a natural phenomenon. Of course, one of its largest components is Roy's voice and choice of songs. Once he abandoned the Red Jones jazzy-type material for the traditional old-time songs, and the crooning for the "old Harp singing style" he developed in the medicine show, a big part of the Acuff Sound was launched to fame.

On programs and recording sessions Roy likes to move from low to high keys, because once he hits a few high notes Roy finds it difficult to go down the scale. Concerning pitch, Roy has some trouble with the slides of the electric steel guitar and, to some extent, even the Dobro. As he puts it, "When Os plays a slide that goes from Beeeee to Zeeeee; I don't know whether to sing the Beeeee or the Zeeeee." To give him the pitch, he always tries to keep a straight guitar between him and a sliding instrument.

Roy Acuff's voice has lost a slight amount of its original quality and has lowered. Also, lengthy breath-holding periods are harder for him, which has meant the almost total dropping from his repertoire of such songs as "Precious Jewel" and "Fireball Mail." Another difficult song for Roy is "Lost Highway." Surprisingly, "Freight Train Blues" is easy for him. He can even do a Jimmie Rodgers type yodel.

But even with these subtle changes, this part of the Acuff Sound has remained relatively constant. So the main variable component has been the band instrumentation. It has changed during the years, and as it has changed, the Acuff Sound has changed.

In the beginning Roy experimented with various instruments but by the time he really began to click in Nashville, around 1941, his band was basically an old-time mountain string band, which features the fiddle and occasionally the banjo, backed by rhythm guitar, mandolin, harmonica and bass.

However, Roy's band differed from this traditional style in a number of ways. Because Roy felt he was not a superb fiddler, that instrument never took the customary dominating lead. This void was filled by the distinctive sound of the Dobro, which became the most featured instrument and basically has been responsible for the Acuff Sound. Roy says, "The Dobro is as important as the sound of my voice." Other instruments not typical of mountain string bands but given roles were the accordion and piano.

In the 1940s Roy averaged about one recording session a year for Columbia. Because the big companies didn't have recording studios in Nashville until the mid-1950s, these sessions were held in such places as Dallas, Chicago, Hollywood, and New York, and they produced hit after hit. At these sessions Roy never tried for perfection and, in fact, proved that it wasn't necessary. "Each time you sing a song, trying to make it better, I think you lose something. My policy in the studio is that once you decide to do a number, put everything you've got into it and don't say, 'Well, we can always do it over.' Let's do it right the first time and to hell with the rest."

While others struggled through take after take, Roy would usually let it stand after one—and earned the nickname "One Take Ache." Art Satherley, Roy's A&R man with Columbia, marveled at Roy's sessions. "He was the easiest man I ever recorded. We once recorded eight sides in an hour and 45 minutes, and that's still a record for the artists I've recorded."

These unpolished recordings were so popular that Roy was often compared with Bing Crosby. The Acuff Sound was in such demand that he recorded quite a few 16-inch transcriptions and some 12-inch V-Discs for the Armed Forces Radio Service toward the end of World War II. The transcriptions were played over the AFRS stations and the V-Discs, along with sturdy hand-cranked record players, were dropped on the beaches after invasions.

Today if a recording sells about 50,000 copies it is considered a hit. But back in those days a record had to sell half a million copies or the company complained. During this period Columbia was rarely dissatisfied with Roy's material, for almost all of the songs sold at least half a million and some of them sold many millions. His record sales then totalled more than 25 million. If regular gold records had been awarded at that time, Roy Acuff could have opened an exhibit at Fort Knox.

By the very early 1950s the songs and instrumentation of country music became less traditional. Having had tremendous success, Roy resisted this change violently, sticking to non-electrified instruments and the old-time songs. But gradually he, too, began to change. First evidence was in the songs he recorded. Art Satherley wanted him to change his style, so his final Columbia sessions of January, May, and September 1951 included "Ten Little Numbers" and "Don't Hang Your Dirty Linen on My Line." These songs definitely were not Roy's style. Sales went down and a mutual unhappiness developed between Roy and Columbia Records. At the end of 1951, despite the advice of Fred Rose, Roy left Columbia.

After a year of nonaffiliation, Roy signed with Capitol in 1953. Rerecordings of earlier hits and a few new titles—"Lonesome Joe," "Sunshine Special," "The Thief Upon the Tree," "What do You Think About Me," and especially, "River of Crystal"—were reminiscent of his old successful style, but in general his Capitol recordings were like his last Columbia sessions. His association with Capitol ended in 1955, and Roy later said, "They wanted me to go. I guess they just wanted something by me on their label."

So by the mid-1950s Roy Acuff found himself still playing to packed houses but with sagging record sales. To rebuild sales Roy felt that, rather than going back to the traditional songs that had been so successful, he should adopt appropriate instrumentation to back up the more modern songs he was then singing.

The band's first electric instrument was Os's screechy electric Dobro. When that was disposed of in 1947, the band returned to its nonelectric composition. This continued until 1956. In 1955 and 1956 the Acuff troupe toured very closely with Johnny and Jack and Kitty Wells. During this tour Shot Jackson, who was playing the Dobro and electric steel guitar with the Wells group, also played the electric steel guitar with the Acuff band. When the two groups parted in 1956, Shot was hired by Roy and officially became a Smoky Mountain Boy. The first electric Spanish guitar was played by Jackie Phelps when he joined in 1961. A few other musicians, such as Jay

Nelson and Jimmie Fox, also have played this instrument with the Acuff troupe. Adding to this modernization, Roy found a little snare drum in an Oklahoma City pawnshop in 1962 and since that time frequently played it with brushes. When these electric instruments were added, Os took up the conventional Spanish guitar and the Dobro—symbol of the Acuff Sound—was put in its case, only to be taken out once or twice each show when the original Acuff Sound was recreated for old-time fans. The Dobro-in-its-case era lasted from about 1955 to 1962.

Deciding to modernize the established Acuff Sound was not easy. Furthermore, Roy really didn't want to do it, but he did so hoping that when the rock and roll era came to an end the trend would be back to traditional country music. "People think that we are getting away from country music, but we really aren't," said Roy, wistfully. "Someday I'll get back to the good ones because the trend will swing back." The decision was distasteful, but Roy made it because he was convinced such modernization was absolutely necessary to keep Roy Acuff and His Smoky Mountain Boys alive professionally.

This era, from the mid-1950s to early 1960s, marks the low point in Roy Acuff's career. Much later, when Jimmie C. Newman mentioned on the Opry that his hit song of "Falling Star" was recorded around 1957, Roy said, in a quip, "That's what I was doin' 'bout that time."

In 1953, Acuff-Rose started its Hickory Label. When Roy left Capitol in 1955 he wanted to switch immediately to Hickory, but Fred Rose advised against it because he felt that people would think Roy was hogging his own company and also that he was recording for his own label because he couldn't get a contract with one of the larger labels. So when Roy left Capitol he switched to Decca and recorded eight songs in 1955 and 1956. The main reason was that the billing of the Acuff and Kitty Wells troupes during these two years was the "King and Queen of Country Music." Two of the eight songs were duets with Kitty Wells. In this period, Roy recorded 12 hymns for MGM, vaguely reminiscent of the old Acuff Sound.

On October 29, 1957, Roy finally realized his four-year wish and made his first session with Hickory. This produced "Once More"; a heavy promotional campaign led it to become the first Acuff title on the charts in many years. Generally, the Hickory sessions of the late 1950s and early 1960s only demonstrated that Roy was still clinging—after a decade—to the modern Acuff Sound. By this time, it became clear to Roy that his modern sound wasn't helping him professionally.

So Roy began a middle course, one which he sometimes continues today. It isn't the old or the modern, it's midway. While it includes the drum and electric instruments, the old Dobro is back in prominence and more of the songs are in the old traditional style.

In fact, much to the delight of Os, Howdy, and all of the old-time music fans, the old Acuff Sound returned on June 12, 1963, when "all the electricity was unplugged" and Roy recorded 12 songs, 11 of which he had never recorded before: extremely old traditional country songs, for which he composed the arrangements. Roy made the selections from childhood favorites. No one knows who wrote most of them. Howdy feels this session was even better than the old "golden" Acuff Sound of the 1940s.

Two months after this session, Roy recorded another group of songs in a very modern style with a hand-clapping vocal chorus. In an interview in the 1960s, he stated:

> I believe that any kind of music must broaden out and be different, get better. I like to be on stage with drums, and I have no objection to electrified instruments as long as they don't blast them too loud, as long as they play them like they should be played. I'll agree that I can't do too well with the steel guitar. The slides are hard to follow because they don't produce a definite note. But the electric Spanish guitar, if it is played right, it has a bounce and the sound fills an auditorium, and it is acceptable in my act.*

The Acuff Sound of the 1960s was neither old nor modern, but vacillated between the two.

With the dawn of the 1970s, Roy seemed to be leaning more toward the old Acuff Sound. Many performances did not include any electrification, and crowd response had been enthusiastic. Roy felt that at this stage of his career, he had nothing to lose by reverting to the Old Acuff Sound.

A "happening" in Roy's career of the 1970s occurred in August of 1971. Bill McEuen, manager of the Nitty Gritty Dirt Band, a bearded and long-haired group, had the idea of his band recording with some of the old-time country music greats, especially Roy Acuff. McEuen called Wesley Rose, Roy's A&R man with Hickory, and Roy agreed because Wesley asked him. Roy also got information about the group from his son, Roy Neill.

---

* Cherry tape.

"I was a little hesitant," Roy said later, "because I'm not a lover of the hippy class of people." Hesitancy was evident on the other side, too, because McEuen kept the session a secret until the last moment, and then asked the very few visitors to stay away from the United Artists studio until the group and Roy had gotten used to each other. When Roy entered the studio he was polite, but in a cool way. However, when he heard the playbacks of some of the numbers the Dirt Band had been doing, and realized they were good country, he soon became at ease.

The session was historic. Os was there and did three solo numbers, and this session marked the first time that Roy had ever recorded without his band. He had ample help, though. Besides the Dirt Band and Roy and Os, Mother Maybelle Carter, Doc Watson, Earl Scruggs, Merle Travis, and Jimmy Martin were there. Roy refused to do the "Cannonball" and "The Bird," but did record four numbers: "I Saw the Light," "Precious Jewel," "Pins and Needles," and "Wreck on the Highway." Next day the group all joined in on "Will the Circle be Unbroken."

After the session Roy said this about the Dirt Band:

> I was in the studio with them, but I didn't see them. Their faces were covered. I didn't know if I was in the studio with boys 18 or 38 or 48. I couldn't tell. I didn't know if they were boys, men, or maybe girls! You're supposed to know a man by the character of his face, but they had their faces all covered up with something. I'll just tell you they were very nice and they were very interesting, and they certainly knew what they were doing. When I went into the studio I said, "Fellers, they call me One Take Ache, now let's get this over with," and they took me at my word and we did it in one take and that was it. They really were a good group of boys. I would have liked to have seen them. I asked why they objected to being called country. You know, the only thing they said was that the word country can hurt the sales of a song and I agree with them to a certain extent.*

Another reason why Roy consented to the session was because, he said, "I wanted to acquaint the Nitty Band's large listening audience with my kind of music. They came to my style, I didn't go to theirs. Nothing but plain country instruments were used."

Soon after the session, "I Saw the Light" came out on a 45 rpm and it became the first Acuff number to hit the charts in a long time.

---

*This is a compilation of several sources, but especially of Steve Goldstein, "Opryland to Politics to Yo-Yos . . . An interview with Roy Acuff," *Country Music*, October 1972, p. 38.

This recording even won him a Grammy nomination for "Best Country Vocal Performance by a Duo or Group." The awards were presented in March 1972, and even though Roy lost to Conway Twitty and Loretta Lynn's "After the Fire is Gone," the nomination marked an important event in Roy's career. *Record World* of January 1, 1972, had a story entitled, "Roy Acuff, Young America Folk Hero," which said that Roy was playing college campuses and that an Acuff revival was budding.

The entire session was released on a three-record deluxe LP, "Will the Circle Be Unbroken." Its artistry is apparent, and within a short while it had grossed a million dollars; and early in 1974 gold records were awarded.

Furthermore, on December 7, 1973, Roy had made what turned out to be another remarkable session. Howdy and Os were the only Smoky Mountain Boys in attendance, and Roy Neill, Roy's son, was one of several backup singers, which was the first time he joined his father in a session. Two of the songs were "Old Time Sunshine Song" and "Back in the Country." The latter one hit the charts immediately, quite possibly making Roy Acuff, at age 70, the oldest artist to be so honored. Encouraged by the success of this session, Roy recorded again, one year later, on December 5, 1974, using virtually the same personnel. His latest session, though, on December 17, 1975, included his entire band. What's evident is that the Acuff Sound of the 1970s is one marked by flexibility and success.

Hindsight, always clearer than foresight, is not just the province of historians. They like ifs and might-have-beens because history is a speculative business; other people like to speculate about could-have-beens. Roy admits that he modernized late, reluctantly, and only halfway. But he believed then, as he does now, that adding a steel guitar, which he says never went well with his act, was an absolute necessity. And if he hadn't, his career would have ended—by the mid-1950s his popularity was less and a few Opry sponsors were hesitant to have him host their shows, because he was "too old-timie."

Trudy and Powell Stamper, two of Roy's most respected and trusted friends, feel that he should have either modernized early and totally or stayed strictly old-time country. They also point out that if Roy had chosen the latter course, he would have benefited from the bluegrass/folk/hootenanny popularity of the late 1950s and early 1960s.

Oswald has a different view. He has always been very much

against any trend away from authentic old-time hillbilly music, and strongly felt then, and feels today, that Roy's career would have been better if he had never used electricity or drums.

As evidence, Os cites Roy's appearance on March 28, 1970, at the International Country and Western Music Festival at Wembley Pool in London, England. On this occasion, even though Roy was only one of a dozen big-name stars, the Acuff segment literally stopped the show. It was the most enthusiatic audience before which the gang has ever played. The applause and shouting were so great that plaster fell off the walls. This crowd especially appreciated Os and his Dobro. After the show when Charlie Walker, who had predicted the Acuff triumph, said to Os, "You really put it to 'em," Os grinned and replied, "I put a little o' that unamplified Dobro to 'em."

Furthermore, Os feels that Roy does better performing slow numbers, and that most of the fast songs are "no account." Oswald says "We never got bad mail about our playing until the steel guitar. The folks didn't like it. After we got electric instruments, we got bad mail."

Jim Riddle never really cared one way or the other about electricity; but Jim thinks that he can hear better what he is doing without it. Mildred points out that the fan mail always has been, and continues to be, heavily in favor of no electricity or drums.

How would an early and complete modernization have affected the career of Roy Acuff? What if he had continued with the old style? It's iffy. As Roy says, "The past is done done."

A Recording Session

In 1967 Roy decided that another recording session was in order. After a discussion with Wesley Rose, the two decided on a theme. It was personal, and professional. Over the previous ten years some artists, such as Hank Locklin, Floyd Cramer, and the Louvin Brothers, had recorded albums of Roy's songs as a tribute, and so Roy felt he personally owed it to them to reciprocate, even though some of the songs might not be his style.

He brought home the records of these and other stars and played them over and over. While selecting the artists and numbers he wished to record, Roy made up his mind that he wasn't going to imitate, because that would be "crucifying" himself. As an example, he noted Hank Williams' pronunciation of invitation (invertation) in

"Wedding Bells." "That might have been okay for Hank, but if I record the song I'm not going to pronounce it that way."

Before the session in Columbia's Studio B, the Acuff gang had a gathering to determine the approximate "gears" (keys), which usually are A, F, or G. (Although Roy has recorded in every key, it's only approximate because he has said, "One day I might sing a song in A, and then the next day it would be some other way." They do not consider such a gathering to be a rehearsal because, "If you rehearse you suffer, and then you just have to suffer again during the session.")

On the day of the session, the boys were sent over ahead of time "to get their instruments accustomed to it." As the musicians arrived, each got his instrument out of its case and tuned it up. All Jimmie did was to lay out his array of harmonicas on a table.

The room was reminiscent of the inside of a barn; it had a very rough ceiling and lots of soundproofing. Built by Owen Bradley, it was a prefabricated construction called a Quonset hut. Scatter rugs covered parts of the floor. Soundproofed partitions could be rolled to desired locations.

The drums and piano were in place. Each musician, including the bass player, found a location with a suitable microphone, which then was boxed off by the portable partitions. Everyone was seated, except for the twin fiddles.

At this session of July 24, 1967, the Smoky Mountain Boys were: Oswald, on Dobro and sometimes guitar; Jimmie, piano and sometimes harmonica; Jackie, electric guitar; Howdy, fiddle; Larry, guitar and banjo; Charlie, guitar. In addition to the regulars were: Lightnin' Chance, on bass; Buddy Harman, drums, which he played lightly with a brush; and Tommy Jackson, fiddle.

Jackson had an interesting role. He was designated as "leader," and in this capacity he and Wesley Rose, the A&R man, directed the session. Of course, everyone felt free to make comments or suggestions at all times, but Jackson and Rose were the leaders. (Roy is a master at personal appearances, but for recording sessions he prefers to leave the technical leadership to others.)

During the actual recording Roy wanted to occasionally be able to direct his boys with his hands, so he picked a location from which he could see them all, although, due to the partitions, they couldn't see each other. As he sang he stood in front of a music stand, the only one in the room. When an engineer placed a special cloth covering on his microphone Roy asked, "What's that? A muzzle? Oh, that's so I won't pop my P's." As he sang he often kept the beat with his hands and feet. During the session not once did he loosen his tie.

Sessions today usually are thought of in terms of albums, with 12 songs being recorded. They usually last for three, three-hour periods, which can be strung out over three days. This particular session was scheduled for 2-5 P.M. and 6-9 P.M. As things turned out, the boys worked from 2:00 to 8:30, with only a very short break for refreshments, mostly coffee, after the first six titles had been completed. Due to union rules, musicians get paid the same amount whether they work three to nine hours, or on one or all 12 songs. Payment is a flat fee and does not include any subsequent royalties.

The electronic heart of the operation was the control room, where Wesley Rose went during the actual recording of a number. Each microphone, usually placed six to nine inches from the instrument, was connected to its own sound level device so the volume of any individual instrument could be turned up or down at Wesley's direction by the chief engineer.

The recordings were put on tape. In the main control room quarter-inch-wide tape was used for monaural and singles, and an adjacent control room recorded with half-inch-wide tape on three tracks for stereo. During the session several songs were spliced. In this manner, the first maybe having a fine ending and the next a better beginning would be spliced together. Splicing, when needed, is done by the engineers during the session, and a final master tape is available by the time the musicians are through.

Probably the most interesting thing about the July 1967 session was its spirit. Sessions of many artists deteriorate when mistakes require take after take, which tends to make musicians squabble over who will do what on each song. At the end of many hours little is accomplished—everyone has frayed nerves and is at each other's throats. However "One Take Ache's" sessions never have been characterized by this behavior, and this one was especially smooth, even though Roy had never sung any of the songs, with the exception of "Filipino Baby," before in his life.

Before each number, certain decisions had to be arrived at by mutual consent. To begin, which instruments were to be used? Jimmie, for example, stuck with the piano but on good harmonica numbers, such as "Candy Kisses" and "Foggy River," a stall and mike were provided and he switched to his harmonicas, often playing two during a single number. Os used the Dobro whenever possible, it is unsuited to some songs, especially lively ones, and so occasionally he either didn't do anything or played a straight guitar. Such a number was "Moving On," and afterwards Lightnin' commented, "I didn't know Os could play rock and roll." Larry occasionally switched from guitar to banjo and played a wild banjo break on "Filipino Baby." During the playback it prompted some laughter but was kept in when Os said simply, "I like it." Roy would frequently remind the group about the various instruments, saying, "Harp, mandolin? We can do anything we want." He seemed especially anxious that the fiddles and Dobro have prominent roles.

The main decisions were connected with the breaks, kickoffs, and number of verses to be included in each number. Care was taken that most of the songs lasted no longer than three minutes because disc jockeys, with an eye on time for commercials, are reluctant to play long numbers. Occasionally breaks were split between two instruments. Instrumentation was on the basis of what was appropriate and would befit the original artist's style. For example, to get the Ernest Tubb feeling, Jackie Phelps used his electric guitar on "Tomorrow Never Comes." And after many instrumental kickoff attempts for "Don't Let Me Cross Over," it was finally decided that Roy should kickoff the song vocally, just as Carl Butler had done on the original record. But there were no forced attempts to copy the original artists.

The group, sometimes with and sometimes without Roy, usually ran through each song before the actual recording was done, occasionally repeating certain parts so the musicians could get more accustomed to their featured segments. During these times some of the other musicians were idle and there was lots of kidding around. When the group actually was recording a red light would go on and all was quiet and relatively serious. If counting the beat was needed to start them off in sync (synchronization), that was Lightning's job. Roles often would be modified or changed even after the recording process began.

The group literally put their heads together in planning the arrangements for each song. This spontaneous creativity among the musicians is known as a "head arrangement," and is the basis for the Nashville Sound.

Roy selected the order of the songs, moving up the scale of keys because the longer he sings the higher his voice climbs. He had re-

markably little trouble with most of the songs although a few presented problems. On "Tomorrow Never Comes" the low baritone
level was attained by being very close to the microphone and singing
in a very soft voice, which the engineer then adjusted electronically
with the sliding control. There was only one take—Roy said, "That
better do because I doubt if I can do it again." After the playback
there was general joking that "Ernest Tubb will never know." When
it came time to record "Movin' On," Roy said, "This one has me
buffaloed; I just can't move my mouth that fast." At its conclusion
he was kidded about the slowish tempo, but everyone agreed it had
gone well. "Satisfied Mind" was considered a typical Acuff type, but,
surprisingly, it gave Roy trouble. During its recording Jim was moved
from harmonica to piano to guide Roy's timing. On "Filipino Baby"
Roy changed the words "dark faced" to "dark eyed" because he felt
the former might be offensive.

"Don't Let Me Cross Over" was the most Acuffish song of the
session, and before Roy sang it he said, "I believe this is my favorite
of the twelve." Roy left "Uncle Pen" until the last, because he hoped
the band could have some fun with it. (They did.) They were all
directed to sing along on the chorus at their soundproofed partitions,
but the playback revealed it wasn't acoustically correct, and so at the
conclusion of the session they all gathered around an odd-looking
microphone, which resembled a machine gun, and this was used to
dub this vocal track onto a previously recorded take on which Roy
alone had done the singing.

Besides the vocal, Roy's main contribution to the session was acting as sort of a cheerleader. Usually after each take the group would
listen to the playback, which was always extremely loud so each
musician could hear his part clearly. After the very first number, the
playback was met with silence. Roy, wanting to relax the boys and
perhaps shake constructive criticism out of them, said, "Umm. Why
don't some of you bastards say something." This worked, and from
then on suggestions came freely and mistakes were admitted can-
didly—Roy, the musicians, and the control room.

Os kicked off "Send Me the Pillow (That You Dream On)" playing the Dobro, but had many false starts. Then midway through the
first take Jackie "hit a clunker," which also stopped the recording.
After the first complete take, when Roy said "You are all the
judges," Tommy stated that it was ragged all the way through and
they all agreed they could do better. After the second complete take

Roy said, "It's all right from my point of view," and the band was generally satisfied. But the control room wasn't. The next take was "worse than ever!" At this point Roy told them, "Let's wake up and be pert. You all are sleeping with the song." A completely satisfactory take was made, after which Roy said, "if anything is wrong, it's in there [control room]. Don't tell me about it."

Immediately after the session, the master tape was played at the same volume as the playbacks and each musician seemed extremely satisfied. Roy commented that he hoped the album would sell, and then invited the boys over to the dressing room for a drink. Besides the liquid refreshments, Roy feasted on a jar of pickled eggs—bright purple hard-boiled eggs, especially fixed by Nellie. These were particularly appetizing to Roy because he doesn't eat even breakfast, on the day he records until after the session.

The next day a copy of the master tape was brought to the Exhibit, a tape recorder was found next door at Shot's Sho-Bud shop, and everyone stood around and listened to the tape twice. Roy said that "Uncle Pen" was the best. Os, however, said he thought it was the worst. He stuck with Roy's original choice of "Don't Let Me Cross Over" as being the best. Roy got kidded for missing one low note in "Tomorrow Never Comes," and Jimmie got high praise for his fine harmonica work on "Foggy River." The album, Hickory 139, was released a few months later—"Roy Acuff Sings Famous Opry Favorites."

The Precious Jeweled Cannonball Has Never Wrecked

Of all Roy's songs—433 masters, with 341 titles, for six companies—a few have gone beyond a "hit" and have become country music classics. This has happened to at least four. "The Great Speckled Bird" launched his career, it's his sentimental favorite. This song, which was recorded at his first recording session, is his second biggest seller and his most requested number.

Roy's biggest seller is the "Wabash Cannonball." Although the sales of Roy's records are very hard to estimate, it can be safely said that the "Cannonball" has sold well over a million and perhaps as many as 10 million copies, grossing around $5,000,000 at 79 cents a platter. (Some of the dime store labels sold for around 35 cents.) Literally carloads of wax went into its manufacture. The song is Roy's second most requested number—a fan once requested the "Wabash Locomotive"—and in 1965, when someone asked him how many times he had sung it, he replied, "About three times a day, 365 times a year, for 30 years."

The original *Wabash Cannonball* of the Wabash Railroad, says Scott Irby, a railroad buff, was built in the 1880s and was a real speedster of its day. It was lit by oil lamps and heated by potbellied stoves as it swayed across the great plains. Some old railroaders recall it as a Chicago to Kansas City train, others have it running between St. Louis and Omaha, or between Detroit and Kansas City. Soon after the turn of the century the name was removed from the Wabash timetables and did not reappear until 1950, when a streamlined lightweight diesel *Wabash Cannonball* started its run between Detroit and St. Louis. In 1964, when the Wabash Railroad merged with Norfolk and western, the train became known simply as the *Cannonball*, but a public outcry forced the restoration of the full name. Beginning in 1967, and annually thereafter, Norfolk and Western petitioned the ICC for permission to discontinue the *Wabash Cannonball*, but the storied train clickety-clacked along until May 1, 1971, when Amtrak took over all intercity rail passenger service.

Following the tradition of pride Americans have taken in the railroads that opened up this great nation, the song, of which many claim authorship,* exaggerates the run of the actual *Wabash Cannonball* and transforms it into a mythical train that carries its lucky passengers "From the great Atlantic Ocean to the wide Pacific Shore," with stops at such diverse places as Birmingham, New York, Chicago, St. Louis, Minnesota, Springfield, Decatur, and Peoria. So many locations might well substantiate the claim that the song was originally composed and sung by hobos.

At Roy's first recording session of the song, the vocal was done by Dynamite Hatcher. Roy didn't record his vocal until January 1947, so a large percentage of the "Cannonball's" fabulous record sales were not of Roy's vocal at all. When people heard the "Cannonball" on juke boxes, or on their own record players during the height of Roy's career, they were not listening to Roy Acuff's voice but hearing his whistle.

This whistle, which he learned while a callboy on the L&N Railroad was, in Roy's opinion, the major reason why the song became

---

*As is the case with "The Great Speckled Bird," figuring out the true and legal ancestry of this song is very complicated. Several individuals claim authorship, and several publishing companies have published the song. M. M. Cole Publishing Company—Wm. Kindt & Roy Acuff, 1939, 1940; Peer International—A. P. Carter, 1933, 1939, 1960.

so popular. Roy feels the whistle made, almost forced, his fans to listen carefully, and then to wonder not about the song but how he was making the whistle.

The idea of incorporating the whistle into his performances came to Roy early in his career during an appearance at a schoolhouse in Bell Buckle, Tennessee. Roy had sung a verse or two of "Wabash Cannonball" and the band was playing an instrumental break. Just then a train rumbled by and tooted its whistle loudly. The locomotive passed on at the right moment for Roy to resume singing. He soon began using his own whistle between verses of "Wabash Cannonball."

Roy, of course, used the whistle for many other numbers, and to accompany his vocals on personal appearances. Then came the time on stage when Roy's fiddle slipped, for the first and only time, as he was attempting to balance it. This necessitated some bridge work and, as he later explained, "The dentist pulled my whistle." Jimmie Riddle, whose vocal chords can produce almost any effect desired, stepped in at this time to render the whistle. Jim has done it ever since, except when he is back at the piano and Onie Wheeler performs the primary harmonica chores. During these appearances, Onie also does the whistling.

Roy's third biggest song is "Precious Jewel." It came about while Roy, Os, and Rachel were riding in a car and Roy, while half asleep, thought up the words in half an hour. As he said them, Rachel wrote them down. Roy kept humming the tune to remember it, and when the troupe arrived at its destination, he wrote down the notes. The tune, is similar to "Hills of Roane County," a prison ballad with which he was familiar.

The rumors that Roy wrote the song about a first wife or an early love affair are not true. As a boy, wandering in the Tennessee hills, he often wondered about how the earth could hold all sorts of precious jewels, and yet, when a body is buried, the earth cannot hold the soul. These thoughts returned to him as he was sleepily gazing out of the car window. The true meaning of the song is contained in its last verse.

> This world has its wealth,
> Its trials and troubles,
> Mother earth holds her treasures
> Of diamonds and gold.

But she can't hold the soul
Of one precious jewel.
She's resting in peace,
With the heavenly fold.*

Shortly after its composition, the song was recorded in April 1940. The "One Take Ache" rule was broken because Oswald, who took a big part in the chorus, was suffering from an asthma attack and so a record number of 15 takes was needed. Columbia has released at least two of these takes. On some records Roy says "one" in the first line, and on others he says "girl."

The singing of "The Jewel" requires high notes to be held over long periods. For this reason, despite requests, Roy has been forced to almost totally drop it from his repertoire. For a time he tried lowering the key, but then Os couldn't hit the harmony.

The story behind what is probably Roy's fourth biggest song (although this distinction might belong to "Night Train to Memphis") begins with Dorsey Dixon sitting at his loom on a gloomy morning at the Aleo Textile Mill in East Rockingham, North Carolina.**   As Dixon worked, news soon came of a severe side-on collision on U.S. Highway 1 near Rockingham. After work, Dixon and a coworker, "Pinto" Collins, went to see the wreck. That night Dorsey wrote the words and music to a song he called "I Didn't Hear Anybody Pray" (also known as "Wreck on the Highway"). After teaching it to his brother, Howard, the Dixon Brothers recorded it at their next session, which was on January 25, 1938, in Charlotte, North Carolina.

The initial recording of the song was neither more nor less popular than the brothers' other recordings, It contained eight stanzas, and the second, seventh, and eighth are especially interesting because Roy later deleted them and so they were not on his famous recording.***

Roy first heard the song in Nashville during his early days on the Opry. The fact that Roy was unsure about its origin for years rules

---

*THE PRECIOUS JEWEL, Roy Acuff, © 1943, Renewal 1970. Acuff-Rose Publications, Inc. Used by permission of the publisher. All rights reserved.

**Some of the information about Dixon was obtained from Archie Green, *Babies in the Mill,* Testament Record T3301, album notes.

***These verses inform the listener that Jesus is pleading with them to stop drinking before it is too late, and they are killed in a crash and can't be redeemed. It is not possible to quote these verses, but Dorsey Dixon sings them on *Babies in the Mill,* Tennessee Record T3301.

out the possibility that he learned the song from the Dixon recording.

Roy deleted the third stanza and slightly altered the words of the other five, and also changed the melody. This Acuff version was recorded in May 1942 as "Wreck on the Highway," and soon became a hit. The confusion about the authorship of the song is reflected by the fact that the recording lists Roy as the author and that he is only listed as the arranger in a songbook of the same period.

After the song became a hit Dorsey Dixon wrote to Roy claiming authorship. Roy receives many such letters, and since he fully believed the song was traditional he ignored the letter. During this period, when the Dixon children claimed that their father had actually written the song they were scorned and abused by their playmates who, like Roy, felt it wasn't true.

By 1946 Roy became increasingly conscious that perhaps Dorsey Dixon really was telling the truth, and so he sent Fred Rose to check Dixon's story. After flying to Greenville, Fred met Dixon at the Poinsettia Hotel and soon phoned Roy to tell him that the weaver was undoubtedly the true author. The three mutually agreed Dixon should receive all the royalties accruing as of that date, which amounted to $1,300, and that Dixon's name subsequently would always be listed as the author. The agreement also stipulated that all future royalties (which over the years have amounted to considerably more than $1,300) would go to Acuff-Rose. The song was then immediately published by Acuff-Rose in sheet music form, with composer credit to Dixon. On all of Roy's later recordings, Dixon's name also has appeared as composer.

While "The Wreck" is probably Roy's fourth biggest song, he has sung it far less than the other three. One reason is that Roy believes it to be totally unsuited for performance in establishments where people are drinking. However, his reluctance to perform the song on the Opry or in auditoriums is puzzling.

"The Wreck," along with Roy's other hit songs, was spread to the North during World War II by boys who had heard recordings and radio broadcasts when stationed in military camps in the South. And while "The Bird," "The Jewel," and the "Cannonball" were certainly not loved by those who disliked hillbilly music, these songs seldom were ridiculed. But the whisky, blood, glass, and double negative of "The Wreck" were utterly distasteful to many sophisticates. As the epitome of hillbillyness, "The Wreck on the Highway" also became for many people a symbol of hatred for country music.

However, even though people may disagree violently about their like or dislike of the song, hillbilly music fans will join the music's haters in agreeing on one fact: that "The Wreck on the Highway" is indeed the essence of a hillbilly song. Art Satherley has stated that fine country music must have simplicity of language, emotional depth, and a sincerity of rendition that includes indigenous genuineness of dialect and voice quality.* Satherley and most old-time hillbilly music lovers agree that "The Wreck" and Roy Acuff's rendition of it definitely have all these qualities, and that "The Wreck on the Highway" is therefore the most perfect hillbilly song.

Roy has been very fortunate to have had these four great songs. He frequently gets very emotional when singing them. "These are the kind of songs I can sing every week for forty years," says Roy, "and each time I go at it, it's a little different." These songs have been very good to him, because wherever he goes he can count on drawing a crowd, a significant proportion of which comes especially to hear Roy sing one or more of the "Big Four."

Other entertainers occasionally sing these songs. While Roy is flattered by their interest, these performances slightly irk him and he would prefer that others leave the songs alone. He feels the same way about the many who have tried to imitate his singing style. The best Acuff imitator is Esco Hankins. His records even fooled Roy's mother.

A fact not so well known is that besides the "Precious Jewel," Roy Acuff has written close to 100 songs. A few Acuff compositions that became extremely famous when he recorded them are "Beneath that Lonely Mound of Clay," "Branded Wherever I Go," "Do You Wonder Why," "Just to Ease My Worried Mind," "My Mountain Home Sweet Home," "Not a Word from Home," "Streamlined Cannonball," and "Write Me Sweetheart."

Most of Roy's composing was done during the early part of his career, the 1930s and 1940s. Roy explained the process this way:

> I always get the title first. That's what I start with. Like if I were to hear somebody say, "Will you be true?" Well, that might give me an idea for a song. Then I start to hum a tune until a picture of what I want shapes up in my mind. Then the words gradually come.

---

*Maurice Zolotow, "Hillbilly Boom," *Saturday Evening Post*, February 12, 1944, p. 36.

Roy has composed very little since 1950 because he has felt that his mind is simply not geared to it.

Prior to 1930, the songs played by hillbilly musicians were almost all drawn from the great mass of folk music. But with the coming of the featured vocalists, which was led by Roy Acuff, country musicians began to create music in the traditional styles on which they had been brought up. Roy Acuff's great songs were in the vanguard of this movement.

V

Highways and Byways

On the Road

"Yes, it's a hard life, but I love it. I like one-night stands. I like meeting new audiences. I couldn't stand it if I had to keep on facing the same audience." These were Roy's words early in his career, and while his zest for traveling to one-nighters has dimmed in the past few years, they express what still is basically his opinion.

On tour the troupe occasionally has driven more than 1,000 miles during a 24-hour period and many times 3,000 miles in a week. Roy considers traveling to be the most difficult part of his work and has estimated that since the beginning of his career he and the boys have covered around 100,000 miles a year, which means a total of nearly four million miles.

Touring has taken them to every state in the United States and to most of the Canadian provinces. Their foreign tours, which have been primarily sponsored by the USO, have taken them to every continent except South America and Antarctica. On these tours they have entertained all classes of people and performed on every conceivable type of platform. Round stages, dance hall floors, and the backs of trucks, and from Constitution Hall to bamboo structures in South Vietnam.

Tours, to Roy, are strictly business. He might go sightseeing, but only if it doesn't take too long and isn't too much trouble. He visits in private homes very rarely, and only then at the invitation of a close friend whom he knows can be trusted not to "show him off."

126

Once in a great while, though, he has been known on the spur of the moment to accept invitations from fans to visit or have a meal at their homes.

In their first days on the Opry the troupe traveled in a "woody" station wagon that pulled a trailer. It had a billboard on its top that featured two National Life and Accident Insurance Company shields and the words "Roy Acuff and His Smoky Mountain Boys WSM Grand Ole Opry." By the early 1940s they obtained a cream-colored limousine, with "WSM Grand Ole Opry" written across the top of the windows and "Roy Acuff and His Smoky Mt. Boys" emblazoned on both front doors and the back. It was a stretched-out Ford on a Mercury chassis, with four seats and eight doors. Baggage and instruments were carried on the top. Around 1943 their chief car was a cream-colored Ford sedan with similar lettering. Later this type of advertising was abandoned. During the latter stages of the war, when gas and tires became scarce, the troupe traveled extensively by train.

Probably the most famous transporter of the Acuff band was a chartered DC-3 airliner, with "Roy Acuff's—The Great Speckled Bird" lettered on the fuselage. The plane, officially N25629, was used extensively by the Acuff troupe for four years, in the late 1940s and early 1950s. (Uncle Dave Macon, in a slightly intoxicated condition, was lured aboard for his first flight.) The usual pilots were Mac Rowe and Joe Thurmond, and the charter fee was $120 an hour. By 1952 the cost was considered too great and *The Great Speckled Bird* was no longer used. But prior to this plane and subsequently, Roy's troupe frequently used commercial flights on their tours.

One personal appearance that Roy made without his band was on March 5, 1963, when he played a benefit show in Kansas City. He had driven with some of the performers to the benefit, then afterward was offered the luxury of a return flight. Roy's aversion to flying in small planes saved his life when he refused to fly back to Nashville with Patsy Cline and Cowboy Copas.

After grounding *The Great Speckled Bird*, Roy chartered a few buses and even owned a specially fitted one that he bought from Hank Thompson. (Roy later sold it to Ray Price.) This vehicle was used during the time Shot was with the band—he, with his mechanical ability, took care of it. A driver was never hired; this responsibility fell to the boys, and sometimes Roy. Jimmie Riddle was the only one of the gang who escaped, because when it came his turn to learn to drive the bus, Roy decided he just didn't have the patience to teach him after a hair-raising half-mile lesson.

Private cars have been used more than any other mode of transportation by the Acuff group. For years they had used two or three cars, with an instrument trailer attached to one. But since the early 1960s, when they stopped carrying the big metal bass fiddle, one regular car and a station wagon has been sufficient. For comfort only two ride on a seat, therefore the traveling band seldom numbers more than eight. The lead large model car is Roy's, usually a Chrysler Imperial. For many years it bore a special VIP license plate numbered 109, which Roy considers lucky. He had this plate until recently—since Frank Clement's first term as governor. Roy nearly always travels in this car and usually drives it, and usually is watching the rear-vision mirror for the second car. "Sometimes," says Roy, "it seems like I spend half my life waiting for the other car to follow."

The second car is a station wagon. Jimmie is always in this car and usually the driver. He shadows Roy constantly and because it is felt that the two cars should always remain together, Jim follows even when he knows Roy has taken a wrong turn.

When they reach their destination they gas up so they'll be ready to go as soon as the show is over. Unpacking is done haphazardly. But when they pack, one person is in charge and the rest hand him the instruments and suitcases as requested.

In most cases, the troupe would rather drive to the next date immediately after a night's engagement rather than sleeping and driving on the next day. For one thing this insures their arrival. Roy Acuff and His Smoky Mountain Boys have missed fewer dates than perhaps any troupe on the Opry, and they can always be depended upon to arrive well in advance of the show. The number would certainly be under ten and more probably four or five. A few have been missed due to blizzards, and one was missed because of the 1965 automobile wreck.

Another reason why the band leaves right after the show is so they can have what sleep they get right before their next job. When the end of a tour finds them far from Nashville they usually will return by taking shifts at the wheel, rather than checking into motels, even if the Opry is several days away. If they do spend a night at a motel, Roy rooms alone if there is an odd number; if not, he rooms with Os. Years ago Roy always roomed with Os because he didn't like to be left alone in a room. Eating is done at crazy hours, and frequently on the run at hamburger stands.

Traveling is certainly the hardest part of their job, and until 1965 about the only evidence of all the miles was a few dented fenders and scratched sides. But once, on a steep grade, the brakes went out on the second car. The driver, Howdy, shouted to Joe Zinkan, his front seat passenger (the rest were asleep in the back), "The brakes have gone!" And Joe said the only possible thing he could say: "I'm with you." Once, in 1965 when the group stopped in Flint, Michigan, to get gas, a band member got thirsty and wandered away. They drove on and after about 10 minutes they discovered he was missing. Back in Flint it took four hours before the troupe found the lost member happily quenching his thirst.

An embarrassing situation involving booze occurred during a four-hour layover at the Memphis airport. Roy had given Jim a bottle of whisky to keep. Jim rolled it up in Roy's overcoat, which was on the ticket counter. When boarding time came, Roy grabbed his coat and the bottle hit the floor with a tremendous "splat" in full view of a huge crowd. Roy gasped, "Jesus Christ!" and ran like mad.

Although the band has played in many "marginal" dance halls and in beer joints, it has never been involved with fistfighting during· a performance. However, they have been involved in robust activity with obstreperous bullies while relaxing after a show. In those tussels Roy was usually the star performer. In July 1966, though, just one year after the wreck, he was less fortunate as half a uniformed base-ball team ganged up on Roy and the boys near Lima, Ohio, in an argument about how the cars were parked. Two of the group gave special attention to Roy, one holding and the other beating him.

Generally, their road experiences have been more humorous, like being stopped by police. Once the entire band, consisting of six, was in a station wagon pulling a trailer filled with instruments. Tommy Magness was driving and the others were sound asleep. An officer pulled them over to tell them that the trailer lights weren't working. Tommy, trying to wiggle out of a ticket, said, "I'm so sorry, Officer. I had no idea those lights weren't working. Why just before I got in the car I looked at them and they . . ."

At this point Jess Easterday, roused from his sleep, spoke up from the dark in the wagon. "Tommy, I told you more than two weeks ago those lights were out." Tommy finally broke the night's sudden great quiet. "That's a lie, Jess Easterday. You never told me no such thing. I wish you'd keep your big fat mouth shut!"

The officer must have been an Opry fan, because he didn't give them a ticket.*

On another occasion, Jim's car was stopped for speeding but when he told the officer, "I'm in Roy Acuff's band and I'm simply following him, he's up ahead," the officer raced up the road with siren screaming. Roy later reported that he had indeed been stopped, but all the officer wanted was to shake his hand. In Brinkley, Arkansas, Roy was stopped by an officer for passing him on the wrong side. When Roy explained that he was in a hurry, the policeman escorted Roy back to the court—at 90 mph—to pay his fine.

For the audience, an Acuff show is very entertaining, but for the troupe, show after show can get dull. Wherever they go they are faced with the same questions: "Where did you play last?" . . . "How long did it take you to get here from there?" . . . "How did you make it so fast?" . . . "How long are you going to be here?" . . . "Where do you go next?" . . . "How long will it take you to get there?" . . . "How will you make it so fast?"

Occasionally, their audiences provide entertainment. Before one Grand Ole Opry Tent Show Roy noticed an elderly couple dressed in formal evening clothes who came very early and sat in a front row. Roy's experienced eye immediately assessed the couple as hecklers, and he watched them carefully. As the show started, they were a bit ill at ease, but they soon limbered up. After the performance the couple came backstage, and said that while they had expected to see grand opera they had never had such a good time in their lives. There have been other incidents when people confused opera with Opry.

Very few hecklers have bothered Roy during his career; of those who do he handles them expertly. Even so, he has had one embarrassing moment. Once Roy answered a young man who was giving him a bad time by saying, "About two weeks ago someone was yelling at me just the way you are now. I called him an idiot and I'm calling you one." After the show he was approached by a woman, who said, "That boy is my son and he really is a mental idiot." After that Roy has never called anyone an idiot, and has subsequently used the story to quiet other hecklers.

---

*WSM, *WSM Official Grand Ole Opry History-Picture Book*, volume 2 (Nashville: WSM, Inc., 1961), p.11.

One of the Acuff troupe's most memorable experiences was their entire tour, in the summer of 1950, with Senator Dudley LeBlanc's first Hadacol Caravan. LeBlanc, a sometime Louisiana state senator, was the inventor of Hadacol ("They had to call it something, so they called it Hadacol"), the largest selling patent medicine of all time. Os remembers the tour with affection.

> The Senator spent a tremendous amount of money. All expenses were paid. We couldn't hardly buy a toothpick. It was a real caravan. The lead car was filled with Old Forester whisky and we had a party every night. We played all over the South. Every county or town had a queen, and if the queens wanted to stay they could so we kept accumulating queens. As we entered a town we would sit on a flat truck and throw out chewing gum and candy to the kids. The admission to the shows was a Hadacol box top. When we played a city, Hollywood stars would join. During our stay with the tour Harpo Marx and Mickey Rooney came. It was the last of the great medicine shows. That was the doggonest tour I've ever been on! It was amazing the amount of money that man spent!

The "last of the great medicine shows" went out again the summer of 1951 with Minnie Pearl and Hank Williams. After a few months it folded.

On the road the Acuff troupe has performed sometimes alone, at times with local talent, sometimes with well-known non-Opry stars, and is frequently teamed with one or more of the other Opry acts. Such teams usually last through the tour, but one existed for two years.

In January 1955 the Kitty Wells/Johnny and Jack troupe joined Roy Acuff and His Smoky Mountain Boys to form a unit show, which lasted until January of 1957. During this time the acts were practically inseparable. Even when they were in Nashville they generally played on the same Opry segments. They toured throughout the United States and Canada, playing in many leading auditoriums and breaking attendance records.

Humor and many pleasant memories characterized this tour. Kitty especially remembers two. In Toronto, Canada, while relaxing in her dressing room, she had slipped off her stage heels and was wearing slippers. Then she heard her introduction and rushed out. Roy soon joined her on stage—wearing her heels. On another occasion an electrician was working outside her dressing room door, squatting astride Os's Smodge Pot. He accidentally connected it. When it went off he flew through the door of her dressing room as if shot from a cannon. Kitty's astonished comment was, "Lord, have mercy! I thought I was gonna die!"

"If I had my preference, I'd just play the small towns. I don't like big cities; don't even like to visit them because of the traffic and everything. Seems like you can't ever get anywhere, even when you know where you're supposed to be going."* This is Roy's basic opinion, but he has played in the biggest cities many, many times.

The most notable engagement of the Acuff/Wells/Johnny and Jack show took place in the nation's largest city from the fourth to the tenth of November 1955, when they "played the Palace." Appearing at the Palace in New York is the traditional height of ambition for many acts in the field of entertainment. This unit show was the first country music troupe to play on Broadway at the Palace. The appearance was very successful, grossing $31,000.

Roy much prefers to play auditoriums or theaters than dance halls or even well-known clubs. In the first place, auditorium shows are far less exhausting. They rarely last more than two hours, and if the show includes other stars, Roy's troupe can concentrate all its energy and talent on a short but carefully presented performance. Club dates, though, frequently require the troupe to perform for sometimes four separate hours. Because these performances are interspersed with those of the house band, they usually do not end until one or two in the morning.

Besides the length of the show, there's also the atmosphere. In an auditorium the audience is awake and appreciative, so Roy and the boys enjoy presenting a rousing show that includes skits and antics attracting the audience's full attention. Roy can draw from his full repertoire of songs without worrying about making a sad drunk sadder or maybe have a wreck on the way home. He also feels free to sing religious numbers, which comprise a very large part of his repertoire, knowing that his audience will accept and respect them.

But the atmosphere of a dance hall or a club is quite different. People are dancing and drinking, so Roy tries to avoid religious or sad numbers. At such a place the first show is usually typical, with costuming and skits, and the jokes are slightly more risque than they would be in an auditorium. But as the evening wears on the attention span of the audience deteriorates and so, for the later shows, those in

---

*Jack Hurst, "Roy Acuff: Still the King!," *Nashville Tennessean*, October 21, 1965, p. B11.

the band in costume, even Os, return to casual clothes and there is no real attempt to put on a regular Acuff show as such. Roy usually ends up singing song after song. If the audience is reluctant to use the dance floor during the show, Roy will invite them to do so, although this is more of a bluff because he prefers their attention, not dancing. In fact, Roy likes the audience to come right up to the stage and watch the show, rather than to sit at their tables and drink. This closeness is more personal and a bit like his medicine show days.

Shows put on by Roy Acuff and His Smoky Mountain Boys are family-type, clean-cut performances requiring audience attention. Roy's wariness of the noises and distractions of dance halls and clubs was justified by what happened during a club engagement in June 1952. Even though some of the older and wiser Opry people, including Roy, felt that it was a mistake from the start, they made the decision to take the act East.

On March 26, 1952, Roy and Hank Williams were on the "Kate Smith" national television show. The show was a smash hit and it gave an idea to the man who ran a famous supper club in New York City. Robert K. Christenberry was the manager of the Hotel Astor Roof and he needed a replacement of some kind for the big-name bands that had not been drawing full houses for the Roof. He also happened to be an old Tennessean and connoisseur of country music. So the "Grand Ole Opry" was offered a summer's engagement at the Hotel Astor Roof.

Governor Gordon Browning even accompanied the Opry stars in their chartered plane and personally launched the show's opening with a solo of "Tennessee Waltz." Red Foley played the first two weeks, but the show was a flop. Although Roy tried to salvage the situation during the following two weeks, it soon was evident that the New York nightclub crowd didn't provide the rapport between artist and audience that is needed by Roy's uninhibited country act. Also many of New York's true country music fans could not afford to go to the Astor Roof. The engagement was called off by mutual consent after four weeks. Roy later said, "They tried to make a New York show out of us, and we won't change the Grand Ole Opry for anybody."*

Nevertheless, this engagement blazed a trail. In due time country

---

*Emily Coleman (editor), "Country Music is Big Business, and Nashville is its Detroit," *Newsweek*, August 11, 1952, p. 84.

acts have had success in New York night spots. (Roy himself returned to New York's Taft Hotel for a week's engagement in early February 1968. This time the show went very well.)

The next extended club date of note occurred in the fall of 1960 when Roy was offered a week's booking to play at the Showboat, a downtown Las Vegas club. Roy was quite apprehensive and he meant it when he said, before departing, "Well, I'm going out there and do country music in my own way, just like I've always done it, and if they don't like me, I'll just come home."

On the first two shows Roy refused to sing hymns. The Showboat management called "D" Kilpatrick, who had booked the appearance, in Nashville. "D" called Roy and persuaded him to present a normal Acuff show, which always includes hymns. From then on everything went smoothly. At the end of the last show on September 5, Roy gave this speech:

> You know, this has been one week of real pleasure for me and the boys and little girls. We've had a lot of fun; we've enjoyed it. I have to frankly admit before I came out here I was a little leery of coming into the place and playing. I'm a country boy and we're all country children, believe me. We—[applause]—thank you. It was a completely strange business to us, but it's become a part of us, we love it. We have become acquainted with all the gentlemen and the ladies that work out on the floor out here, and they have certainly been gentlemen and ladies to us. They have spoken to us, treated us as we were one of them and we're not always treated that way. You've been so kind to us that I hope that we'll have the opportunity and the pleasure of visiting with you again sometime. I want to talk for a long time about my visit here at the Showboat to our people back home in Tennessee on radio station WSM. It's been wonderful. Thank you. Good night.

The following year, in mid-September, Roy returned for an equally successful engagement at the Showboat. He also celebrated his fifty-eighth birthday at a party the management gave in his honor.

When he played the Flame in Minneapolis in February 1962 Roy still was suspicious about extended club dates. But Roy's act was well received.

Roy returned to Las Vegas to perform at the Mint, from December 17, 1963, to January 12, 1964. It was another successful engagement.

Two years later he accepted a club date in Chicago for February 1966. To the audience in Rivoli Hall, he said:

Seems like we're going out into the larger cities more than I'd like to. I'm really not a club act like they'd like to have here. I'm not good at this. I might have some hesitation about singing some of the numbers I love to sing in a club, some of the religious songs and ballads. I'm a little leery of putting them over to people who are drinking and having fun.

But soon he was hearing individuals in the delighted audience express their enjoyment of the show: "He's real country" . . . He's the most country I've ever heard" . . . "He's the most country you can get."

From February 13 through March 1, 1967, Roy starred in a large Opry show in an engagement that carried more prestige than any to which Roy or the "Grand Ole Opry" had ever played. The troupe performed at the Headliner Room at Harrah's in Reno, Nevada. As leader, Roy was given the luxurious penthouse, which was so large that its dressing room was as big as most bedrooms. Two maids were in attendance and his meals were served there. Despite the rumors at the gambling tables prior to the show that it would be a flop, the engagement was a tremendous success.

Roy returned to Nevada for an extended engagement in February 1971. He and Waylon Jennings headlined a three-week show at the Landmark Hotel, which looks like the Seattle World's Fair Space Needle and is located just off the main Las Vegas strip. The troupe had a very good reception.

Roy and the gang have been on 21 overseas tours beginning in November 1949. These tours to distant places around the world have been to entertain the troops, and usually were sponsored by the USO. Roy considers servicemen to be his most appreciative audience and he's frequently played to crowds that equaled those drawn by the biggest stars, such as Bob Hope.

A common misconception is that Roy was overseas and toured the fighting fronts during World War II. The fact is that he was at the peak of his popularity during the war, and was well known in the military camps here. For example, in Florida the Camp Banning newspaper, *Bayonet,* reported on November 17, 1944, that a GI performed so well that he was known as, "The Roy Acuff of the 63rd."

Even though Roy did not go overseas during World War II, his fame did. Bill Graham (later to become a WSM executive) was in India and tossed a coin to a boy to sing a song. Much to Graham's amazement, the song was "Night Train to Memphis." And Richard Cornish remembers an incident while he was a marine stationed on New Guinea. They played their records, most of which were Acuff,

over a series of loudspeakers in the evenings when the volume would
be turned up extremely high. One evening, three terrified Japanese
soldiers came into the marine camp and surrendered. When asked
why they gave up, rather than continue to hide out on the huge
island, the three replied that the Wabash Cannonball must be a super-
weapon—they preferred surrender to being hit by it.

Before and during the war Roy's records were played on Japanese radio stations and sung on the streets of Tokyo. Because he was
regarded as a major American personality, his name was used for
propaganda purposes to enrage our GIs. In 1944, the troops who
were recapturing the Philippines heard only two battle cries distin-
guishable in English: "Damn President Roosevelt" and "Damn Roy
Acuff." By 1945, the Japanese army had come up with another version, on Okinawa. In a suicidal banzai attack against a marine position, the enemy soldiers rushed forward yelling, "To hell with President Roosevelt, to hell with Babe Ruth, to hell with Roy Acuff!"

Besides Japanese and marines the Pacific Theatre of war had a
famous occupant, Ernie Pyle, the journalist and war correspondent.
After the marines had pretty well secured Okinawa, he moved on
with them to another island, Ie Shima, where he was shot and killed
by an enemy sniper on April 18, 1945. Men killed in action usually
were buried without coffins in a combat zone, but one was fashioned
out of packing cases for this beloved war correspondent. Weeks later,
after the fighting had subsided, the cemetery was pathed and fenced
and crosses were erected. Before the rifle salute was fired, at the
memorial service, one of Ernie's favorite songs was honored—one of
his buddies sang "The Great Speckled Bird." (In 1948 his body was
transferred to Hawaii's Punch Bowl Cemetery, where it now lies
between two unknown soldiers.)

Roy's continuous popularity among servicemen resulted in Roy
being starred in the productions of numerous films and transcriptions, such as *Country Style U.S.A., Country Music Time, Leather-
neck Jamboree,* and *Here's to Veterans.* These are used for recruiting
and for veterans' information.

However, the most important result of his military popularity has
been the official request that he make overseas tours. Roy and his
troupe enjoy them, but for the most part these excursions are very
difficult and exhausting. Roy donates his own services on these
tours, receiving only per diem pay, which is a daily allowance covering living expenses. In addition to the per diem pay, each band mem-

ber receives his full salary. If it is a USO tour, the USO pays the salaries. On some tours, Roy personally has met his band's payroll. Though the work is hard and the monetary gains nonexistent, the other rewards more than compensate for them. These overseas tours have been a very important part of Roy Acuff's life since 1949.

Details of Roy's overseas tours are presented in Appendix A.

In August 1970 when Roy introduced a Medal of Honor winner on the Opry he said, "I've traveled to Vietnam several times to do what I can for the soldiers and our country, but compared to what this man has done, I feel as if I have done nothing. This man is a true American." Despite Roy's typical understatement, he considers it "a duty and a pleasure" to entertain the men who guard our nation's security.

He thinks of it as a duty because he is a loyal American, and because he was in the generation of Americans that was too young to fight in World War I and too old to see combat in World War II. The pleasure comes from the enthusiastic response always given him by the boys in the armed services.

On August 8, 1965, the night before he was released from the hospital after the auto wreck, Roy stated that he didn't want to stop his personal appearances, but even if forced to stop he would continue to entertain servicemen. "I would rather appear before the troops at some overseas post," said Roy, "than make a public appearance next week in Kansas City." Later in 1965, when asked what events in his long career have given him great thrills, he replied, after some reflection, "The shows we've done overseas for the boys in the service. Those are all great. They seem to appreciate them so much." Though other entertainers have received more public acclaim for lesser efforts, no other has compiled a more impressive record entertaining the troops.

Country music, too, has gained from Roy Acuff's foreign excursions. These trips have contributed significantly to its internationalization.

The response of the people in foreign lands to country music has pleasantly surprised the troupe. Roy speaks of it:

> It astonishes us more each time we visit a non-English speaking nation to see how much they know of our country music and its stars. I do not believe language is a barrier where country music is concerned. Evidently the simplicity and direct sincerity helps project the message in our songs.

Perhaps this explains why the people of other countries seem to prefer Roy's traditional style, which is so sincere. One reflection of Roy's influence in Europe was apparent—in an article, "Roy Acuff vs Dialectic Materialism," discussing the popularity of country music, which appeared in Prague, Czechoslovakia.

Roy's records can be heard world-wide over the Armed Forces stations and the people of Australia, Canada, England, Germany, Japan, and New Zealand can buy special foreign releases of his records at their local record stores.

In private tours, such as to Japan in 1964, Roy brought country music directly to the Japanese people. Even on the military tours his shows are seen by many natives of the country.

Once in France during a military show, half the building was given to Frenchmen and our servicemen had the other half. Roy explains:

> They had an interpreter and it was very interesting. I would sing my song or tell my little jokes and the boys would come up with the big laughter and then half a minute later you would hear the French people come up with their laugh after the interpreter had given them the gag. He followed us in our songs and jokes and everything.*

In doing his share to internationalize country music, Roy has covered an astonishing amount of ground. His crowds have ranged from elegantly gowned and bejeweled customers paying $6.60 in Washington's Constitution Hall to Oregon loggers, tired from long days of work, who paid $1.20 each for the privilege of standing in a seatless dance hall. And the number of people in his audiences have been impressive (except in Tennessee, which has proved the truth of the Biblical phrase, "A prophet is not without honor, save in his own country"), whether the engagement is at home or abroad. Roy has often played to more than 15,000 admissions, as well as opened vast new territories for country music. Down through the years promoters would rather have Roy because, "Roy Acuff can outdraw anyone." It's been said that "a thousand people know Roy Acuff, the fiddler, for every one who knows Fritz Kriesler, the master violinist."

Roy has played before, behind, and directly against some big-name acts. Frequently they would have 2,000 people and across the street Roy would have 5,000. In 1951 in Houston, Texas, Roy filled the 12,000-seat Coliseum two nights in a row, and the nearby City

---

*Stone tape.

Auditorium, which featured a Sigmund Romberg production, was less than half full.

This drawing power, which has always been a surprise to Roy, didn't diminish during the rock and roll of the fifties. For example, on February 18, 1956, Ohio State sponsored a "Greek Week" show in Columbus's main auditorium. This Saturday show featured Pat Boone, one of the nation's biggest stars, but the auditorium had a crescent of empty seats in the back. The following night, a Sunday, the Roy Acuff/Johnny and Jack/Kitty Wells show filled every seat in the auditorium. At the time Roy's records weren't selling and he hadn't had a hit in several years, but the loyal crowds came.

Roy Acuff's largest crowd was on July 4, 1944, at Happy Johnny's Baltimore Park. Cars were jammed for seven miles down the highway and the troupe was caught in the jam. When Roy asked a police officer the reason for the tie-up, he was told, "Roy Acuff is playing the park!" Identification got him a police escort and the group was on time for its performance—before over 20,000 fans.

A custom of the Acuff troupe has been for the boys to sell songbooks and pictures during intermissions. Roy purchases the books and gets half the gross; the other half is divided among the boys. Os remembers that at Baltimore Park, when the money overflowed his pockets, he tied the bottoms of his pants to his ankles. The subsequent sales completely filled the legs of his overalls. Jimmie recalls that his share of the songbook sales for that day was $80. At the time his weekly salary was about $50.

Earlier, in 1944, when the band was in Hollywood making a movie, Roy played to one of the first of his giant gatherings. Foreman Phillips had converted the Venice Pier into a country dance hall and brought in big-name entertainers. Bob Wills drew 8,600 to his show, but was topped by Roy who set the record of 11,130 paid admissions—and authorities were afraid that the pier was going to collapse. Various articles have listed the Baltimore crowd at 50,000, the Venice Pier audience at 17,000. But crowds, like record sales, are hard to document. It was also in this period that the troupe succeeded in almost filling up one side of the Orange Bowl on two successive nights.

Admission then to Roy's shows seldom cost more than one dollar. Even so, the crowds represented his major source of income. By 1942 and 1943 he was making between $50,000 and $100,000. In his peak years—1944, 1945, and 1946—his income reached about

$200,000 annually. At times it was as much as $10,000 a week. But by 1949 it had declined to around $150,000.

Except for the early part of his career, Roy usually has received straight payment for personal appearances, seldom working on a percentage basis. In the 1940s, $20,000 gates were not unusual, and even after all his expenses, Roy often netted in excess of $5,000 for a single performance. In 1970, a Roy Acuff show commanded up to $1,500.

An incident concerning payment for a show was remembered by Spot. They were in Texas, playing personals on their way to the West Coast tour of early 1947. When Spot gave Roy a $3,000 cashier's check made out in Roy's name, Roy asked, "What's a cashier's check?" Spot explained. The next night Spot was going over the funds with Roy and said, "With that cashier's check I gave you yesterday, the total is . . . ." To that Roy inquired, "What cashier's check?" They both looked but couldn't find the check. Payment was cancelled, of course, and before they reached Los Angeles the check was made good. The incident taught Spot that his brother was not a good businessman: there are bank notes and there are musical notes.

Roy distinguishes between a manager and an agent: an agent is simply a booker while a manager takes care of everything. Various managers have worked with Roy off and on during his career. Ollie Hamilton, Ford Rush, Oscar Davis, and Frankie Moore worked in connection with the 1946 tent show and the 1959 Australian tour. Joe Frank helped Roy in his early career and was an official manager in the late 1940s. In the early 1940s Colonel Tom Parker, who was based in Florida, wanted to manage Roy. When Roy wouldn't leave the Opry, Parker took Eddy Arnold under his wing. Roy has absolutely no regrets about not teaming with Parker. Most of Roy's close associates feel that he has never had the benefit of a really skilled personal manager for any substantial period, and that his career would have been even more successful had he been able to find such a person. Roy, on the other hand, feels that he has had fine managers at all times.

Beginning around 1950, personal appearances began to have a decreasing importance in Roy's total income. The reason was that wise investments were beginning to flower.

Over the years the business venture that has netted him much more than personal appearances, movies, or records has been his 50 percent interest in the Acuff-Rose Publishing Company. Other investments include stocks, most notably in the National Life and Accident Insurance Company, and real estate, much of which is in downtown Nashville. The parlaying of funds into a fortune can be attributed to Mildred's business ability.

Understandably, Roy Acuff doesn't like to talk about his wealth. Once when a WSM questionaire asked if there was anything it had left out Roy wrote, "Yes, you didn't mention money–thanks." Of his wealth he says, "Oh, I've made money, made mistakes, too. The more money you have the more you have to worry."

Until very recently Roy continued to pursue an active "on the road" schedule, despite the fact that personal appearances accounted for only a fraction of his income. What this indicates, of course, is his love of entertaining people.

He Did Hear Somebody Pray

"It's rough driving all those miles. It's a lot of responsibility and there's always the possibility of a wreck." On July 10, 1965, the inevitable caught up with Roy Acuff and His Smoky Mountain Boys.*

The boys had a date on Saturday night, July 10, in Terrell, North Carolina, about 300 miles from Nashville. Under normal conditions the gang figures it can drive 200 miles in four and one-half hours, but it was raining and so they left Nashville at 7:30 A.M. to allow themselves plenty of time.

The leading car, a cream-colored Chrysler Imperial, besides Roy should have contained Benny Martin, Onie Wheeler, and June Stearns. The trailing blue Pontiac station wagon should have had Os, Shot, and Jimmy Fox as passengers with Jimmie Riddle driving. However, Jim was tired and so, in consideration of his seniority with the band, Roy asked Onie to trade cars with Shot and drive the station wagon.

As things turned out, Onie and Shot did switch but Os drove the station wagon. Os's passengers were Onie, Jimmie Riddle, and Jimmy Fox. Roy drove the first car carrying June Stearns and Shot. Benny Martin cancelled at the last minute.

The two cars proceeded in the rain from Nashville and about 60 miles later the rain worsened as they pulled into Smithville, where the group went to a small cafe for some coffee. As they left in the

---

*Some of the material for this chapter was obtained by talking to the persons involved. Some was obtained from newspapers, especially Nashville's *Banner* and *Tennessean*.

pouring rain a kindly old gentleman called, "Roy, you be careful. It's dangerous out there!" Os turned over the wheel of the station wagon to Onie and joined the Jims in trying to catch some shut-eye. Roy continued to drive the Chrysler, with June Stearns, who always tried to sleep at every opportunity, dozing in the back and Shot sitting in the front seat. Both cars contained complete sets of seatbelts, but they were unused.

The two cars continued along State Highway 26. By 10:30 in the morning they had covered almost 100 miles and were about seven miles west of Sparta. Roy, who was not driving very fast in the pouring rain on the little two-lane highway, decided to pass what he thought was one extremely slow-moving car. As he pulled out, the one car turned out to be two and then Roy saw another car approaching over a rise. He applied the brakes to ease back into his own lane but the Imperial skidded out of control. As Roy saw that a head-on collision was shaping up he decided that the least damage would be done if he steered into the ditch on the left side of the road. As he turned in that direction the smashup occurred.

The right front end of Roy's Imperial collided with the left front end of the westbound 1963 Ford owned by Edward Blish, a laborer with the Corps of Engineers, who was en route to his home in Smithville. Roy's car came to rest in the middle of the road and Blish's landed in the ditch. Both automobiles were considered total losses.

The most serious injury was the skull fracture sustained by Shot when his head hit the windshield as he was thrown forward from the "suicide seat." He also suffered breaks in both jaws, 18 broken ribs, a punctured lung, and a contused kidney.

Roy, upon hitting the steering wheel, suffered 2 pelvic fractures and a broken collarbone. One whole side of his rib cage was crushed.

June Stearns had a broken ankle. She was lucky.

Eddie Blish's jaw and teeth were smashed, which resulted in temporarily hampered breathing. He also was not wearing a seatbelt.

At the moment of impact Roy was knocked out for a few moments. When he regained consciousness, he wasn't breathing. In great pain he forced himself to take a breath. After he had accomplished that feat, he knew he would live. The next thing he remembered was Shot crying that he was dying and June moaning. When later asked if by any chance he thought, even for an instant, of "The Wreck on the Highway," he replied, "No, I did not think of the song. There was no time to think of things like that." During the following rescue efforts, Roy passed in and out of consciousness. June was asleep as the collision was developing but later reported, "I woke up when the car started spinning. It was probably a good thing I was asleep, or I might have been hurt worse than I was."

When Onie, trailing behind in the station wagon at about 100 yards, saw what had happened he shouted to his three slumbering passengers, "Roy's had a wreck!" As the Pontiac pulled up Jimmie Riddle was the first one out and he dashed to Roy. Roy's first words were, "Help Shot."

Great confusion made the rain-soaked scene even more jumbled. Eddie Blish, jaw hanging down, was standing beside his car. Jimmie Riddle, Os, Onie, and Jimmy Fox tried desperately to free their three companions in Roy's car. Os, semi-hysterical during this period, later described their efforts:

> The whole right side of Roy's car was caved in. The metal was sticking midway into the car, and the glass was broken out on that side. The doors wouldn't open. So then we tried to open the doors on the left side. They were also jammed. We knocked out the glass. I honestly don't know what we used to get into them from that side. I guess we must have used our fists, because Jimmy Fox cut his hand badly trying to get out glass.

As the four ran from one side of the car to the other in their futile efforts, Roy, who was more painfully though not as critically injured as Shot, kept telling them that his greatest concern was for Shot and that they should help Shot in any way possible.

Shot, solidly pinned by the jagged metal, which had been pushed in from the right side of the car, kept screaming and moaning and saying he couldn't breathe. Os later said:

> Time and time again Shot grabbed me and tried to pull me down to him as he was looking up at me and screaming "Oswald." But we couldn't do anything except try to comfort him as he sat there in blood, screaming. The most terrible thing that can happen to a man is to look in a person's eyes like that and not be able to do anything. We just couldn't get into the car.

Roy said, "Shot must have died three times."

The boys have described this period as the most agonizing 15 minutes of their lives. During this time Jimmie went to a nearby house and told the people to phone an ambulance and when that call went in, the state police and a wrecking crew were automatically alerted. Upon the wrecker's arrival, it took another 15 minutes to get the car doors open. Then the ambulances, belonging to the Hunter

Funeral Home, took the four casualities to the White County Hospital in Sparta. Soon Oswald phoned Mildred and she and Roy Neill immediately drove to Sparta, as did Billy, Os's 26-year-old son.

When the injured arrived at the hospital, Blish was given emergency treatment and then, accompanied by his wife, was flown directly to the Veterans Hospital in Nashville.

By two o'clock that afternoon, Dr. Donald Bradley, having made a preliminary evaluation, described Shot's condition as "critical" and stated that Roy was only in "serious" condition. Mildred said, "Roy is doing a little better. He is conscious and lucid. They all seem to be doing a little better than when they were first brought in." However, Dr. Bradley announced that Roy and Shot would not be moved to Nashville for further treatment for some time because, when speaking of Roy, "Every time we move him his blood pressure drops and he goes into shock."

During the next hours State Trooper Eddie Cantrell, investigating the accident, talked to Roy, who gave him the full story. Cantrell said of this interview, "His voice was weak and not very loud but he seemed to know what he was saying." Meanwhile, Dr. Cleo Miller, a close friend and personal physician to Roy ever since Roy's arrival in Nashville in 1938, was rushed to Sparta via highway patrol escort.

Upon his arrival, Dr. Miller consulted with Dr. Bradley. The result was that an earlier decision to keep Roy and Shot in Sparta was reversed, because Dr. Miller wanted the advantages of Nashville's superior medical facilities. So the two were rushed to Miller Clinic in Nashville in separate ambulances under police escort around 6:30 P.M. June, however, elected to stay in Sparta overnight. "I plan to return tomorrow," she said. "I'm just a little shook up and I've got a sore foot, it weights about 20 pounds."

On Sunday, July 11, Dr. Miller announced that the conditions of Roy and Shot remained "serious" and "critical," respectively, and that further X-rays would be taken Monday to determine their full injuries. Concerning Roy, he ended on a hopeful note: "Roy isn't injured as badly as we first thought. Unless complications develop he should mend pretty well in about six weeks, which is in plenty of time for his planned trip to Vietnam in December." Dr. Miller added that Roy was in a great deal of pain.

Visitors and newsmen came in droves. Shot wasn't allowed to have any visitors, and Roy was only allowed to see members of his family and the press for a few brief minutes. Most of the visitors, including Minnie Pearl and the Wilburn Brothers, crowded around June, who had just arrived from Sparta, until a nurse shooed them out. (June continued as a hospital patient for about a week.)

Sunday evening, when newsmen were allowed to see Roy, he continued to express concern over Shot while minimizing his own injuries. "I'm going to be all right. I'm not uneasy about myself. I have good doctors and they're taking care of me—and the nurses, too."

On the subject of the wreck itself he said:

> I kept warning the boys about their driving. Maybe I should have been the one that warned myself, because I was under the wheel. We do 100,000 miles a year and I think I'm qualified to drive an automobile. It's just one of those things. I've been very fortunate.

One of the groups of newsmen represented the CBS Morning News and they shot some film that was used on the national TV newscast the following morning. After again explaining the cause of the wreck, Roy asked rhetorically, "You know that song which talks about the 'Wreck on the Highway'—the one that says nobody was praying. Well, that song is wrong, 'cause there was somebody prayin'— it was me."

On this same Sunday three members of the Carter Family were involved in an auto mishap as they were driving through Ohio. Mother Maybelle later said, "We had been listening to radio stories about Roy Acuff all the way so we were being real careful."

For about the next ten days Roy was still not allowed to have visitors, except his immediate family. (Mildred slept at the hospital during Roy's entire stay.) People would come, and when they were told they couldn't see Roy they would simply stand outside.

But the mailmen and other delivery services weren't standing around. They had work to do—a tremendous influx of mail, abetted by Dizzy Dean's announcements nationally of Roy's condition plus address on his weekly baseball broadcasts, yielded everything imaginable. The first few days saw the delivery of dozens of telegrams, and in succeeding weeks Roy received 70 pots of flowers and thousands of cards and letters. Some came from foreign fans, such as the packet of letters forwarded by the Commonwealth Broadcasting House in Brisbane, Australia. One fan sent $5, and stated more money would be forthcoming after her campaign to raise funds to pay Roy's hospital bill. A large amount of mail came from servicemen.

On July 22, Roy cancelled all his road trips for the remainder of the year, with the exception of the Vietnam tour. In Vietnam he later said, "I could have gotten up sooner and gone back to work. Instead I just laid there and healed because I had this trip coming up and I didn't want to miss it."

Beginning the twenty-second, Roy and Shot began to perk up and Dr. Miller announced that Shot, even though he had been critically injured and almost died, would be going home before the end of July, but that Roy would have to wait longer because of his broken bones. (As things turned out, however, Shot was held over for additional tests and he and Roy went home the same day.) From their separate rooms they communicated via notes. One of Shot's read, "I am enjoying it here—*now.*" Roy had to get Mildred's help to decipher most of Shot's correspondence: "He is a terrible writer. When he gets out of here I am going to enroll him in a penmanship course."

As Roy showed improvement, the question of retirement came up many times. About the future Roy said, "I think my personal appearances, with the exception of the Opry (if they want me) and shows for charity and the GIs, are over. I think the wreck was a warning that my luck—my traveling luck—was running out. I had a premonition it was going to happen."*

However, toward the end of July Roy was doing plenty of traveling—scooting all around the hospital in his wheelchair. On July 31 he started to use crutches, and within a week he had mastered them and abandoned his wheelchair.

On August 9, after six weeks of hospitalization, Roy and Shot went home. Roy, determined to make his first appearance on the Opry within three weeks, soon threw away the crutches and used a cane. During this time he made frequent visits to his Exhibit.

The Smoky Mountain Boys weren't idle, either. For a long time the band, billed simply as "The Smoky Mountain Boys," had made many appearances without Roy, and on August 13 and 14 they played shows in Savannah and Valdosta, Georgia.

After two months of determined recuperation Roy's big night came on Saturday, August 28. Backstage he told well-wishers, "Let's forget about the accident; I'm not an invalid." To prove this he twirled his cane, which he had been leaning on while commiserating

*Red O'Donnell, "Shot Shoots Off Note—He Has To," *Nashville Banner,* July 23, 1965, pp. 1-2.

with Mother Maybelle, as he stepped onstage to standing applause. Roy then traded his cane for his uke as he steamed into "Tennessee Central No. 9." Shot was there, too, but June Stearns was still home recovering from her broken ankle. (June never appeared with the group again.)

When the commercial was being read after this first song, Roy amused himself and the audience with his Yo-Yo technique which, like everything else on that triumphant night, seemed unchanged by the accident. Roy then shut his eyes and sang "The Great Speckled Bird."

After strolling around the stage (in his checked coat, maroon tie, black slacks, and white shoes) with only a slight limp, he returned to the microphone and gave thanks. It included the people of Sparta who assisted his troupe, all his fans, his doctors, and, especially, Dizzy Dean. He ended by saying, "Above all I want to thank you for the many prayers you said for us."

Backstage when he was asked how it felt to be back, Roy said, "It's part of my life." And then, upon further thought, "It is my life." The King, twirling his cane on his finger and balancing his fiddle bow on his nose, was back in his domain.

Two months later, when newsmen clustered around Roy during the October disc jockey convention, he said, "I don't like to complain about the accident." When pressed further he said, "My hip was broken in the wreck but it doesn't hurt me at all. But my legs and ankles, which didn't get broken, hurt worse than anything else. I reckon they must of got jammed or something." Roy admitted that he still needed to take his time going up and down stairs and was consciously trying to eliminate the limp from his gait. (Getting rid of this limp took him a year.)

December found him in Vietnam. Shot, however, couldn't go. (In the year following the accident Shot had many operations to restore his fitness, and continued to have various troubles for some time.)

During the last half of 1965 Roy intended to cut down on his road activities. An article early in 1966 quoted him as saying, "We were burying them around here like animals for awhile. I don't even like to talk about it. I and all the other singers who haven't been killed yet are lucky and ahead of the odds. During my career I have traveled around 100,000 miles a year. But I'm thinking about cutting down."

Think about it was just that, for Roy, as soon as he was able to drive, got in his car and took it for a spin. Seatbeltless. Roy can't bring himself to use them because they make him feel trapped. He does, however, feel that Shot but not he would have benefited by their use.

Not surprisingly, Roy played an extended club date in Chicago in February of 1966. And later that spring, he went on his traditional Hap Peebles midwestern tour.

In Chicago he was asked about his accident and the others that had befallen country acts. He rested his head in his hands and rubbed his eyes wearily, then said, "It is weird enough for me to wonder whether I want to continue or not. But country music is bigger than ever and all over the country there are folks to be met." He added proudly, "I'm the oldest performer on the Opry who's still traveling."

On July 28, 1970, Roy was involved in another, although comparatively minor, automobile accident near Kingsport, Tennessee. It happened while he was on his way to Knoxville to play a campaign date for Tex Ritter, who was running for the Senate.

Roy stopped the Chrysler Imperial when his passenger, big Joe Green, whose 8-year-old son also was along, indicated a desire to eat at a restaurant they had just passed. Roy was beginning to back around when the car was struck first on the left front and then left rear by a huge milk truck with a long trailer. Roy's car landed in a ditch and the milk truck's cab was upside down in the middle of the road. Milk was spilled everywhere.

Three of the seven people involved were slightly injured and were treated at a nearby hospital. Roy received a bruised kneecap and chin, and a cut that went through under his lower lip.

Roy proceeded to the Knoxville rally that night, his only handicap being slight discomfort when balancing his fiddle bow. The following day he drove home to Nashville, with his car's hood tied down and the battered fenders bent away from the wheels. The unperturbed Roy, who certainly wasn't crying over spilled milk, later said, "People kinda looked at me, but I just looked right back at them."

Portrait of Roy, taken in 1974. (*Photo courtesy Roy and Mildred Acuff*)

High school yearbook photograph of Roy.
(*Photo courtesy Roy and Mildred Acuff*)

Young Roy Acuff, captain of the basketball team during his last two years in high school. The team fell just short of winning the state title both years. (*Photo courtesy Roy and Mildred Acuff*)

The Acuff children pose with their pet dog **Penny** in this photograph taken at Maynardville, Tennessee, when Roy (*far left*) was 10 years old. Others are (*left to right*): Juanita, Spot, Briscoe, and Sue. (*Photo courtesy Roy and Mildred Acuff*)

Near-legendary western star Tex Ritter poses with Roy in 1967. (*Photo by Elizabeth Schlappi*)

Neill Acuff, Roy's father, the man he admired most. (*Photo courtesy Roy and Mildred Acuff*)

Oswald Kirby, photographed by the author in a 1967 visit to West Covina, California.

Susie and Jimmie Riddle, 1970. (*Photo by Elizabeth Schlappi*)

Entrance to Opryland's Roy Acuff Music Hall in Nashville. (*Photo by the author*)

Acuff memorabilia on exhibit in Roy Acuff Music Hall. (*Photo by the author*)

Roy and his band joined baseball great Dizzy Dean on March 22, 1966, in Jackson Mississippi to play a benefit show for tornado victims. Onie Wheeler (*second from left*) is flanked by the Nelson Brothers, along with Jimmy Lunsford, Dean, Roy, and Roy Neill (*seated*). (*Photo by Jimmie Riddle*)

Roy holds son Roy Neill, flanked by Ollie Hamilton (*left*) and Joe Frank in this 1948 photograph. (*Photo by Jimmie Riddle*)

The 1922 Central High School football team, showing halfback Roy Acuff (*back row at left*). (*Photo courtesy Roy and Mildred Acuff*)

A group of musicians at WNOX in Knoxville about 1934. The photo is somewhat posed, since all of the group did not perform together. They are (*front row, left to right*): Clell Summey, Bob Wright, and Roy; (*middle row*) Bill Norman, with fiddle; banjo player unknown; Archie Campbell (*behind microphone*); Roy's brother Spot; and Red Jones; (*back row*) Jess Easterday and Sam "Dynamite" Hatcher. Sitting at the right is announcer Lowell Blanchard. (*Photo courtesy Roy and Mildred Acuff*)

Mama Acuff (*third from right*) is flanked by her children in this photograph, believed to have been taken at Dunbar Cave on Mother's Day in the 1950s (*left to right*): Spot, Juanita, Roy, Mama Acuff, Briscoe, and Sue. (*Photo courtesy "D" Kilpatrick*)

Roy flashes a smile from the doorway of his airplane, dubbed "The Great Speckled Bird." (*Photo courtesy Roy and Mildred Acuff*)

Roy and his band in a show in Vietnam in 1967. (*Photo courtesy Jimmie Riddle*)

Roy and his band in their appearance at the International Country and Western Music Festival at Wembly Pool, in London March 28, 1970. Although Roy was one of a dozen big names appearing, his segment literally stopped the show. The enthusiasm of the audience actually shook plaster from the walls. Appearing with Roy (*left*) were Jackie Phelps, Oswald Pete Kirby, and Charlie Collins. (*Photo by Godfrey Greenwood*)

Roy takes a punch in *Smoky Mountain Melody*, a 1948 motion picture by Columbia. Big Boy Williams holds Roy's hat and coat at left. Roy enjoyed the fighting scenes in his movies and once remarked with a grin: "I got beat up bad in some of them!"

Speaking from a flatbed truck, Roy carries his gubernatorial campaign to the people of Tennessee in October, 1948. (*Photo courtesy Jimmie Riddle*)

View of Roy in 1972, with construction on the new Opry House seen from his
back yard. (*Photo courtesy Jean Thomas*)

At a 1963 benefit show, Roy fiddled while the Nashville Symphony Orchestra played. (*WSM Photo by Les Leverett*)

Roy and the Smoky Mountain Boys in 1977 (*left to right*): Charles Collins, Pete Kirby, Howdy Forrester, Roy, Onie Wheeler, and Gene Martin. (*Photo courtesy Roy and Mildred Acuff*)

Roy as he appeared in the Republic film, *Night Train to Memphis*.

Roy promotes a sponsor's product. The Royal Crown Cola Show was one of the Grand Ole Opry's finest segments. (*Photo courtesy Trudy Stamper*)

Wife Mildred meets Roy as he returns from U.S.O. Caribbean tour in January, 1960. Mildred's straw hat was brought by Roy from Cuba. (*Photo courtesy Roy and Mildred Acuff*)

One of Roy's early bands in Knoxville. Male members are (*left to right*): Red Jones, Clell Summey, Jess Easterday, and Roy. The woman in the front is unidentified. (*Photo courtesy Roy and Mildred Acuff*)

Another photo of Roy's early band in Knoxville, probably taken about 1936. Members are (*kneeling*) Jake Tindell; (*standing, left to right*) Jess Easterday, Roy, Red Jones, Clell Summey, and Kentucky Slim, the latter also known as "Little Darling." Kentucky Slim never actually played with the band as far as Roy can remember. (*Photo courtesy Elton Whisenhunt*)

The band that Roy brought to the Grand Ole Opry in February, 1938. Members are (*left to right*): Clell Summey (*also known as Cousin Jody*), Jess Easterday, Imogene Sarrett (*known as Tiny*), Roy, and Red Jones. All but Easterday quit in 1939 and Roy organized a new band. (*Photo courtesy Trudy Stamper*)

Roy's band in its prime in the early 1940s. Members are (*left to right*): Oswald, with white topped Dobro; Jess Easterday, bass; Roy; Rachel, banjo; and Lonnie "Pap" Wilson, guitar. Lonnie and Oswald had joined Roy's band in January, 1939, and Rachel followed in April of the same year. With the later addition of Jimmie Riddle in 1943, the essential part of Roy's greatest band was complete. (*Photo courtesy Trudy Stamper*)

Roy performs his specialty in the early days. (*Photo courtesy Trudy Stamper*)

Roy provides President Richard M. Nixon with instruction in the art of spinning a yo-yo. Nixon attended the first show in the new Grand Ole Opry House on March 16, 1974. (*WSM photograph by Les Leverett*)

VI

Acuff-Rose and More Fun

Two Blind Pigs Searching for an Acorn

In 1942 Roy Acuff found himself to be moderately successful. His first songbook was having phenomenal sales, his radio shows were going along nicely, and he was doing quite well in personal appearances in the surrounding states. So Roy and Mildred began to consider the possibilities of making an investment.*

> Mildred and I were wondering about some way to sometime have a little something in our lives. You see, we wanted to accomplish more than just what I could bring in. If you bring it in, it's good to be able to put it in the bank, it's good to be able to take it home. But if you've got something that you can lay your hands on when you go to getting old, when the gray hairs start up in your head—that's what we were looking for.

As Mildred and Roy discussed the matter they began to wonder if perhaps an investment in a music publishing business might also solve the difficult situation concerning Roy's compositions. Until 1940 the only music licensing agency that handled performing rights was ASCAP, the American Society of Composers, Authors, and Publishers, and this organization was not interested in country music. As a result, the compositions of Roy and of other country music artists frequently were pirated by recording companies and music publish-

---

*Much of the material for this chapter was obtained from Roy Acuff's speech at the dedication of the new Acuff-Rose building on July 10, 1967; talks with Wesley Rose; and from Lee Zhito, "A Handshake and a Promise," *Billboard*, February 3, 1968, 25-page center section.

ers. The process of correctly protecting the composers by copyright was extremely difficult and took specialized knowledge, which the young country artists didn't have. Then on October 14, 1939, a group of broadcasters formed Broadcast Music, Incorporated (BMI), to give country writers a chance to profit from their creativity. There was much competition between ASCAP and its fledging rival. During the BMI-ASCAP fight many men came from New York and offered substantial sums to buy Roy's remaining non-pirated songs, but he wouldn't sell. Instead, he privately published his first songbook in 1941. But despite the great success of this book, Mildred and Roy felt that Roy's compositions, as well as the work of other country artists, needed a real publishing company, one that they could call their own. Roy began looking for someone who knew how to start such a company.

In Nashville, Roy frequently met Fred Rose in the WSM studios. Fred had a daily piano program, and Roy opened the station each morning with his early show. The two also went to the building on various kinds of business. Roy had run into Fred on other occasions, such as when he had brought "Pins and Needles" to Roy at his home in the trailer camp. However, these were only casual meetings. Roy later said, "It was a voice, possibly from the higher ups," that prompted him to consider Fred as a partner.

Roy had no particular knowledge about the music publishing business but felt that maybe Fred did. Before he directly approached Fred Rose, though, Roy asked the advice of many men. Among them were the Opry stage manager, Vito Pellettieri, and the WSM station manager, Harry Stone, both of whom knew Fred and the music business better than he. From them he learned Fred Rose's background.

Fred was born in Evansville, Indiana, on August 24, 1897, and as a youngster he moved to St. Louis. By the age of seven Fred had taught himself to play the piano, and before he was ten he was performing professionally. When he was 15 he left for Chicago and sang and played in small taverns and restaurants, finally in night clubs. At this time he made some piano rolls for the QRS Company and records for Brunswick. At 17 he began to write songs and in his "pop" career he composed many favorites, such as "Red Hot Mama" (for Sophie Tucker), "Honest and Truly," and "Deed I Do." He joined ASCAP in 1928.

Next he was traveling as a pianist in Paul Whiteman's band, and gained star status in "Fred Rose's Song Shop," which CBS featured in a 15-minute spot each Sunday afternoon. At the end of his CBS contract, in 1933, he came to Nashville and transferred this program to WSM.

Beginning in the following year, he began jumping about the country—from Hollywood to New York to Chicago. During this time he had his financial ups and downs and frequently sold songs for a pittance just to keep body and soul together. Later he barnstormed as part of a trio called the Vagabonds. One rainy night around 1937, as they were headed for Fred's home town of Evansville, the trio took a wrong turn and wound up in Nashville. Harry Stone couldn't use the trio as such but put Fred back on his old WSM piano show and used the others as a duet.

Even though Fred was in a country music center, he still was performing his pop music and was, for the most part, not very impressed with the country style of music. However, in 1940 he left Nashville briefly and went to Hollywood to write 16 songs for Gene Autry, including "Tears on My Pillow," "Be Honest with Me," "Yesterday's Roses," and "Tweedle-O-Twill." This was Fred's first country music venture.

Fred, however, remained unconvinced about the merits of real old-time hillbilly music. Then, in early 1942, he happened to wander backstage at the Opry and as he looked out on the stage he saw Roy Acuff singing, "Don't Make Me Go to Bed." As Fred looked more closely he saw that tears were streaming down onto Roy's shirt, and realized country music had a great deal to offer when properly performed. That night he went away from the Opry a changed man.

During the depth of the Depression, while in New York, Fred became devoutly Christian Science* and afterward attributed his success to its teaching. Fred's blunt manner caused some people, including young Joe Lucus (who was to become a major Acuff-Rose executive) to be almost afraid of him. His seeming brusqueness was because he always gave a straight answer to any question. However, everyone of whom Roy asked advice said that Fred Rose was not only talented but straight and of sterling character, and that Roy

---

*Fred Rose had very poor eyesight and Roy was constantly after him to purchase glasses. Fred acquiesced to the point of buying a pair at the drugstore. Joe Lucus claims that the Christian Science must have rubbed off on the staff, because before Fred's death there was hardly a day lost to sickness; after his death, the staff began getting colds and the flu.

could never find a better or more trusted man with whom to go into business.

"When I finally approached Fred* he thought I was just kidding. He didn't take me very seriously. I don't believe that he could believe anyone would have that much faith in him. But I guess I kinda got to him. After discussing me with some of the fellows, he returned after two or three weeks and asked, 'Roy, were you serious about a business proposition in the music industry?'

"I said, 'Yes, truly, I am. I want to invest a little bit in it.' "

It was in this way in early 1942 that Roy, Mildred, and Fred Rose began a series of talks in hopes of deciding whether Roy and Fred should enter into a partnership in the music publishing business. During these discussions Fred told Roy that he wanted to go to Chicago and talk with some of his friends, especially Fred Forster, who owned a music business and was manager of another. Roy said, "Go right ahead, do whatever you want to," so Fred went to Chicago. When he got back Fred said, "Roy, Mr. Forster says that he will do everything he can to help us. Did you really mean what you said?" "Fred," replied Roy, "all you've got to do is to let me know that you want to go into business and I'm ready to fulfill my part of the deal." At this point Fred Rose went back to Chicago and talked with Mr. Forster again. Upon returning Fred said, "If you're still serious and will do as you promised, I'll do my part. Let's get it started."

Roy's part of the deal was to provide the new partnership with a financial base, but Fred never mentioned any specific amount of money. So late in 1942, Roy went to the bank and simply transferred $25,000 from his account to the newly established account of Acuff-Rose Publications. (The story that Roy gave Fred the money in a paper sack is a myth.) This fund was primarily created to provide for Fred's expenses while he was getting the business started. Roy told him, "You can withdraw part or all of the money any time you wish. I am putting it in and I hope that you'll have success in what you do. I'll never bother your business."

Roy later said of the transaction: "The truth is that Fred Rose never touched the initial money that I put in. He didn't have to. He was writing songs at that time and I had songs; and he took them all and got started."

---

*The story that Fred initially approached Roy is untrue.

A few of the 1942-43 Acuff-Rose copyrights were "Home in San Antone," "Pins and Needles," "I'll Reap My Harvest in Heaven," "Low and Lonely," and "Fireball Mail."* So the production of the firm's first two songwriters, and not the initial investment, actually launched the company. Roy Acuff and Fred Rose smiled over this many times.

At this time, December of 1942, besides simply shaking hands, the two made a formal promise. Because this had been a period when publishers were notorious for "taking from and never giving anything back," Roy and Fred agreed that the firm would be scrupulously honest—that the writers would always get their royalties and that no one connected with the company would behave in a shady way. They also agreed that the business would go out of its way to help deserving talent. These were their plans and their principles and as they were sealed with a handshake, Roy Acuff and Fred Rose became partners.

Twenty-five years later, when asked about what stood out most in his memory of Acuff-Rose, Roy, after considerable thought, said:

> There was one thing we had in common, Fred and I, and that was the fact that honesty must prevail in every phase of business.
>
> Back in those old days there was quite a complaint from the artists because they felt that publishing and recording companies weren't just as fair to them as they should be. It seemed that there was always the feeling that the artists weren't getting 100 percent justice.
>
> Fred and I both realized this and our agreement was that if an artist came to work with us in any respect no matter how small, that if we couldn't pay him off with a check or hand him a dollar bill, that postage stamps would be the next best thing for change. And that has actually happened. We have sent stamps out. That is true and I know that to be true. My sister has written a few songs for the firm and there was a time when maybe her numbers weren't going too well—maybe after awhile they had dropped off—let's put it that way, and they sent her some pay in postage stamps.**

When the firm opened for business early in 1943, its address was 2403 Kirkman Avenue, which was Fred Rose's home. Its sheet music was printed and sold out of Chicago by the Forster firm of Adams, Vee & Abbot, Inc. Fred Rose, long an ASCAP member, requested an affiliation for Acuff-Rose, which was the first company in the world

---

*Of this song Roy said that while Fred wrote it, he put the extra "bye, bye" onto the end of Fred's line of "Let her bye," and this put the song over.

**Bob Loflin-Roy Acuff interview. July 10, 1967.

to exclusively publish country music as well as being the first music publishing company of any sort in Nashville. When ASCAP took what Fred considered to be too long a time to approve his request for membership, Acuff-Rose affiliated with BMI. The firm did business at the Kirkman address for about a year, in which time many songs were copyrighted.

In 1943 Fred Rose rented an office at 220 Capitol Boulevard from the National Life and Accident Insurance Company. It had one large room and a closetlike passageway, which was used for storage. Soon Acuff-Rose songs were becoming so well known that ASCAP suggested that Fred Rose create a subsidiary company with which ASCAP could affiliate. So Fred created Milene Music. The title was a combination of the names of Mildred, Roy's wife, and Lorene, Fred's wife. From that point on, all of Fred's songs belonged to Milene Music. During his career Fred Rose often wrote songs under pseudonyms simply because he thought it created a better impression. Two of these names were Bart Dawson and Floyd Jenkins.

In April 1945, Wesley Rose, a successful accountant with Standard Oil in Chicago, drove with his wife and young daughter to St. Louis to visit an aunt. He had no intention of making a side trip to Nashville to visit his father, whom he hadn't seen in ten years, but his aunt prevailed on him to do so. Wesley consented, with some apprehension, because he was afraid that the long separation had created barriers. However, Fred Rose was cordial and the two discovered that they had a warm relationship. At Fred's suggestion, Wesley checked the Acuff-Rose books and found they didn't balance. It was apparent that an accountant putting in only one day a week on the books just couldn't do the job correctly. Wesley suggested that his father find a new accountant who had more time, and returned to Chicago.

During the next few months Fred visited Chicago occasionally to see Fred Forster, who was still publishing and shipping Acuff-Rose sheet music and songbooks, and do some recording. While in Chicago Fred made social visits to his son. After several months Fred offered Wes a job with the firm. Wes, whose job with Standard Oil was an excellent one, was very reluctant to accept, saying that he didn't know anything about the music business. To this his father wryly replied, "The music business is full of people who don't know anything about it!" When his excuse didn't work, Wesley made what he considered to be exorbitant demands. He stated that his relationship with the company must be set up on a close-friend rather than a father-son basis, and furthermore that he was to have the last word in all business decisions. To Wesley's great surprise his father accepted all these demands without question, stating that he really wanted to just be a songwriter anyway.

In December of 1945 Wesley joined the firm and took over its complete management. He soon proposed that the Chicago operation be transferred to Nashville. Taking his son's suggestion Fred went to his partner and said, "Roy, I now believe that the company can take over the business that we are doing out of Chicago with Mr. Forster." Roy consented without question. The operation was moved and the first field promotion manager ever used in the country music industry, Mel Foree, was hired to direct it.

In 1946, when all the Chicago paraphernalia moved in, the Roses were forced out of the large room and into the passageway. Then a room at a nearby business college became available, and Fred came again to Roy. "We need another room," he said. "I know where we can rent one and add to the one room we already have and thus have two rooms." Roy answered, "It's your baby, you nurse it. Take it wherever you want to!"

By 1948 the firm had grown to the limits of its quarters and Fred and Wes began looking for a new home. In searching, they wandered south down Franklin Road to an area that was (at that time) far from the downtown activity. Here they rented one section of a block-long one-floor retail store complex, which also included a hardware store, a tobacco store, a vacuum cleaner shop, and a beauty salon. Although the owner offered to sell the whole section of stores for $30,000, Wesley worked out an agreement by which the expanding firm could also rent the other stores one at a time as they were vacated. In time, Acuff-Rose did overflow into all parts of the complex, finally buying the land and building for $85,000.

This arrangement provided enough space and the firm grew into a giant corporation in the 1960s. Visitors to its headquarters, though, having heard about the firm's great size and being fully impressed by its accomplishments, were astonished at the sight of the shabby green-awninged buildings of Acuff-Rose. What they saw stretching along the block looked like a cheap shopping center. This contrast became even more apparent when sumptuous buildings of many country music firms began to spring up along Nashville's downtown Music Row.

So in 1967 the caterpillarish cheap shopping center was transformed into a butterfly—a beauty. The new multimillion dollar headquarters of Acuff-Rose was dedicated on July 10. Its facade of backlighted stone tracery was cantilevered from black granite walls, and utilized a design concept new to the Nashville area. In fact, the intent of the building's architecture was to be an aesthetic comment on the stature and vitality of the music business in Nashville.

The growth of Acuff-Rose has had dramatic high points through the years. In 1948 the firm copyrighted its biggest hit, "Tennessee Waltz." Another big tune was, "I Can't Stop Loving You." Acuff-Rose and Milene Music were joined by incorporation on October 2, 1961, by Fred Rose Music, which is another BMI firm. The corporation is one of the world's few complete-line publishing companies. It is just not a holding company for copyrights. The firm still prints sheet music, and employs a special staff to promote the products of songwriters.

On an October day in 1946 Acuff-Rose found its greatest songwriter. WSM had converted one of its early studios on the fifth floor of the National Life Building into a recreation room, and since their Capitol Boulevard office was only a few blocks away, Fred and Wes often played Ping-Pong there during the lunch hour. One day a skinny kid and his blonde wife, Audrey, walked in. Their game was interrupted when the young blonde woman, who did all the talking, introduced her husband as a songwriter. She explained that they had not had any luck in New York and she hoped that Acuff-Rose would consider publishing her husband's material.

After the table tennis game was finished, the four walked a few doors down the hall and Hank Williams sang six of his compositions. Wesley, who was learning fast what country music was all about, really flipped. (He and Hank Williams were to establish a brother-like rapport.) Fred, also, could see that the young man had great potential and he immediately bought the six songs and signed Hank to an Acuff-Rose writer's contract. Later that day they went to Fred's house and Hank recorded the songs on a disc recorder Fred kept in his attic.

At this point the Roses were interested in Hank as a songwriter, not as a recording artist. It was hoped that the firm could place Hank's future compositions with other companies. Fred was also looking for material for Molly O'Day and the six songs were purchased with her in mind.

Two months later Fred received a call from a small New York

company, Sterling Records, which wanted to cut two sessions, one country and one western. Fred selected the Willis Brothers, then known as the "Oklahoma Wranglers," for one session. Wesley suggested Hank for the second.

The first session was held in the WSM studios on December 11, 1946. It was produced by Fred Rose who also served as A&R man. Hank, who had left his band at home in Montgomery, Alabama, was backed by the Willis Brothers. Four songs were recorded, for which Hank was paid $250. The four songs sold surprisingly well and so, on February 13, 1947, Hank recorded four more in the same manner, for which he was paid another $250.

Hank was content with his new financial status and returned to Alabama to fish. Fred Rose, however, was anything but satisfied. He took the eight Sterling sides, plus some Williams's recordings that he and Wes had made on the attic recorder, to Frank Walker who was starting the MGM Record Company. An agreement was signed, which stated that all the sessions would be recorded in Nashville and that Fred Rose would be completely in charge.*

In this way the Roses found themselves not only actively involved with publishing music but with recording it. Prior to this time Fred, especially, had made himself very useful at some of Roy's sessions, but the Rose's first in-depth involvement with directing or producing sessions began with Hank Williams.

These first sessions for Sterling and MGM were possibly the first recordings made in Nashville. They were not formally arranged, they were head sessions and were the beginning of the Nashville Sound.

Since Hank Williams's recordings did so well, Mildred suggested to Fred that a recording company be formed as part of Acuff-Rose. The idea was to create a label that would accommodate artists who weren't able to find room on other labels. Wes suggested the name Old Hickory because its connection with Andy Jackson would give the new label a dignified regional flavor. Fred settled upon plain Hickory. Hickory records were first recorded in a rather primitive studio in the "shopping center." Hickory's first release was Al Terry's "Good Deal Lucile," which became a hit. Terry probably

---

*Fred Rose was A&R man for all of MGM's country material, and upon his death Wesley took over the job. He was in charge of Roy's mid-1950s MGM session at which he recorded 12 hymns. MGM and Acuff-Rose have had a close connection over the years, and in late 1973 MGM and Hickory merged.

never would have recorded had it not been for this new label. Then as the major record companies moved their studios to Nashville, Hickory utilized those. In 1967, as part of the new building, its completely new and modern recording studio came into its own when Roy opened it with his Hickory session of March 5, 1968. Acuff-Rose thus became the first Nashville publisher to have its own recording studio. Actually, Acuff-Rose has done all its recording in Nashville, and has turned down talent who wanted to record elsewhere.

The company's most spectacular growth has been in its international expansion. A "One World of Music" concept was begun in November 1957 with the opening of an office in London. Through such organizations as Acuff-Rose International and Acuff-Rose Far East, the parent company has firmly established all categories of its operations around the world. It controls song catalogs and it represents talent in such places as the British Isles, Germany, Australia, Italy, France, Switzerland, Norway, Spain, Japan, South Africa, Belgium, and Israel. At the dedication of the new building in 1967 the spectators had to dodge around scores of flagpoles, holding international flags, that were especially erected on the block-long sidewalk for the occasion.

Wesley Rose attributes the growth of the company to the production of its artists and songwriters. However, in this statement Wesley is being much too modest. Primary responsibility for the firm's tremendous success must rest with the men who recognized and developed the capabilities of the country music artists—namely, the company's founders and present operators.

Many people give Fred Rose the most credit for the company's success. One way was, naturally, by putting in his own songs. He never considered himself to be arty; songwriting was a job to him, but it was a job into which he put his heart. Furthermore, he would write for a particular artist. Roy said, "When he started with me, he wrote strictly for me." How this would happen was occasionally unusual. For example, Fred would go to many of Roy's sessions and sometimes Art Satherley, the A&R man, would tell him that they needed one more song. Fred would go out in the hall and come back with a completed song within 30 minutes. "He was just that fast," says Roy. One song that resulted from this type of creativity was "Thank God."

An even greater contribution was Fred's remarkable ability to find and develop new talent. It was perhaps his most precious gift to Acuff-Rose. Fred would never turn down an aspiring songwriter. And if he thought the fellow had even a little bit of talent, Fred would do everything in his power to make the man a success, frequently taking the writer's songs and reworking them. During this process he would often do two-thirds of the work himself, and then hand the material back to the author with no strings attached. Money meant little to Fred Rose, he simply wanted people to make a success out of their lives. Here Hank Williams was the classic example of where Fred's assistance went beyond simple polishing. He shaped and reshaped most of Hank's songs, but usually refused to share authorship. Without Fred Rose's guidance, it is extremely doubtful that Hank Williams would have ever reached maturity as a creative being.

Fred Rose, one of a very few individuals to emerge from a non-rural background and make a success in country music, is indeed a man to whom Acuff-Rose owes a great debt. And when he died of a heart attack around 8:00 P.M. on December 1, 1954, the world of country music was deeply grieved.

"You could depend on every word he said," Roy said of him. "He never told a falsehood. He would kid around with you, but never when it came to business. He was strictly serious then. I could really sum up Fred Rose in one very meaningful word: sincere."

Fred lived by the poetic line he loved: "Let me live in my house by the side of the road and be a friend of man." The title of one song he wrote for Roy is on his headstone: "I'll Reap My Harvest in Heaven."

The deaths of Hank Williams and Fred Rose could have endangered Acuff-Rose but for the company's administrative talent, people like Bud Brown, Dean May, Jean Thomas, Mel Foree, and Joe Lucus. When the latter was a young printing company salesman he tried to do his business with Acuff-Rose whenever Fred and Wes were out of town because of their outwardly forbidding manner. But Fred got to know him and mapped out a plan whereby Joe could gain enough experience to eventually join the company. During this process Joe's uninsured car was involved in an accident with that of a Nashville judge. He kept anticipating the bill with trepidation but it never came. Years later Joe found out that Fred had secretly paid it, but he could never get an admission from Fred.

One of Joe Lucus's fondest memories of Fred Rose concerns

Fred's philosophy of business. In its early days Acuff-Rose, like all companies, would run hot and cold. When it was cold, Fred would close down the office and take the staff of five to lunch. At the meal he would tell them that Acuff-Rose was God's business, that it would exist long after they all were gone. And sure enough, not long after one of these little speeches, the company would perk up and run hot again.

The firm has continued to draw top administrative people. In 1947, Wesley talked an old school pal, Bud Brown, into joining the firm as comptroller. In 1956, Wesley persuaded his brother, Lester, who was a boilermaker in Chicago, to join the firm. For four years Lester was the road manager to the Everly Brothers and then joined the Hickory staff. "D" Kilpatrick, Howdy Forrester, and Bob McCluskey have been a few of Acuff-Rose's other fine executives, of which the most talented of all is Wesley Rose.

Although Wesley was never an entertainer or officially a song-writer, he has been very successful in taking over his father's respon-sibilities. As A&R man for Hickory sessions and in day-to-day deal-ings with songwriters, Wesley Rose has proven his ability to carry on the Acuff-Rose policies. Like his father, Wesley has never accepted a penny for his guidance of many performers; in fact, his contracts with artists state he will accept no management percentage. Under Wesley the chief policy of the firm continues to be writer develop-ment.

As an A&R man he goes into every session convinced that he is going to record the nation's next number one hit tune. Also, he works with both country and pop artists. However, Wesley is a pas-sionate advocate of pure country music (and also its history: under his direction the firm donated $1,000 to the John Edwards Memorial Foundation).

But it should be pointed out that if Wesley has the choice of re-cording a country song to which Acuff-Rose owns the rights or a country song that is not owned by Acuff-Rose, he usually will pick the former: Wesley Rose prefers "Acuff-Rose Country" to just plain "Country."

Whenever a country artist wants to change his style Wes tells him, "Don't do it." He explains, "I've been fighting this battle for years. I tell my boys to keep their eyes off the pop market and concentrate on making good country songs. If they're good enough they'll make their way anywhere."

Like his dad, Wesley, has earned praise and trust from many artists. Don Gibson's remark is typical: "Without Wesley Rose I wouldn't know how to operate."

Wesley's remarkable ability to deal with musical talent has certainly been of great benefit to Acuff-Rose, but his major contribution has been in the firm's business affairs. This has been his primary responsibility since December 1945. After the death of his father, Wesley set the company on a course which carried it through its major growth and brought it to its present eminence.

At the dedication of the new building Wesley said:

> We've had more than our share of success and the fun that went along with it, and it really was fun, folks. I've had the distinct impression that someone must be watching over us and I will be forever grateful and forever humble for this fact.

God undoubtedly has been watching over Acuff-Rose, but so has Wesley Rose. Of course, other personages also have been responsible for the success of Acuff-Rose. Two names so far have not been discussed—Mildred and Roy Acuff.

Mildred has been Roy's business arm and has guided his investments. In fact, when the partnership papers were signed in December 1942, the firm was formed officially as a partnership between Fred Rose and Mildred Acuff.* It was felt that owning a publishing company might hamper Roy's career as an artist. Another reason was that Mildred played a large part in urging Roy to approach Fred and to make the initial investment. In the beginning Fred made her a part of the company, and with its incorporation she became its secretary. Mildred has an office in the new building, where she signs checks and attends policy meetings. At these meetings Mildred usually agrees with Wesley's decisions, but occasionally offers ideas of her own.

Roy has never interfered with the company's business or policy decisions in any way. He rarely goes to the building. In fact much time is spent explaining this dissociation to fans who think he is a song publisher. However, he frequently sends someone to Acuff-Rose. On one occasion he called Wesley and told him he wanted to send a friend over, and asked, "What's your address down there?" Wesley told him, "You can look it up in the phone book!"

---

*As of January 1, 1952, Wesley shared his father's half and as of his father's death, he purchased the remaining Fred Rose portion.

Roy is the first to admit that he has taken no part in the success of the company and he claims no credit. He explains:

> I never took any active part in running the company. I was an enter-tainer; had to be on the road. This was strictly an investment for me. I left it all up to Fred. I have not had anything to do with it except the name; I lent them the name Roy Acuff. I give credit to the Roses and the other working personnel for all the accomplishments. I give them all the credit.

This is a typical, modest Acuff statement, but it's atypical be-cause it isn't quite true. In the first place, Roy underplayed the importance of his name. When the company was founded, Roy's name was more famous than Fred's and ever since that time, espe-cially in the beginning before the company's reputation was estab-lished, artists have been drawn to the firm by the name of Acuff, which has and does connote success, reliability, and honesty. Second, through the years Roy's travels have brought him in contact with many young talents, and if he thinks highly enough of their abilities he sends them to Acuff-Rose. He does so without making any prom-ises, because he does not want to put the firm on the spot. Some of the performers sent by Roy have developed their talent with Acuff-Rose, and Wesley considers the forwarding of such artists to be Roy's greatest contribution to the company. A case in point would be Hank Williams.

Around 1937, when Hank was just beginning to organize his band in Montgomery and Roy was trying to make the jump from Knoxville to Nashville, Roy's songs were Hank's favorites and his first performances were almost entirely his imitations of Roy's material. Hank idolized Roy from the beginning of his career and patterned his style after that of The Smoky Mountain Boy.

Roy jokingly says he first met Hank when Oswald was in the Cub Scouts, but in a more serious vein he says it was in the early 1940s when Hank and Audrey made it a point to attend any Acuff show that played near Montgomery.

Roy's fondest memories of Hank are when he would saunter into the dressing room and just hunker down in a corner—he never would sit in a chair—and push his hat back on his head and the two would simply talk. Then Hank would say, "Here's one of your songs, Roy, and I'll even play it on the fiddle to be sure it sounds like you." Then the two would sing some Acuff songs together. After a time, Hank would tell Roy, "I have wrote another song. Would you like to hear it?" And Roy always would.

Roy later commented about Hank's singing: "He would sing his songs and he would sound in his singing a whole lot like me. He'd sing my type of songs; and he loved my type of songs. And he, truthfully, would copy me to a great extent. I guess in a way he idolized me as a country artist." Country music scholars have, indeed, felt that Hank Williams's style revealed a strong Acuff influence, and that Hank and Roy were more alike on stage than any other pair. This can be seen especially in the way Hank copied Roy's pronunciation of certain words, such as "care" and "worry."

Roy found himself taking a liking to Hank and after his own performance he would often go the the honky-tonks or fairs where Hank and Audrey were performing. Sometimes Roy was just a spectator, on other occasions he actually participated. "I would go out on stage and perform with him and Audrey and he'd sing my songs and I sung his. We'd sing them together."

Besides approving of his delivery, Roy also appreciated Hank's songwriting abilities. "He could get ideas for songs so quick, and once he did he could solid write them, too." So Roy was one of the very first to appreciate Hank Williams and the two grew very close. Hank once said that Roy Acuff was one of the few people who never let him down. Of Hank's later life, Roy has sympathy: "Of course, something turned his life later on. I guess it was all that money and people crowding in on him. He was just a simple country boy who came too far too fast. He just didn't know how to handle himself."

Roy did not tell the Roses about Hank because, at the time Hank walked in during their Ping-Pong game, neither had ever heard of him before. It is probable, though that Roy suggested to Hank that he go to Nashville and seek out Wesley and Fred.

At the start of Hank's recording career one of Fred's main problems was to talk Hank out of imitating Roy and to establish a style of his own. This individual style appeared with the recording of "Lovesick Blues." However, Hank always retained much Acuff influence.

During his 29-year lifetime Hank wanted Roy to record some of his songs, but Roy recorded very few. Years later Wesley approached him with the idea of recording a Hank Williams album. At first Roy was reticent, saying, "I don't know whether I can do Hank justice or not. I had so much friendship for Hank that I don't want to destroy any part of his works." The more he thought about it, though, the more he began to feel that it was a good idea. He finally got downright excited. "I've always loved Hank's songs and I got to thinking that maybe Hank, if he were living, would have wanted me to do it and would have appreciated my efforts. And besides, this might be my chance to give a small tribute to a man that gave so much of himself to country music." The album, entitled "For the First Time— Roy Acuff Sings Hank Williams," was recorded on June 6, 1966.

After Hank's initial recordings, the next step was to get him on the Opry. Roy went to Vito Pellettieri and asked him to speak to Harry Stone, saying, "Vito, it would really be a feather in you cap if you could get this boy on the Opry." Finally, on June 11, 1949, a guest spot was arranged and Roy introduced the tall nervous kid on the show. "I was glad to take Hank under my wing. I introduced him to everyone backstage and then brought him out on the stage and introduced him to the crowd. You might hear it a lot of ways, but that's the way it happened."*

Of Roy's considerable contributions to Acuff-Rose, one big fact must be considered: there wouldn't be any Acuff-Rose had it not been for Roy Acuff. He was the entrepreneur who took the initial gamble. When Roy put up the $25,000 he wasn't thinking he would lose it, "I wasn't really afraid to lose the money. With Fred Rose, I never thought I would." However, Roy has admitted, "I had to take a chance on what might happen to my money. It was a gamble."

Prior to the founding of Acuff-Rose, country music consisted largely of handed-down materials. With Acuff-Rose a monumental transition began, one that took country music out of the hills, so to speak, and into the world by publishing and promoting it. In the process Nashville, Tennessee, has been transformed from "Athens of the South" to "Music City U.S.A."

Did Roy and Fred ever think their venture would turn out so well? "Not at all. I only thought possibly it might do good. But I never had any idea it would turn out like this, grow this big. At the time Fred and I were like two blind pigs searching for an acorn."

Fun Instead of Profit

While Acuff-Rose Publications has certainly publicized Roy Acuff's name, its major result has been to rain financial rewards upon Roy and his family. However, through the years Roy has invested in

---

*Some of the preceding material about Hank Williams was obtained from the Cherry tape and from Roger Williams, *Sing a Sad Song the Life Story of Hank Williams* (New York: Doubleday and Company, Inc., 1970) especially pp. 36, 44-45, 80.

some spectacular ventures, the main effects of which have been to give him pleasure and publicize his name.

Immediately after World War II many country-music parks sprang up around the nation. Strangely, none were in the South. With this in mind, Roy and Joe Frank, his manager at the time, went to Clarksville, Tennessee, to look at Dunbar Cave. Roy wanted something close to Nashville, and his original intent was to rent the resort or perhaps work out a deal involving a percentage of gate receipts.

The historic old resort, whose 200 acres had long since depreciated—tangles of weeds and dilapidated buildings—was owned by the citizens of Clarksville. The principal owner was the town's mayor. The mayor, believing that a country-music park would not be a success, refused all deals except a straight sale. So late in 1947, after some bargaining over the price, Roy made a 10 percent down payment of $12,000 and agreed to pay the balance over a ten-year period. (Within six years all the payments had been completed.)

The next step was a reconditioning to fulfill its intended purpose, "a pleasure place for plain folks in which they can do anything that is decent and comfortable." While Dunbar Cave was made presentable very quickly, opening for business in the spring of 1948, the remodeling projects were extensive and varied and continued for years. The 30-room hotel was used, but it was antiquated and soon torn down. It was later replaced by a few tourist cabins. Dunbar Cave, especially during the late 1940s and early 1950s became something of a retreat for Roy and his boys and their families, and they took great pleasure in the resort and its natural setting.

Visitors were charged an admission varying from a dime to 20 cents, "just to make them appreciate it." Once inside, each attraction had a slight additional fee. A 15-acre lake provided fishing and boating, and there was a block-long pool for swimmers. Sometimes special events would be scheduled, such as parachute jumps by men at nearby Fort Campbell and coon dog field trials. The latter event was conducted in two ways. The first was to put the raccoon in a sack, drag it a few miles, and hang it in a tree. Then the dogs were let loose. The first one reaching the coon was declared to be the line winner and the first one that barked was the tree winner. Sometimes a coon was put on a log, which was floated out in the lake. The first dog to drag the coon off the log won. Yet the coons were quite successful in beating off the dogs—sometimes 50 dogs would try before the coon fell into the water. Once Roy bought 18 donkeys, plus a bus to haul them. However, donkey baseball was never played and the donkeys were given to Os.

Around 1960, the people of Clarksville requested that Roy develop the rolling hills at the far end of the lake into a nine-hole golf course. He complied, but not being a man to do something half-way, he put in an additional nine holes. For the grand opening, Roy invited Dizzy Dean and others to play an exhibition match. Roy, who was probably the only man in the world who owned a golf course but didn't play, borrowed a putter to use as a walking stick as he followed Dean's foursome around. As he strolled along he would sometimes twirl the putter as he does his fiddle and other occasions would find him using it to strike a batter's stance. After the match, Roy said he "got a real kick" out of watching the men play. "They seem to be having such a wonderful time making themselves feel miserable."

One of the main attractions of the resort was the cave itself. For 50 cents visitors were taken on a guided 40-minute tour, in the constant 56° temperature, covering a part of the eight miles of surveyed caverns. During the tour the guide lectured on the usual cave attractions, such as white blind fish, stalactites and stalagmites, and a few pillars that some have formed; and an underground stream, which appears and disappears, and whose clarity reflects the ceiling in such a way it appears to be the floor. In addition, the guide pointed out where Jenny Lind had signed her name with a pine torch after singing on one of the natural bridges. He also regaled his audience with stories of moonshiners (two stills were on display) and of desperadoes. Jesse James was said to have used the cave as a hideout. Once the sheriff thought he had some counterfeiters trapped, and carefully guarded the entrance; however, the outlaws were later found in Mexico, which could indicate a second and unknown entrance.

During the Depression, as a public works project, portions of the passageways of the cave were enlarged so tourists wouldn't have to crawl. And during Roy's ownership a group of skin diving archaeologists and geologists requested permission to explore. Their findings, one of which was an Indian burial place where the bodies of two children had turned to stone, became exhibits.

Caves make ideal fallout shelters: they have a constant water supply and natural air-conditioning. So in the summer of 1965, after returning from the Dominican Republic tour Roy signed an agreement making a portion of Dunbar Cave available as a public fallout shelter, saying that his foreign tours had convinced him of international dangers. Food and supplies to accommodate 2,600 persons for two weeks were stored in one of the underground caverns.

Another of the main attractions of Dunbar Cave was the country music performances. During the winter the open-air dance floor in front of the cave entrance was for the Tuesday and Friday night square dances. The last part of the Friday show featured Roy and the gang and was broadcast over WSM, thus setting in motion a hectic schedule. The troupe would play in Nashville on the "Friday Night Frolic" WSM show from 8:00 to 8:30 and then drive 50 miles to the cave in time to make their 11:30 to midnight square dance performance. During the summer season, lasting from Mother's Day to Labor Day, Roy and the boys presented regular Sunday performances at 2:00 and 7:00 P.M. in the 3,000-seat Country Music Pavilion on the shore of the lake. These shows were performed during the early and mid-1950s and, like the winter shows, for several years were broadcast over WSM. When Roy was on the road, other Opry acts performed at the cave.

Dunbar Cave was a great pleasure to Roy and his group for over ten years. Then, in the late 1950s, Roy began to lose interest and offered the refurbished resort to the state of Tennessee for $185,000 because, as a state park, it would be "run by the right people." Nothing came of this. Subsequent attempts at sale failed until, finally, the golf course was sold to the city of Clarksville in July 1964. In the spring of 1967 a business group agreed to purchase the rest of the resort for $200,000, due to various reasons this deal was not consummated. The cave property finally did leave Roy's ownership in 1973 when the state purchased it.

Dunbar Cave and the surrounding Clarksville area had meant even more to some members of Roy's family than to Roy and his boys. After Roy left Knoxville his parents moved from Raleigh Street to 610 Atlantic Avenue and then to North Broadway. Even though Neill Acuff passed away in 1943, Roy's mother continued to live in Knoxville until the mid-1950s, when it was decided that she should be closer to Nashville and so she moved to Dunbar Cave and lived in a lodge at the end of the lake. Whenever the gang would come up, they would congregate there. But when Roy developed the golf course, this lodge, which had been called the "Clubhouse" for years, actually became one and so Roy built his mother a little house nearby. During her short time at the resort he also built her a peacock hatchery because she loved the birds so much.

Roy's mother only enjoyed the little house about a year. In 1961 she broke her hip, and in 1962 she was moved to the Greer House at Hendersonville, where she lived for seven years. When Roy returned from his August-September 1969 Vietnam tour, he was informed that his mother couldn't last. She passed away on September 17, 1969, while Roy was on tour in Kansas. Ida Carr Acuff was buried in the family plot at the entrance of Spring Hill Cemetery.

At one time or another all of Roy's brothers and sisters lived near or around Dunbar Cave and all, except Sue, at some time took an active part in running the establishment.

Spot Acuff married Gladys Ashton. Their offspring are twins, Roger and Shirley, born in 1938. After acting as one of Roy's managers in 1946 and 1947, Spot went back to Knoxville but soon returned and was the chief manager of Dunbar Cave from its beginning in 1948 until his heart attack on October 14, 1961. Upon his recovery Spot was superintendent of several different state parks, finally settling at Henry Horton State Park, which he managed from 1964 until his death from a second heart attack on August 28, 1971. Claude bore a striking physical resemblance to Roy; all one had to do was imagine a redheaded, freckled-face Roy Acuff. The qualities of their speaking voice were also very similar. However, Spot was much more easygoing and jovial—a joy to be around.

At one time Roy's older brother Briscoe helped to manage the cave, and when the mother vacated her little house, Briscoe lived in it for awhile and then moved into a trailer on cave property. Briscoe, who never married, is reserved and quiet, but very easy to talk to.

Juanita has lived near the cave but not actually on cave property for years. At times she helped to manage the establishment. Juanita married Captain Hartsell D. Phillips, who was stationed at Fort Campbell, on December 29, 1956, in the Clubhouse. After giving his sister away Roy rushed back to the Opry, appearing for the first and only time on that show in formal clothing. Her husband later retired as a major and was connected with some of Roy's food enterprises. Juanita wrote the songs "It's All Right Now" and "Ten Little Numbers."

Unlike her sister, Sue married early in life. She married Robert L. Allen, Jr., and their son Bob was born on October 31, 1931. Sue prefers classical music and doesn't know much about the Opry, but her favorite song of Roy's is "Easy Rockin' Chair." Bob Allen, on the other hand, started playing hillbilly music at the age of six and had his own radio show while in the navy from 1951 to 1955. The Allens spent most of their married life in Tampa, Florida, and Sue still lives there. However, even before her husband's death in 1963, she would often spend summers helping out at the cave.

Besides members of his family, a few of Roy's associates have also called Dunbar Cave home. Ollie Hamilton was employed there for a time and Ford Rush, after working on a northern radio station, returned when Roy offered him a little house at the cave.

Roy Acuff is a born collector. His collections have accumulated in several ways. One has to do with fans, who send him countless items pertaining to his hobbies. Some gifts are very valuable, but all are treasured and a proper place is found for every one. Roy has said, "If somebody gave me a toothpick, I'd still have it." Another way Roy collects is on his travels, especially from foreign lands. Roy also is a regular visitor to Nashville's huge monthly flea market.

Probably Roy's first hobby was the collecting of miniature liquor bottles, each full and with seal in place, and he has accumulated around 2,000. Many of them are intricate and made of blown glass. A related collection is miniature oil lamps.

Around 1945 WSM announcer Louis Buck gave Roy a hand-painted necktie picturing a flock of ducks. At first he refused to wear it, saying it was much too flashy. But soon a lot of ties came in and Roy was wearing a different tie for each broadcast and personal appearance. Besides the usual animals and flowers, Roy's collection of maybe 250 includes portraits of himself, his family, and his troupe. Many of these portraits were painted by the sister of Grant Turner, a WSM announcer.

Roy's collecting turned international in the 1950s, when he began to collect dolls dressed in native costumes. By the start of the 1960s Roy was collecting musical instruments and coins from many lands. These collections, in turn, led to the addition of numerous old-time disc and cylinder record players, plus a very fine collection of U.S. coins. But Roy Acuff the Great Collector was having a storage problem. For this and many other reasons Roy purchased an old stone theater with a high roof in the Great Smoky Mountain resort town of Gatlinburg, Tennessee, and proceeded to partition the theater horizontally. The top half consisted of motel-like rooms with kitchens; the Roy Acuff Hobby Exhibits occupied the first floor. The enterprise opened in 1963. Roy explained the concept:

> I started thinking about this when I joined the Grand Ole Opry years ago. I wanted to show all my friends that I took enough interest to keep the things given to me over the years.
>
> I also began collecting oddities I came across while traveling around the country and around the world. It's a personal thing. For instance, my father's fiddle is there. Things like that. My boys are well represented in write-ups and pictures. It's just like walking through a hobby shop—only this one's filled with things I've chosen. I find it difficult to explain exactly what it is. People don't understand, and the only way they can really appreciate it is to go through it.
>
> The Exhibit will grow. We'll keep adding to it. I feel that in the future it will mean even more to the public. It takes time to establish something like this.

The Exhibit remained in Gatlinburg for two years under the management of Mildred's brother and sister-in-law. Because the crowds there were only seasonal, and because Roy likes to be near his pet projects, he paid about $100,000 for some property downtown and around the corner from the old Opry House and moved his collections. The Roy Acuff Hobby Exhibits opened in early 1965.

The Exhibit itself was only a part of a large complex of multipurpose rooms in a two-storied building ending at the same alley that led to the Opry's backstage area. An added benefit for Roy and his boys was their private dressing room so close to the Opry.

Upon entering the Exhibit a tourist immediately found himself in the salesroom, which contained an unbelievable array of souvenirs as well as some worthwhile items. It did a land-office business on Saturdays as people from the long line of Opry ticket seekers, which stretched around the corner and past the Exhibit, dashed in and out.

It was the fortunate tourist, though, who paid the one dollar admission fee to the actual Exhibit. Some visitors called it a shrine, others a museum. One person might fancy the liquor bottles, another the musical instruments. Also the visitor could see literally gobs of such Acuffish material as songbooks, records, and awards. Of special interest was Roy's gold record from Columbia, and a replica of his Hall of Fame plaque. Other relics concerning country music and Opry history were also on display.

One item was the fiddle that Uncle Jimmie Thompson played on the first Grand Ole Opry broadcast in 1925. The instrument was given to Roy on the Opry stage in 1963 by Thompson's niece, Mrs.

Eva Thompson Jones. At the time Roy thought it was an outright gift. However, the fiddle became the subject of litigation in April 1969, when Mrs. Jones sued Roy for its return, claiming the fiddle was being "unlawfully detained." Roy was given the choice of returning the instrument or paying $15,000. The matter never went to court and Roy still owns the fiddle.

Making certain that each fan upon visiting the Exhibit saw the item that he or she may have given to Roy was one of his constant chores. And this, like Uncle Jimmy's fiddle, could be a headache because space was limited. But Roy loved this pet project, and any fan who visited the Exhibit had a good chance of meeting and talking with him.

When plans were first developed for Opryland, Roy was assured that space would be provided for his Exhibit. In accordance with that promise, WSM built the Roy Acuff Music Hall, which is an attractive three-room building near the entrance to the park. In the spring of 1972, everything pertaining to music from the old Exhibit was moved there—WSM owns the Music Hall and leases the instruments from Roy—and Opryland opened on May 27. Because the Music Hall is not as spacious as the old Exhibit building, there was no room for Roy's other collections. However, plans are currently under way to expand the Music Hall so that it will be able to house Roy's other collections.

Floods during March 1975 damaged Opryland, and most of the Music Hall was under water. However, before security guards ordered them out, Roy and his boys had time to rescue most of the instruments. A large piano and a metal nickelodeon could not be moved. Most other instruments left when time ran out were later repaired.

As is the Music Hall, Roy himself is one of Opryland's main attractions. And because Opryland has enabled Roy to see his fans without traveling, he has cut down his touring almost entirely since its opening. Many park visitors approach and inquire, "Roy, when are you going to come and see us?" To this Roy loves to answer, "I've been to see you, now I hope all of you will come here and see me."

Dunbar Cave and Roy's collections have taken up much of his time for over 20 years. In addition to these pleasurable activities, there have been other Acuffish enterprises. In the late 1940s a Roy Acuff Square Dance Hat went on sale. A man by the name of Harrison tried to start a comic strip called "The Roy Acuff Story." Currently a Yo-Yo made by Duncan bears Roy's picture and autograph.

During his career Roy's name has been connected with a variety of prepared foods. In the early 1940s, Cherokee Mills of Nashville put out Roy Acuff Flour, which was marketed for a short time throughout the South. Colonel Tom Parker helped Roy market the flour in Florida. Starting in 1968 Roy received a percentage of sales when a firm used his name to advertise its mild and hot sausages, which were called Roy Acuff's Smoky Mountain Sausage—King of Country Sausage. Although the sausage was excellent, this enterprise fizzled after a very short time.

During the middle and late 1960s, many country music stars permitted the use of their names in the establishment of fast-food franchises. So early 1969 saw the beginning of Roy Acuff Food Systems, Incorporated, with Roy as the honorary chairman of the board. At first he was very enthusiastic about the project and purchased a few shares of stock, and urged his boys to do the same. The new firm planned to establish a coast-to-coast chain of Roy Acuff Cannonball Kitchens. They were to be decorated in turn-of-the-century railroad decor, with appropriate art prints and memorabilia: each "kitchen" was to be a veritable museum of American railroading and its dining areas to be reminiscent of the opulent dining cars of the 1890s. The menus, unlike those of other fast-food chains, were to appeal to the entire family, serving everything from steaks to hamburgers.

Ground was broken in the spring of 1969 for what was to be the first of five Nashville kitchens, which officially was opened the following September. This—and it turned out to be the only Roy Acuff Cannonball Kitchen—was in operation for about a year. In April 1971 a stockholders meeting was held to sell the land, which was considered the company's only real asset. Other fast-food enterprises were folding at this time.

VII

Off to Hollywood

"In the Movies There's Nothing to Hold You Up"

Roy Acuff's preference for live audiences has reasons both personal and professional. Much of his success as a performer depends upon entertainer/audience rapport, which, when established, is so mutually enjoyable that a show becomes memorable to all who participate. At the other extreme, movie-making has no spontaneity—but a film reaches enormous audiences. Thus, for the benefit to be gained from publicity national in scope, Roy and the boys went to Hollywood on eight occasions to make movies.

His films, five with Republic and three with Columbia Pictures, were all B movies filmed in the 1940s, with shooting schedules of two weeks. They were made in the Saturday matinee cowboy Western formula of that era, and all did well at the box office.

Although many of them had a Western theme, with Roy occasionally wearing a cowboy hat, he never really bowed to studio demands that his troupe be depicted as cowboys, evidently feeling that such an image projected on his country band would subject them to ridicule and make them appear ignorant. This policy was made crystal clear to the movie moguls during the filming of the first, *Grand Ole Opry*, and it rarely deviated. In fact, Roy kept the country music image to such an extent that scripts frequently referred to the group as "hillbilly," and Roy once was called the "King of Corn."

Roy played himself in all his pictures because he was considered a personality rather than an actor. In *Grand Ole Opry* and *Sing*

Neighbor Sing he had good roles but shared the spotlight with others. His parts were small in *Hi Neighbor, O' My Darling Clementine,* and *Cowboy Canteen*; many early advertisements barely mention him. When these pictures were rereleased in the later 1940s, however, the advertisements were redone and prominently mentioned Roy's name. In his last three films, *Night Train to Memphis,* and most especially *Smoky Mountain Melody* and *Home in San Antone,* he had starring roles.

All of Roy Acuff's movies were quite pure: he never drank whisky or smoked in the pictures and, to the villain's bilious consternation, the toasts were drunk with coffee cups. Roy did use his fists—although not as successfully as in Knoxville—in some of them, especially the last three. This was the part of his acting career that he probably enjoyed the most. Later, in thinking over his movies, he proudly said, "I got beat up bad in some of them!" There was little love interest, especially on Roy's part, although he fell in love with but failed to win the girl in *Night Train to Memphis.*

Os is the only member of the band who worked in all of Roy's films. Jess worked in the first six and Rachel in the first five, which carries each through their general tenure with the band. Joe and Tommy went to Hollywood with the band regularly after they joined, appearing in the last four movies. Lonnie performed in six, only missing *Sing Neighbor Sing* and *Night Train to Memphis,* which were filmed while he was in the navy. Jimmie Riddle worked in *Clementine* and *Cowboy Canteen* when he first joined the band, and received a deferment allowing him to perform in *Sing Neighbor Sing.* However, he missed the making of *Night Train to Memphis* while he was in the service, but later when he resumed his duties with the band, he worked in the last two films. Velma Williams appears to have made three, *Hi Neighbor, Clementine,* and *Canteen,* and Oral Rhodes none.

Roy and his band averaged three songs per film. Each song was recorded separately prior to the filming of the scene. During the actual shooting, the recording was played back and Roy and the band pantomimed.

Although the feature films in which Roy appeared were quickies and had formula plots, the story behind the story for each one had it own dramas and amusing scenes. Here now is what went on in the eight movies.

1. *Grand Ole Opry*. Republic Pictures (copyright 6/25/40).
Filmed in May 1940.
Band members: Roy, Os, Lonnie, Rachel, Jess.
Songs: "Down in Union County"
"Wabash Cannonball"
"The Great Speckled Bird"

At some time in 1938 a representative of Republic Pictures came to Nashville to prospect the Opry. Later when word from Hollywood had it that Gene Autry was being considered for the starring role, the Opry people thought the project had been dropped. However, in 1939 when the Opry went network, the studio came to its senses and decided that the movie *Grand Ole Opry* should, after all, star Opry personalities. Roy, Uncle Dave and his son, Doris, and Judge Hay were selected from the Opry to appear with such other country acts as the Weaver Brothers and Eliviry.

Judge Hay and Uncle Dave went to Chicago and from there took the train to Hollywood. Roy, Os, Rachel, Lonnie, Jess, and Doris drove to the coast in their stretched-out Ford limousine. Uncle Dave, apparently in the belief there was a shortage of food in California, came to Roy and said, "Roy Boy, I've got a ham that I'd like for you to take out there so I'll have some good country ham to eat in California." Roy consented, not knowing the troubles that were in store. As he explained later:

> I put it in my car and started off with it. We soon found that the border guards were checking everything at each state line. I guess they were looking for fruit flies or whisky or something. Well anyway, everywhere we stopped, we'd have to undo that ham box, knock the slats off, and let them examine the ham. We finally got it out there and Uncle Dave had ham all the time he was working on the picture. Then just before we started back, he came to me and said, "Roy Boy, would you mind taking that box back with you, I want to use it as a hen's nest." So we lugged the box back with us.

When the band reported to the studio for the first day's shooting they were taken to the wardrobe department and issued cowboy and Indian costumes, with the intent of turning them into Hollywood's idea of a real Wild West group. While they were trying on the clothes, Roy, who had been late getting to the studio, walked in.

He stood there with feet wide apart, eyes flashing, and hands fisted. "What's this all about?" he demanded of his troupe.

"The movie folks told us to get into this garb."

"Take it off! We'll wear our regular Grand Ole Opry clothes, or go back home." Then, turning to the studio officials, he added, "We are just a bunch of country boys from Tennessee who have come out here to put on our little country show like we do back home, and we intend to do exactly that and wear our regular clothes. If you don't want us to do that, we will return the way we came.*

There was very little hemming and hawing. And the precedent for a hillbilly act rather than a cowboy act had been set firmly by Roy. In 1943, Roy had this to say about the incident: "I am very annoyed when someone calls me a cowboy. You can see there is nothing cowboy about me. The only cowboy song I ever sang was 'Home on the Range' and that's the President's favorite. I only sing country or folk songs. When I was in Hollywood they wanted me to dress like a cowboy for a picture and I refused. I don't intend for the public ever to see me as a cowboy."

A battle of a different nature was fought during the filming of *Grand Ole Opry*. The opening encounter was noted in Louella Parsons' column of May 7. "Roy Acuff, young hill-billy brought here by Republic from Nashville," she wrote, "is suffering from appendicitis and will be operated on as soon as the picture is finished." The shooting schedule was just getting started. Roy was packed in ice between scenes and during them he performed with a heavily taped side. Then the long trip home, where the operation was performed in Nashville's St. Thomas Hospital. (Due to the surgery, Roy missed one Opry. The following Saturday night he sang "The Great Speckled Bird" while holding onto a chair.)

However, one amusing incident did occur during the filming of *Grand Ole Opry*. It happened while Oswald was riding on top of a trailer. When it hit a bump Os bounced up and when he came down he knocked a hole in the trailer's roof. But Os didn't stop there—his body continued downward through the hole and he landed on Rachel who was inside the trailer. Both were surprised by the unexpected get-together but otherwise unhurt. The director, though, was not amused. The scene was reshot because Os's fall was not in the script.

In Nashville, Roy was questioned about his first movie experience. "Of course I was pleased to go to Hollywood," he said, "but I

---

* Ben Green, "Dunbar Cave Always Reflects Roy Acuff's Love for People," *Country and Western Jamboree*, August, 1957, pp. 8, 34.

was glad to get back to Tennessee. They were all nice to us out there, but it just is no place for us kind of folks. I'm the same Roy you knew back over in Knoxville when I was playing on amateur shows."

Grand Ole Opry was released quickly, unlike some of his pictures, and its world premier was held at Nashville's Paramount Theatre on Friday night June 28, 1940. The final showing of the theater's regular picture, *Four Sons*, ended at 5:00 P.M. and was followed by a street parade and square dances. The actual premiere was preceded by a half-hour broadcast at 8:30 that evening over WSM and was seen by special guest Sergeant Alvin York.

2. *Hi Neighbor.* Republic Pictures (copyright 7/27/42).
Filmed in May or June of 1942
Band members: Roy, Os, Lonnie, Jess, Rachel, Velma.
Songs: "Stuck Up Blues"
"I Know We Are Saying Good-bye"
"Pass the Biscuits, Mirandie"

Roy especially remembers the picnic scene. In it he was to catch Vera Vague (Barbara Jo Allen) and keep her from falling in a stream, then carry her across the stream while balancing on a single-log bridge. Miss Allen was a rather hefty person, weighing about 140 pounds—equal to Roy's weight. To further complicate matters, Roy was required to make the initial catch with his left arm; he would have preferred using his right. In rehearsing the scene, Roy badly sprained his back. A stretcher was constructed on which he could roll Vera across the stream, and the cameras filmed them only from the waist up.

3. *O' My Darling Clementine.* Republic Pictures
(copyright 11/15/43).
Filmed probably late in 1942.
Band members: Roy, Os, Jim, Jess, Velma, Rachel, Lonnie.
Songs: "Fireball Mail"
"Low and Lonely"
"Smoke on the Water"

(This film is not to be confused with the closely titled *Oh My Darling Clementine*, which was shot several years later and starred Henry Fonda.)

As in *Grand Ole Opry*, Roy had a health battle at this time, in this movie Roy appears extremely thin. His role is the town sheriff.

Irene Ryan, who later was to achieve fame as Granny in the

"Beverly Hillbillies" TV show, also appeared in this picture. Many years later, on Saturday night, March 9, 1968, she was introduced by Roy on the Ernest Tubb segment of the Opry. Irene then came back to the dressing room, and she and Roy reminisced about the movie they had made together.

4. *Cowboy Canteen*. Columbia Pictures (copyright 2/8/44).
   Filming completed by April 1943.
   Band members: Roy, Os, Rachel, Lonnie, Jess, Jim, Velma.
   Songs: "Wait for the Light to Shine"
           "Night Train to Memphis"

The earlier *Hollywood Canteen* film had been such a success that Columbia decided to cash in with a cowboy sequel. Roy's good friend, Tex Ritter, suggested him during the casting. Roy enjoyed working with Tex in this film, but—in Roy's and just about everyone else's opinion—it is a most boring movie.

5. *Sing Neighbor Sing*. Republic Pictures (copyright 7/17/44).
   Filmed in April 1944.
   Band members: Roy, Os, Rachel, Jim, Jess, Tommy, Joe.
   Songs: "Easy Rockin' Chair"
           "Not a Word from Home"
           "Sing Neighbor Sing"

Jimmie Riddle never fails an opportunity to play a practical joke. A chance came as he and Roy were walking along a movie-lot "street," which had false-front stores and shops but no interiors. Jimmie pointed to an "ice cream store" and asked Roy if he would like to have a cone. Roy said he would enjoy one. So Jimmie walked over to the store and went inside, then closed the door and proceeded to the back of the movie set. Roy waited and waited and waited for his ice cream cone.

6. *Night Train to Memphis*. Republic Pictures (copyright 4/18/46).
   Filming started October 25, 1945.
   Band members: Roy, Os, Joe, Sonny Day, Jess, Tommy.
   Songs: "Night Train to Memphis"
           "No One Will Ever Know"
           "Glory Bound Train"

Roy considers this his best film. And it is the only movie for which he went to the considerable expense of purchasing a 16mm print.

This film required a stunt man, especially in the scene that called for a dive from a very high rock to rescue the drowning heroine. The stunt man's hat, contrary to the dictates of science and script, stayed on during the entire process and so, when Roy was filmed coming out of the water with the girl, of necessity his hat was incredibly and firmly still on his head.

During this interval in Hollywood the group performed the "Prince Albert Show" in a studio and it was telephoned back to Nashville.

7. *Smoky Mountain Melody.* Columbia Pictures
(copyright 12/6/48).
Filmed from July 15 to 31, 1948.
Band members: Roy, Os, Joe, Jim, Lonnie, Tommy.
Songs: "Tennessee Central No. 9"
　　　　"Thank God"
　　　　"Billy Boy"
　　　　"Smoky Mountain Moon"
　　　　"You Ca De—You Ca Da"

In the opinion of many, including Mildred, this film shows off Roy better than any of the others. It has a lot of action, which includes a wild automobile ride where Roy and "Big Boy" Williams leap from a car and roll down a rocky hillside. Roy, unlike Big Boy, didn't know the trick of putting the hands over the ears to keep out the gravel. During the filming of this scene, the two had to look at the crazily moving road that was projected in front of them in the studio. It made them both dizzy, so each got a fifth of whisky to tame the wild road.

The Smoky Mountain Boys had their troubles, too. In a scene where the boys explain to Roy why they are in jail, Os says, "We're musicians." Lonnie adds, "Yes, we was on our way over to the next county to play at a dance." Then Joe was supposed to say, "Yah, but we made the mistake of trying to cut across this dad-blamed ranch." Somehow it kept coming out as "God-damned ranch." After many shouts of "Cut!" and even more frayed nerves, Joe finally delivered the line in an acceptable manner: "Con-founded ranch."

8. *Home in San Antone.* Columbia Pictures (copyright 4/15/49).
Filmed from November 9 to 23, 1948.
Band members: Roy, Os, Joe, Lonnie, Tommy, Jim.
Songs: "Old Dan Tucker"

"Home in San Antone"
"Freight Train Blues"

The climax of this film was a scene in which two thugs give Roy a working-over in a barn. He is slammed up against a post and a large spike, just above his head, is pounded down. Theoretically, the action was to have been amusing but not dangerous. However, the procedure hurt Roy, and he went to the producer saying, "I'm not going to take anymore of this!" At this point a stunt man was called to double for him.

At the conclusion of this film actor George Cleveland wanted Roy to stay in Hollywood so Cleveland could teach Roy more about acting. But Roy declined with thanks.

Roy's movie career concluded with these eight films. On several occasions some of his movie associates urged him to stay in Hollywood and make films as a full-time career. As an inducement, they offered him a contract for four movies a year at $7,500 per week. There was even talk of Roy and John Wayne working together in films for Columbia, but this never materialized. In 1968 Roy said, "I wish it had, it would have introduced me to a larger audience." At that time, though, Roy was in a mood to stop making pictures.

During the mid-1950s the movie companies tried to lure Roy back to Hollywood. His answer was no. In the late 1960s, the producers of *The Last Picture Show* were considering either Roy or Tex Ritter for the part of the West Texas sheriff. Roy received a phone call, but the conversation was so nebulous he didn't realize the offer was being made. Roy's friend, Joe Heathcock, got the role. Even so, if negotiations had progressed to the script-reading stage, Roy would not have accepted the part, he says, because the film was too sordid for his taste.

While his movies introduced him to a larger audience, which was a major motivation for making them, Roy also enjoyed working with such Hollywood personalities as Big Boy Williams, Allen Lane, Don Wilson, Frank Albertson, Harry "Pappy" Cheshire, George Cleveland, and William Frawley, and other country music acts like Lulubelle and Scotty, the Tennessee Ramblers, Tex Ritter, Jimmy Wakely, the Milo Twins, Doye O'Delle, and Carolina Cotton.

However, in general, Roy found making movies to be a frustrating experience. In the first place, a film can be no better than its script. The plots of most of Roy's films were completely inane. The dialogue written for him and his troupe was frequently so unnatural and in such poor grammar that Roy and his boys had to restate the dialogue and delete many of the errors before they felt at all natural with their delivery. What they were doing, of course, was correcting a stereotyped view of hillbillies and country musicians. An example of this was the changing of the line, "We is musicians that have just played an engagement," to "We are musicians that have just played a dance." This alteration corrects the "is" but leaves "that," which is more indigenous to their speech than the correct "who." The substitution of "dance" was made also for real-life accuracy.

Roy found that the script directions cramped his spontaneous style. These described every physical movement, and used such directions for word delivery as dryly, ruefully, challengingly, and contritely. Furthermore, the hours of waiting, the frequent retakes of scenes for the slightest mistakes, the pancake makeup, and the use of the word "cut!" made him very nervous. So while Roy's acting improved with experience, the projecting of emotions through a machinelike camera to an unseen audience was foreign to his nature. He needed the rapport of a live audience.

In speaking of the mass media, Roy has said,

> Give me radio every time. If you make a slip you cover it up and go right on. In the movies you have to make retake after retake. And besides, in radio, if you get scared you can hang on the mike. In the movies there's nothing to hold you up.*

*Ross L. Holman, "King of Mountain Music," *Coronet*, September, 1948, p. 46.

VIII

Politicking

To Run or Not to Run

When the Grand Ole Opry went on a coast-to-coast network hookup in October 1943, a party was thrown on the stage of Ryman Auditorium. Invited to the affair was Governor Prentice Cooper, a puppet of the Memphis Democratic party boss, Ed "Red Snapper" Crump. But Cooper declined, saying that he would not go to a circus—and that Roy Acuff was bringing disgrace to Tennessee by making it the hillbilly capital of the world.*

About 9:00 o'clock the following Sunday night, some reporters were sitting around the *Nashville Tennessean* office and shooting the breeze about who could be elected governor, since Cooper was going out of office. One of them, Elmer Hinton, the *Tennessean's* state news editor, said, "I'll tell you one fellow who could be elected and that's Roy Acuff." In a burst of newsroom enthusiasm, which was also intended to embarrass Cooper and Crump, they went around the office collecting signatures endorsing Roy's name—and within hours they had 26.

The following day, not knowing whether Roy was a Republican or Democrat, Hinton filed the petition with Russel Kramer, state Democratic Party chairman, which made Roy the first to be entered for the race.** This legal action was without the knowledge or bless-

---

*Maurice Zoltow, "Hillbilly Boom," *Saturday Evening Post,* February 12, 1944, p. 38.

**The gubernatorial term was two years. Some stories state that Roy was actively put forth as a candidate for governor in 1942, but these stories are undoubtedly in error.

ing of any recognized political faction and without Roy's knowledge. Furthermore, no attempt was made to make it public. Hinton considered the petition to be primarily a joke, but he also felt that Roy, then approaching the peak of his career, had an excellent chance to win. Within a short time Hinton and his friends, not able to contain themselves, notified Roy of their little caper.*

As always, the Fourth Estate was on the job and soon the *Sumner Press* of nearby Gallatin phoned Roy, who had just been made aware of his new political status, and he told the paper to contact his WSM advisor, Harry Stone. The paper, with its story confirmed, released the news in an exclusive article on October 15, 1943.

The closing days of October were bewildering for Roy in many ways. He was pressed for a decision, and of that he sighed, "People used to like to ask how I happened to get into the music business and all about my background—but they never asked about my future until this governor business came up."

More baffling to Roy as a Democratic candidate was that his family had always been Republicans; his grandfather being a Republican state legislator. Ever since the age of 21 Roy had voted, usually for Republicans, in almost every major election. This touched on his family, too. While Roy was moving up in country music, his father was progressing in the legal profession. During the mid-1930s he was elected to fill an unexpired term as a general sessions judge in Knoxville. In 1942 Judge Acuff was running for a full eight-year term and Roy played a free show to drum up votes. At the conclusion of the performance he said, "Folks, I've enjoyed playing before you and if you've enjoyed our show please vote for my papa."

On August 6, 1942, Judge Acuff was reelected but shortly afterward an operation for stomach ulcers was necessary. He seemed to be recovering nicely but then worsened; he died on April 29, 1943. The death of his father was a great blow to Roy and added to the confusion he was experiencing at this time. Should he or should he not run as a Democratic candidate for the governorship of Tennessee?

By November Roy began to address himself to this question, although not to answer it.

> Although I have no political aims, if the people of Tennessee want me for their governor, I might consider it. But I won't say yes, and I won't say no. It's an honor, sure. But this governor business could do me a lot of

---

*Elmer Hinton, telephone conversation.

harm. Many people might think I'm getting the big head. There's this about it, if I was governor there wouldn't be any graft. I'd insist on everything being on the up and up. The poor man would have just as good a chance as the fat politician.*

When told that there had been no comment from the Crump camp in Memphis, Roy said, "If they're going to play it quiet, well, so am I. They've got a political machine in Tennessee just like everywhere else, but I could get votes okay too. I played my fiddle to 75,000 people in Crump's home town and they seemed to like it right well."

Crump was playing it quiet and Roy was being evasive, but two of Roy's wisest confidants were doing neither. Harry Stone was saying that he doubted Roy would want to run, despite the claim being made that "In the state of Tennessee you can't beat a fiddler for any office." At this time Roy was the kingpin of the Opry—its meal ticket, so to speak. And for this reason some of the top executives of WSM and the National Life Insurance Company were against his candidacy. Mildred, when asked, confided, "I think Roy had better stick to fiddling."

Perhaps with this advice in mind, by early December Roy was saying:

> I know I'm a good fiddler; but I don't know that I'd make a good governor. I know I can be elected governor of Tennessee if I want to because there's not a man in the state who has any more friends than I have, and friends mean a lot more to me than any political machine. But I don't know if I want the job. I'm pretty well satisfied right where I am, and I wouldn't want any of my friends to think I might be getting the big head. If I went into this thing and didn't keep up my work I'd take a beating financially. So if elected I would continue my work. If a governor surrounds himself with the right kind of help, he has plenty of time.

During this period, the closing days of 1943, when he was asked about specific issues Roy usually said that he didn't know enough to answer. But by early January 1944, opinions began to take shape and reporters were receiving answers to specific questions. Roy stated that he was against the poll tax, the gasoline tax was all right, but he still didn't know about the sales tax. He felt that the sale of fireworks should be limited to small torpedoes or sparklers, and that large displays should be well controlled and only presented at places

---

*Much of the information for this and the following section was obtained from newspaper clippings in Roy's scrapbooks and from the reading copies of his political speeches.

like circuses or fairs. He indicated that politics should be kept out of school affairs. When asked if women should serve on juries he said, "I see no reason why women shouldn't serve on juries. They're fair-minded. My mother was capable of giving us justice. That's all juries need to do: give justice." He expressed a deep and eloquent concern for the aged, whom he described as those "who have reached the hill-top of life and are facing the sunset without means of support." However, on the really crucial issue of his candidacy he would only say, "As for running, I'm leaving it more or less to my friends."

But by this time the wheels of politics were gaining momentum. He received a call from political leaders in Chattanooga, who informed him that if he did decide to run they would string along. After this phone call Roy said:

> Things have gone so far that I may have to run for governor of Tennessee next summer. It is hard to make up my mind what to do. But if I do make up my mind to run, I will carry it through, you need have no doubt about that. It seems that many citizens want a new deal on Capitol Hill. I have received several nice letters from Memphis; but I haven't heard from Mr. Crump yet.

The last statement had been said with a grin, yet Crump still didn't respond to the prompting. But others were moved to take pen in hand and by mid-January big batches of mail were coming into WSM, of which the general tone was : "We know you're the man to beat the Crump political machine—and we're ready to help you do it!"

Again on the subject of Boss Crump, Roy said,

> I do not know Mr. Crump personally. He is no doubt a delightful gentleman, but I am against political machines. If I should run for governor and be elected, I would want to do my best to help the people of my native state and the common people from whom I came and am a part of. If I were governor, Mr. Crump would be welcome in my office at any time, but he would come on the same level as the most humble citizen of my native Union County.

Finally, on January 22, 1944, Boss Crump was heard. A terse statement was released: "I can't believe that the people of Tennessee want a man who knows absolutely nothing what-so-ever about governmental affairs."

In reply three days later, Roy snapped:

> Maybe I don't know so much about state government, but I do know that Tennessee's constitution is as obsolete as a T model Ford compared with a modern airplane. I know, too, that the state's laws are designed to serve a political machine not the people, and if I am elected governor I will

learn enough about state government to see this corrected. I will admit I don't know so much about state government but I do know that the Ten Commandments work just as well in a democratic government as they do in religion. I don't think a man has to know so much about state government to run the state right, if he knows how to pick the right men to work under him.

At this point, Roy Acuff sounded as if he had warmed to the fight and had convinced himself to run for office. But about two weeks later, on the evening of February 7, 1944, he officially withdrew his name as a candidate, saying that he thought he could best serve the people of Tennessee by bringing them folk music.

Before making this decision, Roy considered many factors. Apparently, as soon as the Democrats really became convinced that his candidacy was genuine, they immediately made moves to control him—and he was beginning to feel the pressure. Roy also probably suspected that the idea was tomfoolery. Even so, the primary reason quite likely was financial. The governor's annual salary in 1944 was $4,000 (by 1948 it was $8,000), plus an expense account. At this period Roy's career was blossoming, and his annual income was about $150,000.

Even after his withdrawal statement, Roy was not out of the 1944 political woods. Almost simultaneous with his official Democratic withdrawal came the announcement by a group of Carroll County Republicans that they wanted to qualify him as a Republican candidate. When this was accomplished the Republicans insisted that, although Roy Acuff had withdrawn from the Democratic candidacy, he still was a bona fide Republican candidate. Roy certainly would have felt more comfortable in this new candidacy, but, feeling that the matter was closed, he didn't issue any statements.

As spring wore on, there continued to be more talk, indicating that the matter was still open. A few cynics even suggested that as a Republican candidate in a Southern state he might run not with the idea of winning but with an eye to the publicity value that a losing campaign would bring to his country music career. The people who voiced such talk showed themselves to be totally unaware of Roy Acuff's character, and they also showed their ignorance of Roy's rising career. It didn't need any outside advertising; in fact, the last thing his career needed would have been any kind of an interruption.

Finally, on June 23, 1944, Roy put all speculation to rest when he issued this statement:

To the People of Tennessee:

This statement is being issued for the purpose of setting to rest the matter concerning the probability of my becoming an active candidate for the office of governor, in either the Democratic or Republican primaries, which will be held on August 3rd next.

As is well known, I was first qualified by my friends as a candidate for the Democratic nomination for this office, which action was unsolicited by me, and also, unknown to me, until I was notified of the fact by my friends. Subsequently to this, I received hundreds of letters and telegrams, besides many personal appeals, urging me to become an active candidate. All of these manifestations were appreciated very much by me, but on account of my being engaged in the development of my musical career, and because of my having already made some commitments in connection with my chosen field, I did not feel inclined to acquiesce to the wishes of my friends, and as a result, I issued a statement under the date of February 7th to this effect.

Strange as it may seem, at approximately the same time I issued the statement above referred to, I was qualified by my friends as a candidate for the Republican nomination for this office, which action was likewise unsolicited and unknown to me, until notice was given concerning the matter through the press. After this action was taken, again hundreds of letters and telegrams, and appeals of all kinds, began coming to me, urging me to become an active candidate for the Republican nomination for governor, which appeals have continued to flow into me, despite the fact that I have tried to discourage my friends in their solicitations. It is needless for me to say that these appeals, likewise have all been gratefully received and appreciated very much.

And now, once again, I wish to state to my friends over the state, that while I have been moved greatly by the many appeals made to me, that I become an active candidate for the office of governor of my state, and recognizing the fact that I have been signally honored by these solicitations, I still feel that I should continue to pursue my musical career, through which I hope to bring myself into closer touch with every person of my native state, as well as to add to their entertainment and enjoyment. And therefore, I shall ask that my friends over the state do not consider me further as a candidate for this, the highest office of their gift.

This withdrawal didn't discourage some supporters. In the November election citizens of two counties wrote Roy's name on enough ballots to give him more votes than the two avowed candidates together. And a soldier who had listened to him while in a South Pacific battle zone wrote Roy Acuff's name on a presidential ballot.

In 1946 there was more talk of Roy running for governor, but nothing materialized then.

"I Hope Gordon Browning Will Be
the Next Governor of Tennessee"

In 1948 there was again talk of an Acuff candidacy and on June 30, although his name had not been qualified for the ballot, Roy Acuff made this announcement: "If I am nominated with the help of the Republican Party and my friends in Tennessee I will conduct a vigorous campaign into every corner of the state."

In the meantime, the Democrats were selecting their candidate. The Democratic primary was shaping up as a choice between the Crump machine's Jim McCord, who was running for reelection, and Roy's friend Gordon Browning, who was anti-Crump. On July 4 Browning was Roy's guest at his newly purchased Dunbar Cave. When Roy introduced him to the holiday crowd he said, "My friend, Gordon Browning, the man who I hope will be the next governor of Tennessee." So it was in this bizarre way—as will be seen later—that Roy "launched" his campaign.

Another, more opportune launching occurred in late July when, without Roy's knowledge, a petition was filed by a Republican Party official, John A. Pritchett, which qualified Roy as a Republican nominee for the governorship of Tennessee. Roy received the news by phone while in Hollywood making a movie, *Smoky Mountain Melody*. (By pure coincidence, the villain in this picture was named Crump). Roy pointed out that it would be impossible for him to campaign in the primary, but if he did win that election, then he would make the race. He added, "But if Browning wins and I have to criticize him, I'll withdraw. Gordon Browning is my friend."

Browning did win over the Crump machine in what was considered an upset. And Roy Acuff returned from Hollywood to learn that he had defeated his opponent Robert M. Murray, the mayor of Huntingdon, by a margin of slightly better than eight to two for the Republican nomination. The final vote for noncampaigning candidate Acuff was 81,027, Murray 19,950.

Roy Acuff accepted his nomination with this statement:

The people of Tennessee, voting in the Republican primary on August 5, nominated me as their candidate for governor. I very humbly accept that nomination and feel proud to run in the great traditions of Bob and Alf Taylor.*

---

*Bob was a Democrat and Alf was a Republican. They ran against each other in gubernatorial races and in so doing began the breakdown of the dominance of the Democratic Party in Tennessee. Roy's campaign continued this trend.

I realize that the governorship of Tennessee is a big job and carries tremendous responsibilities. I honestly believe I can handle the job. If I did not think I could serve with credit to my state I would not ask the people to elect me. I am not a politician. I believe in honesty, fair play, and the Golden Rule. I am still old fashioned enough to believe that government run on these principles cannot fail. This I promise the people of Tennessee.

The people of Tennessee have been good to me. I owe them a debt of gratitude and know of no better way to repay them than by honest public service.

Beginning in the early part of September I will visit every county in the state. I personally invite every man, woman, and child, Republican, Democrat, or Independent, to our meetings. I love people and my greatest joy is in entertaining them and making them happy.

Then on the following Saturday night at the Grand Ole Opry, Roy announced:

I do not intend on keeping this matter flying around in the air. I want to announce tonight that I am making the race for governor of Tennessee and making it to win. I have been nominated three times, friends; two times I refused to accept the nomination. I had my reasons and the reasons were good. This year I told them to leave my name on. I feel qualified for the job for I started out as a business and have tried to build it as time passed. It isn't easy for a country boy like me to stand up here and try to make a political speech. I intend on staying up here with you, being one of you, and I promise not to bring politics again to the Grand Ole Opry.

So now Roy Acuff was campaigning actively: "I'm running for governor of Tennessee and I'm running to win. I'm running like the 'Wabash Cannonball' and the 'Night Train to Memphis' rolled into one."

What prompted Roy to enter this race, after declining the offers of 1944 and 1946? He gave many answers during the campaign, and has continued to speak about the subject since then.

His acceptance statement said that he wanted to repay the kindness of the people of Tennessee by giving them public service. And exchanging his then $150,000 annual earnings for the governor's salary of $8,000 would have been financial sacrifice indeed. Some of his later speeches touched on this subject.

Those of you who know me best know that I have not jumped into this race without giving it a lot of serious thought. It was an hour of decision for me, the kind of decision that comes to every man at one time or another. I was pretty busy with my own affairs; after all, a man does have certain obligations to himself, his family, and his business. So there was the temptation to beg off and to take the easiest way out, to say a thing like this is too much trouble.

But, as I see it, a man also has an *obligation* to serve his fellow man if he can; and so many people were asking me to run and they were so sincere and so earnest in it, that I decided I just didn't have the right to consider my own affairs first and refuse to run. It is in this spirit that I stand before you as a candidate for governor.

Another reason was given by Roy two years later:

I didn't much want to get into the race because I was happy trying to make others happy, but I was mighty proud of the confidence placed in me, and it was a great honor. Furthermore, I imagine that every American boy dreams that some day he might become governor of his state and, frankly, I was no exception.

Many years afterward, when asked if he was earnest at the time, Roy said:

Seriously, you might say I was semiserious. However, if I had won I believe I could have handled the job. It would have been a matter of picking the right men to help run the office. It is that way in nearly every business, I think.

Whatever the real reason, Roy Acuff was committed then to making the race for the governorship. In the process of politicking, he was to have his eyes opened a number of times.

During late August, as the campaign was being planned, Roy was confident that his nomination automatically meant complete and total support from every Republican candidate in Tennessee. Roy believed that all who wore the Republican label were running as a team and, therefore, would work with and for each other. Roy thought that all the nominees felt the same way he did. It was in this spirit that he put himself, his money, his band, and his equipment at the disposal of the Republican Party and all its nominees—from Thomas E. Dewey down to the village constable.

Roy's campaign plans were made by advisors, some of whom included Howard Baker, father of the current U.S. senator from Tennessee; Hack Smithdeal; Guy Smith, editor of the *Knoxville Journal*; and, in an unofficial capacity, Powell Stamper, an executive of the National Life and Accident Insurance Company.

Powell and his wife Trudy frequently appeared at the rallies and helped Roy greatly in his hectic campaigning. Trudy later said that her most vivid memory of the whole tour was the adoration on the faces of the people as they looked at Roy. She particularly remembers one little town where a man came over and asked Roy to see his grandmother who, though ill, had been bundled up to make the trip but couldn't get out of the truck. Naturally, Roy obliged.

Roy's political companion was B. Carroll Reece, who had beaten Allen Strawbridge in the primary for the Senate nomination by a margin almost as great as Roy's victory. Reece's opponent was Estes Kefauver, who, like Browning, had defeated the Crump machine. Reece had an imposing political record, having represented a Smoky Mountain district in the Congress for 24 years. Besides this, he had served as chairman of the Republican National Committee since 1946. In this campaign Roy could be considered to be a moderate Republican; Reece was very conservative. Unlike Roy, he was lukewarm in his support of TVA, and his nonunion business background made a labor vote quite impossible. Reece generally attacked the New Deal, Roosevelt, Truman, and the Communists. Roy agreed with him on these four points. (In subsequent years Roy was to agree even more strongly.) After the campaign Roy said that he and Reece had gotten to know each other well, and he found Reece to be "honest, upright, and above all, a straight shooter in every field of endeavor including politics."*

The Smoky Mountain Boys accompanied Roy on the tour. His campaign band consisted of Os, Jim, Sonny, Tommy, Jess, Joe, and Lonnie. Rachel came out of retirement to hit the campaign trail. Roy's campaign entourage thus included Roy, Reece, a large band, newsmen, and advisors. In addition to several automobiles in the caravan, it had a panel truck to carry the sound equipment and a huge truck to carry the stage.

This aggregation embarked on a barnstorming tour of Tennessee that lasted from August 30 through November 1. Generally, appearances were never scheduled after 12:00 noon on Saturdays because the band needed time to get back to Nashville for the Opry; Sundays, likewise were reserved for traveling. Roy usually made two appearances on each campaign day, with the favorite times for these performances being 2:30 and 7:30, but sometimes four were scheduled.

Of the 64 days from August to November, nearly 50 included campaign appearances, which totalled nearly 100 meetings. About 600,000 people attended these rallies, which was two or three times the number that had heard any candidate for governor. And it was a fairly cheap operation. In fact, strategists kept urging that more

---

*Joe Hatcher, in an August 4, 1974, article in the *Nashville Tennessean*, stated that in 1948 Reece controlled the federal patronage in Tennessee, and therefore did not want to see a Republican governor. He therefore chose Roy who, he felt, would draw crowds for his (Reece's) Senate campaign, but not win the governorship.

money be spent because, they said, "You can't win on the pauper's oath." Roy frequently talked about campaign funds during the tour. "Here is a thing I think you ought to know, neighbors. I am paying my own way in this campaign. These boys in the band work for me and I am paying them. I have not solicited a single contribution. I haven't made any trades, deals, or promises. That means that when I am elected I will take no orders except from my oath of office." His funds from the state and national Republican campaign chests were modest. However, Roy undoubtly spent more than his declared campaign expenses of $950.

The campaign was launched at Crossville on August 30 and was witnessed by about 10,000 people. An additional 50,000 attended the remaining nine meetings of that first week. At this point Browning and Kefauver began to take notice. And all over the state old-line politicians were in a dither.

A reporter assigned to the Acuff party sent the following story:

> Boy! I've never seen anything like it. They're really coming out to hear Roy. The thing is, they're coming out clapping their hands and patting their feet to hear sweet mountain music. But they're going home with thoughtful brows and muttering in their beards over the seriousness, the earnestness and the homespun honesty of Roy Acuff. Oh, he still sings and fiddles, but they meet a new man, a plain, sincere man who impresses them as a fellow who wants to be governor to serve the average citizen, to do his best for the people regardless of party affiliation.
>
> It's evident that they are sold on Roy Acuff, as an honest sincere politician, just as much as they were sold on Roy Acuff the troubador. How many of them will come back and vote for him, however, I don't know.

As complimentary as this article was, it touched on some of the weaknesses of the campaign, weaknesses which soon became apparent and which generally put Browning's and Kefauver's minds at rest.

Roy was well received on the campaign trail, except once. It was in the second week of the campaign, September 7, at Kingsport, and the two candidates were pelted with eggs, tomatoes, and fruit. Roy was hit in the side with a grapefruit and almost left the stage, but Reece persuaded him to return. It seemed that the reception had been deliberately staged by hoodlums; however, no arrests were made.

There were hecklers, though. One occurrence was one of the final days of the campaign when one smart aleck yelled, "You're nothing but a sideshow performer!" To which Roy snapped, "I'm sorry, son, you've got me mixed up with someone else. Frankly, I've always been the main event!" (Roy remembered this and used it with good effect in his final speech. He just changed the original sentence, in which he said, "I'm not in the sideshow in the governor's race, either. I'm the main attraction" to "I'm one of the main attractions.")

Except for Kingsport, Roy was enthusiastically received on the campaign. Actually, it would be more accurate to say that his music got this reception.

While Roy's appearances were listened to by more than any other political programs in the history of the state, it soon became evident that most of the audiences came for the music and not the speeches. Reece was sometimes the victim of this audience preference. His little jig and Jew's harp playing couldn't match the Acuff Sound, and on one occasion he was booed off the stage in the middle of his speech because the crowd wanted to hear Roy sing. This happened in Clarksville on October 18.

But Reece wasn't the only victim of this type of treatment. Toward the end of the campaign Roy decided to lengthen his speeches from 15 to 30 minutes. It proved to be unfortunate. The day of October 25 was a rough one for Roy Acuff. His first appearance was in Woodbury at 12:00 noon and the crowd began to leave half way through his lengthened speech. At the 3:00 P.M. Smithville appearance, Roy continued to speak as the crowd dwindled, until a congressional candidate placed his arm around him and told him it was time to quit. The big 7:30 rally in Sparta was reported in the *Nashville Tennessean* this way:

> Roy Acuff, hillbilly entertainer, found here last night that he could not hold his crowd for a full 30 minute political address. The experience apparently rattled him. The crowd here began to empty the grandstand at Austin Athletic Field early in Acuff's speech. Acuff's anxiety apparently increased as the audience diminished and his irritation evidently resulted in his charge that the newspapers are "making fun of me and my music."

The subject of speech length was brought up, along with many other topics, in some memoranda to Guy Smith. These gave suggestions how Acuff and Reece could improve their campaign. One stated that Roy should always limit his speeches to 15 minutes, which was not followed. However, the campaigners did follow some of the suggestions, such as Reece should be more enthusiastic in his support of TVA and talk less about the New Deal; Roy should try and bring out a new point of voter interest every few days, and especially show his union card; that the spoken word is not enough, therefore more money should be spent on mailings of political pamphlets, especially since the opponents had much greater newspaper support; and Democratic votes must be vigorously sought.

Much of the memoranda, though, contained devilish political stratagems. Examples were that Roy should refer to Browning as "Mr. Truman's candidate"; that "allegedly" crooked gambling and liquor deals of the treasurer of the state Democratic committee should be exposed, expecially to church people; that Roy should denounce the Open Shop Act, of which he approved, to gain more of the labor vote; that the two candidates should make a special effort to help Republican nominee Tucker defeat Congressman Gore; and that literature pinning the CIO brand on their opponents should be sent *only* to farmers and small businessmen. The upshot was that Roy never acted upon these stratagems in either his campaign or speeches—it was a matter of character.

Frequently Roy's addresses began unpolitically, with a statement sort of easing into the subject at hand. For example:

> I'm still the same Roy Acuff you have known for a long time. I don't claim to be a new Moses found in the bull rushes; nor a Pied Piper to rid the state of rats; nor a new St. Patrick to drive out the snakes. I guess I'm the first candidate for governor you've ever heard who is not going to tell you that if you don't vote for me your crops will fail, the roof will cave in, your well will run dry, and the whole state of Tennessee will be doomed forever more. I just want to talk with you man to man and then you make your decision.

Roy then spoke a lot about the Ten Commandments and the golden rule; however, it is inaccurate to say, as did many national magazines, that his campaign was based solely on these two masterful statements of moral conduct.

Though he frequently mentioned that he would be the governor of the "common people and the masses," his addresses usually reflected his moderate Republican views, and stated that he would try to have a business administration free from political manipulations and entangling political alliances. "At the outset, I intended to be different," he said. "I am not going to make promises which neither I nor any other man can fulfill. If that is necessary to be elected, then I certainly will not be."

Every time Roy appeared at a rally he discussed some specific issues with the people. His stand on these issues was formulated at the beginning of the campaign and it never deviated. These promises were precisely phrased, with care taken to inform the electorate exactly where the money was coming from.

Most of Roy's speeches were written by Powell Stamper and typed. Being accustomed to audiences, Roy delivered the speeches very well but usually read verbatim, only occasionally seeing fit to pencil in changes or additions. As happens to every entertainer or speaker, a foot-in-mouth blooper occurs. Roy was no exception, and one blooper of his is remembered by Jimmie Riddle. On one occasion Roy meant to say, "If I've ever done anyone other than good, I don't know about it," but actually said, "If I've ever done anyone anything other than bad, I don't know about it."

The following section comments on the voting issues. Also given is a resume of Roy's statements about them.

TVA. Roy equated being for the Tennessee Valley Authority with being a loyal Tennessean.

> I don't know anybody in Tennessee who is not for TVA. Saying you favor TVA is like saying you favor religion. Everybody is for it, and that means me and Carroll Reece, too. I want it thoroughly understood that I am 100 percent for TVA and I want its benefits extended. I would like to see electricity in every farmhouse in Tennessee, and the soil conservation benefits, which are a part of the program, extended to more of the farms. I want to see more industry brought into Tennessee to utilize this great source of electric power. Yes sir, I'm for a bigger and better TVA!

Roads. Being a much traveled man, Roy knew what good and bad roads can mean to both an individual and the public.

> One of my main ambitions as governor will be to lay out a program for building roads that will exceed anything we have ever done in the state. By this I mean not only the main highways, but also the farm-to-market roads. We have some fine roads and highways but there is yet a lot more to be done. More roads and highways mean more progress for Tennessee. I believe we have the basis for financing a program of road-building, and such a program will have my fullest effort as governor. I will do everything I can to make Tennessee's system of roads and highways the best in the South.

Tourists and parks. Roy talked about tourists and considered tourism to be a great asset. He pledged himself to the preservation of the great system of state parks and recreational facilities, and to their improvement, whenever possible, for the pleasures of Tennesseans and the attraction of visitors.

States' rights. Roy was for them once he became convinced that the people were for them.

Poll tax. As in 1944, Roy was greatly opposed to the poll tax and pledged that if elected he would lead a drive for its repeal. In the early part of the campaign he took special pains to inform some people, who, due to complex laws, might not otherwise have known that their poll tax was paid.

Labor. Roy often took out his union card and waved it, saying:

> The best way I know to tell you how I stand is to tell you that I am a member of the American Federation of Musicians, an AFL union, and have been for 12 years. And so are all the boys in my band. In these years I have never been involved in a minute's labor trouble of any kind. So naturally I believe in organized labor, and in its legitimate rights and privileges, and in collective bargaining. And, incidentially, as far as I know, I am the first candidate for governor you ever had a chance to vote for who carries a union card!

Sales Tax. In 1948 as in 1944, this was a perplexing issue. The Tennessee sales tax was the subject of great debate. It was passed primarily for the benefit of the schools. But by 1948 many people were saying the sales tax was bringing in more money than was needed for the things it was intended to do; therefore, according to some, a surplus was building up in the state treasury.

> It wouldn't be right for me to say I'm for the sales tax as it is now, or for changing it, because *I don't know*. The only way a man could really know is to get in there and make a study of the whole thing; see how much money the sales tax is bringing in and what is being done with it. Then we'll decide *together* what to do about it. If we find we don't need all the money the sales tax is bringing in them I'll be for cutting it down; and if we don't need *any* of it, we'll cut it *out*!

Schools and education. Roy was in favor of the best schools that the people of Tennessee could afford. He believed in hiring the best teachers the state could get and paying them a living wage in keeping with their training, their experience, and their responsibility. The "best schooling" also included good, nourishing hot lunches for all children, whether they could pay for them or not; and free textbooks, at least through grammar school and, if possible, through the high school grades. He also commented that as an entertainer he had seen the inside of many schoolhouses, some of which were good and others in need of repair, and still others lit by oil lamps. He proposed that all school buildings be brought up to standard. Roy suggested that his proposed improvements in the education program could be paid for by the extra money that the sales tax allegedly was bringing in.

Taxes. On the general subject of taxes Roy said:

> There is one thing for all of us to remember. The state doesn't give its people anything except what is has taken away from them, either by taxes or by borrowing, which is just postponed taxes. The state could keep on trying to give more and more to its people until taxes and borrowing went clear beyond control. I don't want to be that kind of governor. I want the people of Tennessee to have every service and every advantage there is to be had. I believe that for every dollar you pay in taxes in the state of Tennessee, you are entitled to a full dollar's worth received, I believe that the cost of government should not be so high that in return for your tax dollar you get back only 40 or 50 cents in service from your state. I am committed to an administration that will have economy as an important part of its code. By that I mean a capable person in every necessary state job.

Benefits and old age pensions. Roy must have felt very strongly about these issues because some of his finest eloquence was heard in his discussions of them. Sometimes old folks came up and talked to him during the campaign, saying that they were getting as little as $8 to $12 a month. "I think we have been pretty stingy with our old folks," Roy stated. "The rest of us have gotten pay raises in the last few years and they deserve one, too." Then he talked about blind and dependent children: "I think it is just as much our obligation to give these unfortunate folks some chance at security and happiness as it is to give our children the right kind of education. I don't believe there is an able-bodied younger man or woman in Tennessee who don't agree with me." He also wanted to increase the retirement benefits for older teachers: "Let's not devote all our attention to the younger and more active teachers and ignore those who have given their lives to the cause of education." And, as usual, whenever he proposed that the government spend more money he raised the question of where it was to come from. In this case, he felt these benefits could be financed through the reported sales tax surplus or simply through more economy in government.

Tax on churches. In 1947 the Tennessee legislature passed the Employment Security Act, which stated that as of March 1949 orphan homes, churches, hospitals, and other institutions which "exist only to serve the helpless and needy" were subject to a tax. "I think the whole plan is wrong," Roy stated. One of the first things he planned to do as governor was to work for repeal of this law.

Veterans' bonus. When speaking of those who served during World War II, Roy said:

> Some left school, some left jobs, all left home, and they gave up from their lives one or two or four or five years they'll never get back. I think these young men and women are entitled to something from their state to partially repay them. Mind you, I can't promise to guarantee a soldiers' bonus; that wouldn't be honest. It would take a lot of money for even a small one of $250. But I do promise that I'll appoint a commission, made up partly of veterans, to study the matter and, if the means can be found, then I will ask the legislature to pay.

Bipartisan cabinet. Roy promised to appoint a cabinet containing both Republicans and Democrats that was honest, capable, and trustworthy. "If you elect me governor, the first thing I will do is to surround myself with the best qualified men and women I can find in Tennessee to be in my cabinet. In making these appointments I shall welcome the advice and assistance of all the people of my state." He further pledged that his administration would be one of cooperation, in which the government would represent the people, not just one party, and in which there would be a united effort working to the good of the state. Further, he said:

> There are many efficient men and women now working for the state and they need to make a living as well as the rest of us. Their jobs should not depend on politics.
>
> And right here I want to say to you good people, you send as your representative and your senator to the legislature of Tennessee whoever you choose. I have no requests to make of you that you choose your members of the legislature to suit me. I can work with anybody you send there, and we will have no problems along that line. To these things, I pledge my heart and my hands. I want that kind of a spirit of cooperation to be recorded in history as the spirit of my administration as governor of Tennessee.

Voting. All during the campaign Roy said that voting was not only a duty but a responsibility and a sacred privilege. He also stated that people should vote their convictions and not necessarily follow party lines; that voting should be for the better man and for the betterment of Tennessee.

> Let no one tell you how you can vote November second. Regardless of how you voted in the primary, you have the right to vote for whomever you please in the November election. This is still a free country, so vote for me if you feel like you can. But if you can't vote for me, then vote anyway, and let's make this election a free and open expression of the will of the people of the great state of Tennessee.

Davidson County Machine Coldmere Club. One reason why Roy went to such great lengths to tell the people that they should vote their convictions was to counteract the powerful influence of this machine, and this undoubtedly was the spiciest issue of the main campaign.

Now, I want to tell you folks about a meeting some of the politicians had in Nashville last week.

They had it at a place called the Coldmere Club, the same place where the mayor of Nashville had his barbecue right after the primary. The mayor was there the other night, and some of the other members of what they call the Davidson County "organization."

Well, one fellow got up and said: "This man with the fiddle is getting some enormous crowds in other counties. It's up to this organization to cast 50,000 votes and help out our cause in some of those counties."

Now that's what he said, and since I'm the man with the fiddle, and since we've got another one of those big crowds here today, I guess he must have been talking about you and me. He served notice on you, and on all the good folks in the big crowds we have been having everywhere we've been, that the Davidson County machine intends to see to it that you have no voice in choosing the governor of this state.

For a bunch of politicians who were talking so righteous before the primary about the evils of machine politics, they seem to have had a change of heart. They now seem to think machine politics is all right, so long as it is their own machine doing the politicking.

But they are wrong more ways than one. In the first place, the people all over this state, in both the small and large counties, are going to choose their own governor—the same people who have made up these enormous crowds. And they are not going to take orders from anybody.

And in the second place, the machine isn't going to get all the votes in Davidson County by a whole lot, because a lot of fine folks in Davidson County are going to vote for the man with the fiddle on November second.

And then there was another fellow got up at that same meeting last week, and here is what he said: "The railroad men are still working harder than ever. Why, we're even turning off our radios on Saturday nights."

Now, first of all, I've got a lot of friends who are railroad men, and who are not turning off their radios on Saturday nights, either. And to those who are, I want to assure them it will be perfectly safe to listen on Saturday night because there will be no politics on my programs on the radio. But if they are that scared, I suggest they turn off their radios on the night of Tuesday, November second, because the news that will be coming in that night they are not going to like.

It's going to take a lot more than turning off radios to head off the sweep of votes in Tennessee on November second, when my people go to the polls to elect their governor. You know, an ostrich who sticks his head in the sand and thinks he is hid, can lose a lot of tail feathers!

Up until the final weeks, this speech served up the only zest to an otherwise bland campaign. Roy and Browning were friends and, although Reece and Kefauver occasionally attacked each other, the gubernatorial opponents seemed to be boxing with big soft gloves. Roy's unpolitical character prevented him from attacking Browning and, once Browning became convinced that Roy's huge crowds came just to hear his music, Browning had no reason to hammer away at Roy.

As the campaign rolled along the Democrat newspapers began to get a little feisty. (In Nashville the *Banner* supported Roy while the *Tennessean* backed Browning.) And as it entered its final days Browning himself couldn't resist the impulse to start taking potshots to make a sure victory even more certain.

These barbs were of two types: they attacked Roy's qualifications and his motives for running. When this began, "the man with the fiddle," the man who had received adulation for years, was understandably hurt.

As Browning and the papers began needling Roy about being a fiddler, this "issue" got retaliatory thrusts in Roy's speeches.

Some of the people who have been active in this campaign, and especially some of the newspapers, have tried to make fun of me by calling me a hillbilly fiddler; and have used various other forms of ridicule about me.

Well, friends, I have no apologies for the kind of music I have been bringing to my people for the past 18 years.* It is the folk music of the South, the songs and the hoedowns handed down from the sturdy pioneers who made Tennessee, and I am proud to do my part toward preserving it for the future. My people love it, because it was the music of their parents and their grandparents. That's why three or four thousand of them come to the Ryman Auditorium every Saturday night and thousands of others listen on the radio; not just to hear me but to hear all these other fine boys and girls who play and sing this kind of music. I *am* a hillbilly fiddler and singer, and if that is a crime, I'll have to plead guilty to it. I'll even go farther than that and tell you I am *proud of it.*

I don't really mind their making fun of me because I am a hillbilly musician; but when they do it, it reflects on you good people because when they ridicule me they ridicule the kind of music you like. And I do resent their making fun of the people who love my kind of music and come to hear me play and sing it.

It's just the politics, I guess, when they make fun of me. It isn't my

---

*Toward the end of the campaign Roy frequently mentioned making records for 18 years. This figure is no doubt based on the erroneous date on the gold record he had just received.

kind of politics, and not since this campaign started have I said an unkind word about anybody.

When the subject of Roy's educational background came up, he replied: "Now there are some political minded people saying that it would be just too bad for me to be elected governor because I am not a college graduate." Then Roy proceeded to give the public a history lesson on the educational accomplishments of some of Tennessee's former politicians. He pointed out that Andy Jackson never went to college and, in fact, only learned to read and write after he was married; that Cordell Hull only had one year of college; and he also stated that the present governor wasn't a college graduate, either.

Roy's answer to the charge that he knew nothing about government could be summed up in what George Washington said: "I hold the maxim no less applicable to public than to private affairs, that honesty is always the best policy." Roy stated:

> I have never understood that there was anything mysterious about government. It is our government, the government of the people of Tennessee. There are politicians, of course, who would like to make a mystery of it; who would, in fact, like to make a secret out of it. But it should be something that every citizen in the state can easily understand, and I intend, if elected, to make it just that.
>
> I am not what you might call an expert politician, and you folks know it; but I know honesty and I know efficiency and if a governor follows these he can't go far wrong.
>
> I was raised by the Bible, and especially the Golden Rule, and this is the only way I know. I've tried to follow these teachings in my business, and I know it pays. If that kind of a belief and that way of doing business won't work in the governor's office, then you don't want me for governor and I don't want the job. But it *will* work, and I know it, and I want a chance to prove it.

In answer to the criticism of his qualifications, Roy admitted that, "Unlike some people I do not claim to know everything, but I intend to surround myself with the very best brains in this state."

Probably the most off-base part of attack lay in the criticism of Roy's business ability. Here he felt he was on very firm ground, and he defended himself with a blast.

> Now as to slurs about my business experience and my business ability. I've been in the hillbilly business, if that's what they want to call it, for a long time. I can pay my bills, and it seems to me that the best way to measure business ability is to see what a man has accomplished in his busi-

ness, using his own ability, his own talents, his own self-confidence, and his own initiative. The fact is, friends, that the taxes I pay to the federal government and to the state, the taxes on my business operation which I run myself, are enough to support some of the people who have been writing this kind of ridicule about me.

I feel that I have been quite competent in my business, if I may modestly say that. And I have the competency to serve as the governor of this state.

In responding to questions about his qualifications, Roy frequently said there were probably thousands of men in Tennessee who could be governor, and that a man didn't have to be a lawyer or in public office all his life to qualify. Roy boiled down the job: "I would use simple honesty in everything that is done."

The chirpings by the opposition about Roy's qualifications hurt his feelings, but, after all, they did have some foundation. However when Browning and the newspapers began to attack his sincerity in running for office, stating that Roy entered the race only for the publicity he could get out of it, Roy was chagrined and angry.

The people who seem to think they have a right to dictate the politics of Tennessee are getting pretty desperate. Whenever they go starting rumors, and questioning a man's sincerity, you know they're suffering.

One of the latest they have started is that I am just in this race for the advertising I can get out of it to help my career as an entertainer. That is the most childish thing they've said yet.

Listen, friends, I've done pretty well in my business. I've got a little money and can give my family the things I want them to have.

I don't need advertising badly enough to get into this campaign, travel from one end of the state to the other several times, visit every county in the state, and hold nearly 100 meetings, just to get advertising. You can buy advertising and pay for it easier than that.

If I had been just wanting the advertising I would have run four years ago when both parties qualified me to run, including those who are now questioning my sincerity about this race.

No sir. I'll tell you why I'm in this race. I'm in it because the people of Tennessee have been mighty good to me, and if I can serve them in return, I will be happy to do it.

I'm in this race because I promised the people before the primary I would run if they wanted me to. I left it to them and they put me in this race, and I am not going to let them down either now or after I am elected.

They can question my experience if they see fit to do so, or they can question my qualifications if they want to; those are questions for the people to decide. But they can't question my sincerity towards my people, not for a single minute!

I am going to win this race. The free people of Tennessee, from one end of the state to another, are going to see to that, and then we are going to have an administration in Tennessee under which the people are going to run things. My people know that.

Before going into the campaign Roy stated, "No man, no person, can say that Roy Acuff ever mistreated him, or gave him anything less than a square deal, and if I have an enemy in the world I don't know it." But as the campaign rolled along he came to realize that though true, this statement was one of political innocence—that there's a different sort of maturity you go through upon being a candidate for office.

I suppose I could have gone through life without an enemy in the world had I not aspired to the high office of governor of this state. Naturally, I shall accumulate a lot of enemies now; for the simple reason that I am challenging the claim of certain people to a vested interest in running the government of Tennessee.

Even during the campaign's final days he rarely name-called by implication and never put right name to wrong deed. And so, in his final speech, Roy could say:

Above everything else, I am proud to tell you tonight that I have conducted a campaign without mudslinging, and I am going to take credit tonight for having set the pace of the campaign. I said in the very beginning that I would not have any part in a mudslinging campaign and I have not. The governor's office, and no other office, would be worth enough to me to take my time and go all over the state talking about somebody else. It wouldn't make *me* a better man, and I think the people of the state would have a right to resent it.

This final speech by Roy was given at the gigantic jamboree held in front of the War Memorial Building in downtown Nashville on the night of November 1, 1948. The finale was attended by 20,000 people, who heard Roy's final statement:

Tomorrow, you are going to vote. Vote for the candidate of your choice. Let no man tell you how to vote, because this is a free country and you have a right to vote for whomever you please. If you voted for me in the primary, and now that you have seen and heard me and you want to vote the other way tomorrow, that is your privilege. Mark your ballot any way you care to. It will be counted. You don't have to vote a straight ticket.

If you vote for me, I want to tell you now that I pledge you you'll never have cause to regret it. And for your support I thank you from the bottom of my heart.

Roy concluded by saying what a great honor it had been to run for such a big job, and he added a tribute to Reece.

After delivering this speech Roy returned home to await the results of one of the few gubernatorial campaigns that had nationwide press and radio coverage. Even though Roy entered the campaign feeling that he had at least some hope of victory, the results of November 2, 1948, were no surprise. By 10:30 P.M. he and Reece issued separate statements conceding defeat and congratulating the victors. Next day the tally showed, with 2,232 out of 2,359 precincts reporting, that Roy received 167,944 votes to Browning's 337,899. Later, Roy said that he believed he could have won if he had run as a Democrat, been a puppet, and made campaign promises—but he was very proud that he did not succumb to these temptations. He is further proud that, although he failed to become the first Republican governor of Tennessee since 1920, he received more votes than had any Republican candidate in a Tennessee state race.

While Roy was consoling himself, his better half didn't need consolation. When Mildred was asked if Roy's defeat had been a disappointment, she said; "It sure wasn't. I didn't want him to run in the first place. Of course, some of the things they said about him hurt and made me downright mad, because they were untrue. But I didn't want him to be governor."*

It didn't take Roy long to resume his full-time schedule as a country music performer. The filming of his last movie, *Home in San Antone*, was set for November 9 through 23, and so Roy and the boys were off to Hollywood immediately after the election.

The first of 1949 found him out of state on a tour, from which he sent a telegram to Browning for his inauguration:

> Good luck, Governor. Hope your term nothing short of sensational. I'm in Kokomo, Ind., otherwise I'd be there. Best wishes for success. Regards to your charming wife.
>
> Roy,
> who lost to a better man

Things probably turned out for the best—just as the good Man up above said, "Roy, you're not gonna play baseball," He also probably said, "Roy, you're not gonna be governor of Tennessee."

Roy had a perfect summation when he said, "As governor, I

---

*Elmer Hinton, "Along Came This Feller in a Red Roadster . . .," *Nashville Tennessean Magazine*, April 13, 1958, p. 26.

would have been just another politician. As a singer, I can be Roy Acuff."

He's a Southern Yankee-Doodle Boy

"At least I'm through with running for office, but that doesn't mean I'll ever lose my interest in politics. My dad was a general sessions judge in Knox County, Tennessee, and my granddad served in the Tennessee House of Representatives. I reckon it's in my blood." Although Roy received subsequent offers to run for governor, and flatly rejected them, this action far from precluded his service to the general public.

Roy Acuff always has been keenly interested in the welfare of his and other communities. Proof is that he has played for literally countless benefits. These appearances range from helping a local little league baseball team to a performance before the Lion's International convention in Madison Square Garden. In recognition of helping out with benefit performances he has dozens of letters of commendation and awards. He also has memberships in honorary clubs, such as Full Colonel, Confederate Artillery; Member of the Society for the Preservation and Encouragement of Barber Shop Quartet Singing in America; Admiral of the Commonwealth of Kentucky's Fleet of Pleasure Boats; Honorary Sergeant-at-Arms of the Tennessee Senate; Honorary Modern Farmer; Kentucky Colonel; and Honorary Admiral in the Texas Navy.

Prison audiences in various parts of the country have benefited from Roy's community spirit. For example, inmates in the Davidson County Workhouse, the Tennessee State Prison, and the Nebraska Penitentiary have been entertained by Acuff performances.

On April 26, 1963, a captive audience of a different stripe attended a gigantic benefit performance of the Nashville Symphony Orchestra. The symphony executives decided that all types of music, if well performed, were appropriate and to prove this point, the entire orchestra visited the old Opry House. At the rehearsal, one of the classical musicians, Mrs. Mary Ann Mullins, tried to teach Roy how to play her tuba, but after the lesson, she tactfully suggested he had better stick to balancing his fiddle. During the actual performance Roy Acuff fiddled while the orchestra played country and symphonic selections. The Smoky Mountain Boys even did the Classical Routine.

When the Freedom Train stopped in Nashville in 1948, Roy and

Eddy Arnold recorded a part of a WSM promotional program. In their segment, Roy urged Eddy to vote even when he was opposed to the proposition: "The trick is not, not to vote, but to vote not when the thing you are voting on is something you want not." Eddy then stated that he is going to vote against school taxes. And Roy told him. "Every time you close a school or don't build one to begin with you are laying bricks for your new jailhouse to accommodate those that the school don't take in."

Other public-service programs that Roy has recorded include: "ACS Jamboree," for the American Cancer Crusade; "Are You Ready," for the National Foundation for Infantile Paralysis; the American Red Cross; "Looking for Lester," for Columbia University Press—advising about VD; and "Voices of Vista." These were transcribed and played all over the country—except for "Are You Ready" and for "Looking for Lester"—on various radio stations at different times. These two exceptions are especially interesting because they were recorded only for use in the Southern mountains, and the flip sides had informational programs on the same subjects that were used in the rest of the country. In 1971 Roy made a 30-minute public service film entitled *Teardrops of Nature,* in which he toured Tennessee showing contrasting beauty and pollution.

Roy Acuff also belongs to many community-minded organizations. When he returned from the foreign tour sponsored by the Loyal Order of the Moose he was so impressed that he immediately paid for life membership. However, the organization that means the most to him is the Shriners. Roy and Os are Shriners. Roy belongs to the Alimino Temple in Nashville; his Blue Lodge also is there. He has completed both the Scottish and York rites and shows his pride by regularly wearing a Masonic lapel pin or ring.

In addition to these well-meaning benefits, recordings, and charitable organizations, Roy Acuff serves on boards, such as the Nashville Memorial Hospital's Board of Trust, and frequently donates funds privately and quietly. One good turn was directed toward the Fountain City Baptist Church, which suddenly discovered one Christmas that it was the owner of a huge new pipe organ. Somewhat later the congregation learned about Santa Acuff.

Roy's dedication to charitable activities and benevolent efforts was best expressed after the auto wreck laid him low and when people asked him what he was going to do if he retired. Roy replied,

"More charity work. And, of course, I will always want to entertain the U.S. servicemen."

Roy has attended and also performed at many general political functions, such as when he joined the then Vice-President Hubert Humphrey in dedicating the Barkley Dam at the formal opening of a canal between Kentucky and Barkley Lakes. He and the boys were flown to the dedication in Governor Frank Clement's official plane.

Roy's opinions have been heard in Washington and elsewhere— actually, anywhere he could be of benefit to country music. On February 9, 1953, Congessman Winstead placed in the *Congressional Record* Roy's statements about country music in connection with the making of May 26 of each year "Hill Billy Music Day." On another occasion, Roy's testimony against Senate Bill 2834 (the Smather's bill), which would have killed Broadcast Music, Incorporated, was read before Senator John O. Pastore's subcommittee. Of course, in internal country music politics, Roy has done his part. He has served on the boards and generally has supported organizations like the Country Music Association and the Country Music Foundation.

Roy has spent much time campaigning for candidates of his choice on all levels of government. His function, in the time-honored Southern tradition, has been to draw a crowd; however, if time permitted, he usually remained to hear the speeches and at times delivered one himself. Occasionally, the candidate's campaign committee wrote Roy a check for his services. Roy has quite a collection of these checks—uncashed.

In 1948 Roy Acuff felt that the party was more important than the man, especially if it was the Republican Party. He stated:

> My father and all of my people were Republicans. I was reared by a Republican family. I have remained a Republican all my life. I believe in the two party system of government; and further believe that when I vote in a Republican primary, that it is my duty to support the Republican nominee.

Of course, in his campaign he had to seek Democrat votes in order to win, but forthrightly stated: "If you voted for me in the primary and, after seeing me and hearing me, you don't like me, then vote for the other fellow in November." However, Roy undoubtedly was chagrined by every registered Republican vote he didn't get. Later, with the maturity gained from his campaign experiences, Roy said, "I consider a man's ideas; I don't pick the fellow by the party."

Because the Democratic Party enjoyed almost complete dominance in Tennessee until fairly recent times, it's a small wonder that
Roy, who had become a political realist, has spent much time campaigning for Democrats. The late Frank Clement, a Democrat and
many times the governor of Tennessee, probably received more of
Roy's donations of time than any other candidate. In presidential
elections, however, it's a different matter.

Roy campaigned extensively for Dwight Eisenhower in the 1952
and 1956 election periods. He even made some transcriptions for use
throughout the South. Roy today is firmly convinced that Ike got all
the Communists out of the government during his tenure in the
presidency, thereby slowing up the spread of Communism.

Roy supported the candidacy of Barry Goldwater in 1964 and
helped by campaigning, sometimes on the same stage, with Goldwater. Roy particularly respected Goldwater's frankness, even when
it jarred him. There was one incident of this nature. "When he came
through Tennessee he said the worst thing he could possibly say: that
he was against TVA. I'm for TVA, but I think he should be admired
for saying he's against it."

Roy often campaigned for Richard Nixon. In the fall of 1960,
Roy was on a European USO tour, which prevented his participation
in that campaign. But in 1966 he and Marty Robbins provided the
entertainment at a $25 a plate Republican fund-raising dinner when
Nixon gave a speech on February 4. Mildred attended a tea for Mrs.
Nixon that afternoon.

In 1968 when many Southern Conservatives, including Robbins
and most of the Opry stars, switched to George Wallace, Roy Acuff
showed his Republican upbringing and also his type of conservatism
by really going all out for Richard Nixon. On September 16, 1968,
he was named to head the Tennessee Citizens for Nixon-Agnew Committee, which was formed to mobilize Independent and Democrat
voters in the state. Mrs. Sam Furrow of Knoxville, state women's golf
champion, was named co-chairman. Roy was prompted by Senator
Howard Baker to accept the post, and Roy promised that he would
devote every spare minute of his time to working for the election of
Nixon. He began by making radio and television commercials to be
shown throughout the South, in which he urged the electorate to
vote for "Dick" Nixon.

Roy campaigned extensively throughout Tennessee without
Nixon, and with him in Knoxville. On one occasion Nixon sent a

special jet for him and the boys so they could appear with the candidate in Spartanburg, South Carolina. And Roy was very flattered to next receive Nixon's rare personal invitation to his inauguration—"If I am elected." On the night of November 5, 1968, an exhausted Roy Acuff, ten pounds lighter, took satisfaction in knowing that he had done as much as any man in Tennessee to deliver the state to Richard Nixon. But in January 1969, Roy did not go to the White House because Mildred, at the last minute, was laid up with a bad back.

Roy supported Nixon again in 1972, but made only a few campaign appearances. He continued his support as late as May 18, 1974, when, upon returning from an around-the-world pleasure trip, he issued a five-page press release. (In formulating this, Roy expressed his thoughts to A. C. Dunkleberger, the retired editor of the *Nashville Banner* and also an Acuff biographer, who actually wrote the release.) It was prompted by the great respect and admiration for the United States and its leaders that Roy and Mildred found in all the countries they visited. The release stated, in part:

> The so-called "silent majority" has been silent too long in the face of dangers clearly confronting our beloved country. Here is one American who intends to speak out for truth, honor, and justice. I do not want, for one, to stand idly by and see character-assassins crucify a President, and political malice of that stripe destroy my country . . . . There are those who are trying to undermine this way of life—whether deliberately or just ignorant of what they are doing. There are those playing so recklessly and ruthlessly their partisan game that they would risk this country's going down the drain to achieve their spitework at the President, his official family, and conservatism itself . . . . If impeachment is voted *without genuine, substantial, concrete evidence* as in a court of law, clearly establishing guilt on an impeachable offense under the direct rules of the Constitution, I will personally campaign against any and all Tennessee Congressmen and Senators—Republican or Democrat—who vote for it. This is my pledge in behalf of doing something—a something sorely needed—for my Country.*

Like other conservatives, Roy is sorry that Watergate happened. He deeply regrets this tragedy ended an administration with whose policies he basically agreed.

On April 11, 1970, Roy and Mildred were White House guests for Johnny Cash's concert. Three years later they returned for a much

---

*When excerpts from this press release were printed in the Nashville newspapers, readers wrote "Letters to the Editor." Claude Graves supported Roy's stand. However, Virgil Robertson had this comment: "The Great Speckled Bird has made an expletive deleted out of himself."

more special occasion, the dinner honoring the prisoners of war. On May 23, 1973, Air Force One, the same presidential jet that carried Kennedy back from Dallas, started in California and flew to Washington picking up celebrities along the way. Roy and Mildred and the boys—Oswald, Jimmie, Charlie, Howdy, and Gene Martin—boarded the plane along with John Wayne, who was in Nashville endorsing a friend who had been in a recording session. Already on the plane were Jimmy Stewart and Sammy Davis, Jr.

The following day the POWs were entertained in a 100 x 180-foot orange and yellow tent on the south lawn of the White House. Bob Hope was the master of ceremonies and he presided over a big assemblage of stars, all of whom had voluntarily entertained in Vietnam. Each performer was well received, but the most enthusiastic appreciation was received by Roy and the boys.

When Roy's turn came he sang the "Wabash Cannonball." At the end of the song there was a thunderous standing ovation and Bob Hope called Roy back for an encore, the only one requested that evening. Instead, Roy chose to give a brief speech telling how extremely honored he was to be there and that that moment was the highlight of his professional career. The audience was still cheering when he walked off the stage. After the show, the entertainers and POWs lined up and shook hands with the President and Vice-President.

Then all the guests were invited inside the White House for the largest dinner ever given there. The diners sat at small round tables, which allowed for relatively intimate groupings. Entertainers were mixed with POWs.

Why the tremendous ovation for Roy at the performance? This question was on the mind of at least one of the diners that evening. A year later, at the opening of the new Opry House, President Nixon had this to say:

> Let me tell you something about that POW night. We had some fine Hollywood stars, singing some of the more modern music, that's a little hard to understand. I mean you have a tendency to pay a little more attention to what the girls are not wearing than to hearing the music. But I want to tell you something. I was sitting at that historic evening with six magnificent men who had served the United States in Vietnam and had been prisoners of war for six years or more. All of the stars went on. The modern stars and the older stars and the rest. The one who got the biggest applause was Roy Acuff. And I asked one of the POWs, I said, "You

know, that's rather curious that you'd find that music the type you liked the best." And they said, "Well, you've got to understand; we understood it." They knew it. In other words, it went back a few years, but they understood it and it touched them. It touched them deeply after that long time away from America.

Roy Acuff's politics is also reflected in some of his songs. The first of the political songs that interested Roy was "Old Age Pension Check," which was originally written in 1937 by Ralph Fulton and Sam "Dynamite" Hatcher. The song is a satire on Franklin Roosevelt's New Deal. It describes how frisky Grandma will be, even though she is "old and bent and gray," when her government check arrives. As originally written the song concluded with the following verse:

> For awhile the country sure was upside down
> With this old-age pension rumor going 'round.
> If you want in on the fun,
> Send your name to Washington,
> And that old-age pension man will be around.*

Roy purchased full rights to the song in 1939 and recorded it in July of that year, and re-recorded it over 20 years later. After Roy bought the song, he intensified the satire of the last verse:

> There's a man that turned this country upside down
> With his old-age pension rumor going 'round.
> If you want in on the fun,
> Send your dime to Washington,
> And that old-age pension man will be around.**

During World War II Roy sang many war songs, including "Good Bye My Love—I Heard a Silver Trumpet" and "Cowards over Pearl Harbor," which were written by Fred Rose. Roy wrote "I'd Die for the Red, White and Blue," "Our Prayer," and "Searching for a Soldier's Grave." The latter tells the story of a person who travels abroad to find the final resting place of a loved one. It attempts to universalize the individual tragedies produced by the war when it remarks that beneath each white cross also lies buried the hearts of Americans back home.*** In the opinion of many people this song

---

*OLD AGE PENSION CHECK, Roy Acuff. © 1962, Acuff-Rose Publications, Inc. Used by permission of the publisher. All rights reserved.
**Ibid.
***Bill C. Malone, *Country Music U. S. A. a Fifty-Year History* (Austin: University of Texas Press, 1968), pp. 199-200.

expressed the sorrow and real meaning of the war more than any other.

But probably the best known of all the war songs was "Smoke on the Water" by Zeke Clements and Earl Nunn. Roy neither wrote nor recorded it, but its name is linked with his because the Acuff Opry renditions were so popular. The topics and tense of this song progressed right along with the war. For example, the chorus of

> There'll be smoke on the water, on the land and the sea,
> When our army and navy overtake the enemy."*

eventually changed to

> There was smoke on the water, on the land and the sea,
> When our army and navy overtook the enemy."**

The Cold War wasn't ignored by Roy, either. He collaborated on a song entitled "Advice to Joe" Stalin, and recorded it in January 1951. It starts out, "There's a Communist ambition now to rule or wreck us all," and then advises Stalin that if he carries out his plot he better make sure that when the atomic bombs start falling he has a place to hide because "Uncle Sam will still be living when the smoke of battle's o'er.***

For many years one of Roy's heroes had been General Douglas MacArthur. When Harry Truman fired him on April 11, 1951, Roy in May recorded "Doug MacArthur."

> Once there was a mighty man,
> Sent to far away Japan,
> To defend the liberty of peaceful nations.
> While he did the best he could,
> There were some who thought he should
> Let the Communists take over all creation.****

Roy's self-reliant parents imbued him with traits that would turn him against such programs as the New Deal. On the other hand, the semipoverty of his youth enabled him to feel empathy toward the poor. The result was the moderate Republican who ran for Governor

---

*SMOKE ON THE WATER, Zeke Clements and Earl Nunn, ©1943 and 1951, Adams, Vee and Abbott, Inc. Copyright Renewal 1970 Adams, Vee and Abbott, Inc. Used by permission. All rights reserved.

**Ibid.

***ADVICE TO JOE, Roy Acuff and Earl Nunn, © 1951, Acuff-Rose Publications, Inc. Used by permission of the publisher. All rights reserved.

****DOUG MACARTHUR, Earl Nunn and Roland Johnson, ©1951, Acuff-Rose Publications, Inc. Used by permission of the publisher. All rights reserved.

of Tennessee in 1948, one who had more than just a casual interest in politics or a casual concern for the well-being of his country.

By the early 1950s the menace of communism became apparent to Roy. He feels that its doctrines menace mankind's basic freedoms and liberties, and that at all times its sly advances should be carefully watched.

Although Roy continues to have a soft spot for the underprivileged—witness the many charities in which he is actively involved—he has felt the squeeze of the graduated income tax and feels certain efficiencies and economies must be instituted. Part of the trouble he believes lies with the unions. "I was one of the very first country artists to join the musicians' union. Of course I pay my boys more than I have to, but many musicians would be working for nothing if it wasn't for the union.* So the union has done some good, but I think it and other unions have gone too far." (Roy once introduced the late George W. Cooper, president of the Nashville local, as "The man who *really* runs things around here!")

Roy, like most Southerners, is very proud but also defensive of the South. He even switched, at least partially, his long-time allegiance from the Cardinals to the Braves when they moved to Atlanta because "It's good for the South."

Roy never allowed his boys to use the word "nigger" on stage, and he discouraged the use of "Negro" because "it's so easy to slip." Roy prefers the term "colored" and says, "There is no question in my mind that we must show consideration to the colored people. But this situation, like the unions, has gone too far." The Negro rioting disturbed him greatly and he is worried about the entire country because of it.

In his concern about the future of the United States of America, Roy points to the debasement of our coinage and draws an analogy with the Roman Empire. One time, not long ago while addressing a younger person, Roy drew into a pessimistic mood, typical of conservatives. "This country will fall," he said. "I won't see it, but you probably will see it. They'll keep it secret until the very end."

When asked to describe himself politically he says, "I'm a conservative." But then quickly adds, "Oh, not *extremely* conservative: I'm for TVA!"

---

*In June 1975, Roy was presented with a gold life membership in the American Federation of Musicians, the first living country artist to be so honored. Other life members: Harry Truman, Jack Benny, and Duke Ellington.

A more detailed and much more eloquent description of Roy Acuff's patriotism and political philosophy is to be found in an informal talk he gave on January 1, 1966, at the end of one of his exhausting military tours. This was during a time of racial rioting and antiwar demonstrations.

I have a word or two that I want to speak to you if you will allow me to, just as an American citizen and nothing else. I'm not here as a politician to make a political speech to you. I'm not here as a military advisor in any way to say those things to you. I've never been—the military has never given me any kind of secret information—nothing of that description ever comes to an act like this. And I'm glad that it doesn't. I have no responsibilities in that part of the world. That's their business. But I do want to say this to you as an American citizen, that the un-American things that are going on back home (and I know you hear them over here; you're no different from any other audience we've played for—people either write to you or send you little clippings of the paper) they burn their draft cards or they march on Washington and the Capital. Those are the un-American things and they are done by such a little minority bunch of people that we back home pay no attention to it—it doesn't even phase us what-so-ever. We know that it don't phase you people over here that are the American boys; that you actually can know the truth about it—it doesn't phase any American that lives a true American life. We know that some little fellows took an idiot course and graduated and feel that they are now capable of leading a little march or something. But that is such a little thing that it doesn't make any difference what-so-ever. We realize what you people are here for; we Americans do. We know that you are here to give us protection and we're proud of you. We're really proud of you. We know that you are doing a job over here that must be done. We have a President and a Congress and a Senate and military advisors that tell us what is best to be done and we must do it. And you people here are the ones that are doing it—you in this part of the world. Of course, we have people in the other part of the world that are doing a great job, too. We have a line around the world where we have boys stationed in faraway points—in very distant points where they are remote—where they may be only 12 or 15 boys. I have been many times to offer them a few words and some songs to sing and something to cheer them up.

And you don't know just how proud we people are of you. And our prayers are for you. We're not little people over there in America letting you down over here—we're back of you. We know it's costing a world of money, we know it's costing lives, and we know it's costing much, but you are the boys that are doing it and we're very proud of you. And I'm happy that I could spend just 30 days over here of my time, and to say these few words and to offer you some country music to try to make it a little more pleasant Christmas and holidays for you. So may I in my closing words say in behalf of the USO people, the boys and girls: our prayers are for you. God bless you. We're praying for you to come home. Bye bye.

IX

Country Music Kingdom

King of the Hillbillies

In the 1940s when Roy Acuff gained such enormous popularity, a number of descriptive names were given to him. At various times he had such titles as King of Corn, King of the Grand Ole Opry, King of the Hillbilly Singers, Grand Dad of the Grand Ole Opry, Dean of the Grand Ole Opry, Deacon of Dunbar Cave, Heart of Country Music, Big Daddy of the Grand Ole Opry, and King of Mountain Music. His most familiar title, though, had its origin at a near-riot in Texas.

During World War II, Roy was making an appearance in the Dallas Sportatorium. The big show was a sellout and two distinguished members of the audience, Dizzy Dean and Gene Autry, came backstage to see Roy. As he talked with them a tremendous commotion outside interrupted their conversation. The management asked that Roy go out and try to calm the angry crowd. What Roy found was that the people who had been turned away from the show were trying to tear down a side of the building.* Roy did his best to calm them by assuring them that he wouldn't begin the show until as many of them as possible were admitted. Then he went inside to start the show.

As he began his performance, Roy introduced his two prominent

---

*This happened several times in Roy's career. One incident was in Lexington, Kentucky, when the crowd tore down the front of the theater.

guests to the audience. In acknowledging the introduction, Dizzy Dean said, "Friends, it's always a pleasure to appear on the stage with the King of the Hillbillies." This title seemed to stick better than the others, perhaps because it was a more catchy phrase. So Roy used it, although he said, "I don't know that I really like it. I'm no different from anybody else. I'm not a king, and I'm not on no throne." In subsequent years when the term country music replaced hillbilly music, Roy's title was updated to the King of Country Music.

One reason Dizzy Dean's kingly analogy has lasted is because of its popularity with the press. Here is an example of the fun one writer had with it.*

> The King is Roy Acuff. The potentate receives his admirers, more often than not, at WSM's Grand Ole Opry; though it must be said in all honesty that Red Square is about the only place where he hasn't appeared live. His scepter is a fiddle bow which sometimes, in most un-kingly fashion, he balances expertly on on the end of his nose. His courtiers are bib overalled hillbillies with names like Howdy, Shot and Oswald.

> When Acuff's show is through no witness can be found who will not swear that the King of Country Music is as regal as any Stuart who ever held the throne of England.

Roy and Dizzy Dean were friends for a long time. In the 1930s when Dean was dazzling the National League, Roy followed the newspaper accounts of his pitching feats. In the 1940s when Roy's career was on the rise, Dean, an old-time hillbilly, began to read of Roy's achievements. Dizzy rarely broadcast a game without talking about his "Ole padnar, Roy Acuff" and singing a little bit of the "Wabash Cannonball" (which he recorded on the Colonial label along with "You Don't Have to Be from the Country"). By the 1960s the two were good friends and occasionally would meet during their travels.

Then came a big day in Roy's life. It was on Sunday, June 2, 1963, in St. Louis. A break in a tour schedule gave Roy the chance to see his first major league baseball game. The Giants won 6-4. Before the game Roy met most of the players from both teams, and they gave him autographed baseballs. He sat for awhile with the Giants and their catcher, Ed Bailey, from Strawberry Plains, Tennessee, gave Roy a Giant cap. While talking about all the gifts, Roy said, "Ah gee, it looks like Santie Claus has come."

---

*Jack Hurst, "Roy Acuff: Still the King!" *Nashville Tennessean,* October 21, 1965, pp. B11, 13.

During the first part of the game Roy, sitting behind first base, was asked to stand and be introduced to the crowd and the national TV audience. Toward the end of the game Roy went up to the broadcast booth and talked briefly with Dean over the air. In commenting about his Giant hat he said, "Truthfully I am one of those Redbirds. I love them. I love them all. They have been wonderful, bless their hearts! I've enjoyed it." In answer to Dizzy's request he sang one verse of the "Wabash Cannonball." Then he said that some day he wanted to bring all the Smoky Mountain Boys up to the booth and "We'll just tear up the place—Grand Ole Opry style. There's no two better things go together than baseball and country music."

Roy and Dizzy saw each other on varying occasions. Dean and his wife were Roy's personal guests at many disc jockey conventions. They also made some joint appearances at benefit performances, such as the show on March 22, 1966, in Jackson, Mississippi, for the benefit of tornado victims.

It's regrettable that the two men never toured together—they would have made quite a pair. Roy liked Dizzy because he loves baseball and its people. Dizzy liked Roy because he loved country music and its people. In fact, the two probably wouldn't have minded a bit if the plaques in their respective Halls of Fame were switched.

The Country Music Hall of Fame received its first members in 1961 with the election of Jimmie Rodgers, Hank Williams, and Fred Rose. In 1962 Roy Acuff became its first living member.

An overflow crowd attending the fourth annual Country Music Association banquet at the Hillwood Country Club witnessed Roy's official installation into the Country Music Hall of Fame on November 9, 1962. This is the citation on his plaque:

> "The Smoky Mountain Boy" . . . "Fiddled" and sang his way into the hearts of millions the world over. Oftentimes bringing country music to areas where it had never been before. "The King of Country Music" . . . has carried his troup of performers overseas to entertain his country's armed forces at Christmastime for more than twenty years. Many successful artists credit their success to a helping hand and encouraging word from Roy Acuff.*

In fact, Roy literally was living the words of the plaque because he was in Istanbul, Turkey, on a USO Near East tour. Mildred and

---

*Interesting is that the plaque has spelling errors and one error of fact.

Roy Neill represented him in Nashville. In acknowledging the honor,
Mildred said:

> I am so very sorry Roy could not be here in person to accept this
> honor, which is the greatest tribute to a living country music artist. I know
> Roy would say he doesn't deserve it, but I'm just prejudiced enough to say
> he does. Thank you very, very much.

Acuff the Man

Roy Acuff the man has a demanding conscience and is naturally
energetic, a combination which gives flavor to his personality and
means that he always gives his fans 100 percent for their entertainment dollar. He's a very nervous and emotional person, but over the
years has calmed down considerably. He's also a modest man and has
a humility rare in a person of his stature in the entertainment world.
Actually, it's difficult to get him to talk about himself, especially in
the presence of others. And when he does, he usually downgrades his
own accomplishments while being overly generous in praise of his
fellow performers. A typical statement of his would be: "The woods
are full of fellows who can put on a show like mine, even better. I
guess I got the breaks."

Roy is very loyal to his friends and family. He's easily agitated
when they're slighted. For example, when Spot once was refused
admittance backstage at the Opry because he didn't have a pass, Roy
stomped around, threatened to get the guard fired, and said he would
not broadcast.

The subject of death usually sends him into a temporary depression. These moods, though, are transient. If anyone is mistreated during their course, Roy makes amends, sometimes with a direct apol-
ogy. However, since Roy hates to make apologies or excuses, he's
likelier to show his remorse more subtly, in subsequent kindnesses.

Although Roy loves the roar of applause and the warmth of rapport with an audience, he, like many other great performers, finds it
difficult to get close to people. He also hates to be placed in any
situation that makes him feel obligated. And while having legions of
admirers, Roy has cultivated few intimate friends outside of his family and his band. Once he and Mildred were invited to the home of
close friends for dinner. After the two couples had spent a quietly
pleasant evening, Roy shared a rather pathetic realization with his
hostess when he stated this semi-question: "You invited me here
because you liked me, not just because I am Roy Acuff?"

Roy has been constantly on the go. Ever since the 1940s, though, there has been a stream of statements about his retirement, the majority of them in press releases by show promoters to generate big "last show" audiences. But any intentions of retiring have faded during any actual curtailment of activity. It made Roy miserable, so he always resumed work. "I am missing the road. I am missing the people," he says. "Let's face it I just can't quit. I love the roar of the crowd. Entertaining is the love of my life."

Putting on a show in front of an audience requires a strong ego. Most entertainers have one and Roy is no exception. He was very tickled when Vito Pellettieri, who wrote out and posted the order of appearance for Opry acts, began putting a special notation besides Roy's name. It stated: "The Great Acuff." Roy is also known around the Opry as "The Mighty Acuff." These titles are used by the Opry family with respect, and usually with admiration and even affection. Occasionally, however, the use of them indicates a trace of jealousy. Roy, painfully aware of the inevitability of this feeling, avoids using his considerable influence in an effort to avoid hostility or hurt.

Once, a few years ago, a type of anti-Acuff sarcasm was a left-handed compliment to Roy and his accomplishments. The so-called sophisticates who scorned hillbilly music made Roy and his songs the target of their jokes for awhile. One example was a pop takeoff on the country song "Dear John," which used the line, "Send back my autographed picture of Roy Acuff." And a well-known comedian used this line when everything was going against him: "Oh, I'm going to see a Roy Acuff movie." For a time at the University of California at Riverside a piece of advice to freshmen on how to be popular was this sarcastic bit: "Eat raw fish and listen to plenty of Roy Acuff records." The compliment, of course, is in being selected as the recognized star for any joke dealing with country music.

While Roy certainly couldn't be considered a scholar, he has an intelligent and inquisitive mind. When something really interests him, such as collecting stringed instruments, he studies and becomes well informed. Touring the world has naturally acquainted him with other lands and peoples and history. But the Parthenon in Athens did not impress him. "It is nothing," he said. "It's all falling apart. The one in Nashville is much better." Roy then was reminded that if he were 2,500 years old, he'd be falling apart, too. With startled realization, he replied, "Well, I guess I would be a little frayed around the edges."

Up until the mid-1960s Roy felt it was silly of himself to think of his career as having historical importance. Today, in the seventh decade of life, Roy still is looking ahead and planning the forward course of his career. Part of that is the recognition that he and the many things connected with his career have historical importance, and he's taking an active interest in preserving his contributions to country music.*

Although he's an avid newspaper reader, Roy has read very few books. He also shuns letter writing, saying, "I hate to write a letter worse than anything." In fact, he claims, of the few he's ever written, most of those were to his father. When he feels that the wording of a letter must be expressed in his own way, he will dictate it to Mildred.

The spoken and the sung word are Roy's stock in trade, of course. However, he occasionally mispronounces words—and with amusing results. For example, during performance introductions, the people are out in the superbs, electric guitars have resignators, and bands become aggravations instead of aggregations. Roy is aware of most of these Acuffisms and perpetrates them deliberately. Once, upon being corrected about the pronunciation of discography, he said, "Now that I have learned to say it, I shall always denounce it correctly."

Roy's sense of humor is evident on the stage, where he always jokes with his band and, sometimes, with the stage crew or the audience. It is also apparent in his daily life: he finds humor in even the most commonplace matters and loves to needle his friends.

Roy is fastidious about his clothes and possessions. On the road his jackets are carried in an apparel bag that he alone handles. It usually is placed on top of the other luggage and no one unloads the trunk until Roy personally picks up this bag. As for his other possessions, Roy is a firm believer in "A place for everything and everything in its place." At the Roy Acuff Music Hall as at his old Exhibit, he personally supervises the placement of each item—to the inch. If someone suggests improving an arrangement, and if Roy agrees, the change is made immediately and exactly. In the Acuff household, all

---

*In 1954 I started collecting all types of Roy Acuff memorabilia. After 22 years my collection was huge and included anything and everything that pertains to Roy's career. In April 1976, I donated this collection to the Country Music Foundation Library & Media Center—Country Music Hall of Fame & Museum in Nashville. The Media Center has built a special room to house the Roy Acuff Collection.—The author.

pictures are straight, all clocks run to the second, and (long before the energy crisis) all lights are turned off when not in use.

Roy has been photographed thousands of times, but he still has not quite gotten used to flashbulbs. A major reason for this is that, frequently, after the picture is posed, the flash apparatus fails to work. If Roy is wearing eyeglasses, he usually removes them, even if the picture is to be of him reading something. Nor does he appreciate tape recorders. Roy answers the phone by saying, "All right."

He doesn't mind if casual acquaintances call him "Roy" or "Mr. Acuff." However, if one is around him for an appreciable time, he will insist that the person call him "Roy," because to him "Mr. Acuff" will always be his father. He also signs autographs "Roy Acuff" even when a fan he knows well requests "Roy." He never writes gushy sentiments, such as "love" or "yours forever," that are common to the most casual autographs of some other stars.

Over the years Roy Acuff has had more than his share of health problems. A very serious affliction appeared in the latter part of 1942 when Roy had pain in his legs and ankles and a loss in weight. It developed in Hollywood during the filming *O' My Darling Clementine.* Roy noticed that his left foot and ankle were swollen. The symptoms were diagnosed as Buerger's disease, thromboangiitis obliterans, an uncommon circulatory malady that attacks men who smoke heavily. (Although specific therapy still is unavailable, one supportive treatment is to quit smoking.) He was told that unless he gave up tobacco his legs might have to be amputated. Here was an old habit come to roost. Roy had started smoking cornsilks out behind the barn at a very early age. In fact, when his dad offered to buy Roy and Briscoe a horse if they refused to take up the habit, the boys turned down the offer. However, even though Roy had developed into a chain smoker, he had no trouble making a decision. He immediately gave up cigarettes and hasn't had one since.*

The circulation in his legs improved for a time but then his left foot began to numb and freeze to such an extent that he wore two wool socks on it. An operation was advised. Dr. Cleo Miller made an incision around Roy's waist and, next to the spinal cord, snipped some nerves associated with the blood vessels in Roy's left foot, thus enabling the blood to circulate more freely. Since that operation Roy

---

*Roy's father drank moderately, but was a heavy smoker. He always said smoking was his main fault, and he tried to give it up many times. Roy believes smoking is what killed him.

has had some aches in his legs and ankles and, occasionally, wears comfortable orthopedic shoes; but the Buerger's disease is considered to be arrested.

Late in 1975, Roy had stomach and chest pains. His doctor prescribed a medication, which reduced the symptoms enough that the doctor said it would be all right if Roy played six show dates around Waco, Texas. This trip lasted from March 28 to April 4, 1976, and was comparatively easy because the troupe traveled in a luxurious bus. However, the symptoms persisted during and after this tour.

Roy played three Opry shows the following Saturday, April 10. During the performances his condition worsened and, early the next morning, he drove to Miller Clinic. The initial diagnosis was exhaustion, but it was soon discovered that he had had a heart attack. Tests revealed, though, that his condition was not serious enough to demand surgery, and, after two weeks in the clinic, he was advised to recuperate at home.

Following a few weeks of thoroughly quiet rest, he ventured to Opryland for short periods to be with his friends and fans. Finally, tests showed that he had recovered sufficiently to resume his career, but on a limited basis. Roy's first performances were two matinees at Opryland on Wednesday, August 11. He sang the opening song for each program and acted as emcee. He was nervous, especially during the first show, and a little weak, but extremely happy. Roy returned to the Opryhouse the following weekend, August 13-14, for his regular evening Opry shows.

However his euphoria lasted only for a while. October again found him in ill health and he was hospitalized on the 13th. Tests revealed a gall bladder condition, and he underwent surgery on the 21st. After a month's recuperation Roy returned to the Opry feeling better than he had felt in more than a year.

At present, Roy is playing a full schedule of Opryland shows, and he's spending a lot of time in and near his Music Hall conversing with fans. It's quite likely that as he continues to gain strength an occasional tour might be added to his activities.

Even earlier in his life Roy had gall bladder problems. He has also has been plagued by hernias. He catches colds and develops sore throats easily, and, like many singers who consider viruses to be major enemies, he is careful to guard himself against the threats of cold weather and air-conditioners and to frequently use extra blankets at night. With all these aches and pains—including some hearing loss—it's little wonder that Roy is mildly hypochondriac and carries an assortment of pills, mostly vitamins, in his ukulele and fiddle cases.

Tea is Roy's favorite drink. He has never liked the taste of either coffee or liquor, but he likes the effects of both. As with smoking, Roy began using alcohol at a fairly young age. Being moderate in drinking habits is especially difficult for an entertainer: most performances are at night and many are in places where alcohol is served. When there is a pattern night after night of crazy schedules and rigors of the road, relaxing with a drink or two is frequently the result.

During much of his career Roy Acuff could be considered a heavy drinker. Unlike some other entertainers, though, he was able to keep it under control and audiences were rarely if ever aware of it.

Quite a number of phobias and foibles have been attributed to Roy. Generally they are outgrowths of his complex and nervous personality and most of them have diminished with the years, such as his claustrophobia. It used to be so great that, many years ago, he knocked down a hotel room door when he was left alone in the room. Nor was he able to sleep alone or in the dark. On the road Os was his roommate and had to learn to sleep with the light on. Roy isn't particularly fond of elevators, either, especially if they are automatic, but he's usually able to ride in them with only a little concern.

Roy doesn't hate cats, has nothing against them, and wants to like them. He's just scared that one will jump on him. He remembers that in Maynardville someone threw a "red-eyed" cat on his mother, and it clung to her breast so tightly that they had a hard time getting it off. In Knoxville the boys learned of his fear and exploited it: as he was driving his car, one of the gang threw a cat in. Roy exited quickly and the moving auto continued on its way. Another incident happened one night when he was a callboy for the L & N Railroad. Roy suddenly awakened to find a "friend" ready to throw a cat in where he was sleeping. Roy grabbed a stick and would have injured the boy, even though he was actually quite fond of him. At the present time Roy is able to stand cats in the same room with him, just as long as they stay on the floor. He even brought himself to gingerly pet a friend's two black Persians. But he stayed awake that night thinking of their "big yellow eyes."

Roy says he has extrasensory perception (ESP). "It scares me how any little thing I want seems to fall into my lap. Like for instance there was this certain doll I wanted for my collection, but I couldn't get it. On the very next tour I saw one from a bus and jumped off the bus and bought it."

In Harrah's Reno penthouse, he believes definitely that he had a psychic experience:

> I was half asleep one afternoon and a voice said to me, "Go downstairs and play the 50-cent slot machine." I got right up and went down and put in a 50-cent peice. Immediately money came pouring out and lights started flashing and horns started tooting. A man came up and said, "Just a minute." I was scared, I thought I'd done something wrong—broken the machine or something. But all he wanted to do was give me the payoff. Then I put in another 50 cents and all the commotion happened again except that no money poured out because the machine was empty. I didn't even stay around for the payoff. I ran right back upstairs again. Hunches like that scare me. I get a lot of them. Sometimes I follow them and sometimes I don't.

When asked if he knew what ESP is, Roy said, "No, but whatever it is, it scares me."

It's apparent that Roy Acuff is a very interesting and unusual individual, as well as being one of the most respected men in the entertainment field.

Roy's eccentricities (if one can even call them that) have diminished with the passage of time. The result has been a mellowing into a kind and gracious human being. One of Roy's close associates has said, "It took Roy 60 years to grow up, and he has grown into one of the finest men in Nashville."

"She's Done a Lot More for Me Than I Can Ever Do for Her"

Being married to the King of Country Music and keeping track of the "affairs of state" that surround him requires such qualities as super-patience, super-tact, super-meticulousness, and super-resourcefulness. Roy Claxton Acuff waited 33 years to choose a wife—and on that Christmas Day in 1936 he made the most astute decision of his life. At the altar he obtained a lady who has absolutely devoted her life to him and the maintenance of his career.

Earlier, in somewhat less than a castle, we left Mildred enjoying the adventurous life of the trailer camp during the early days before the King was crowned. One weekend in 1943 Roy's parents came from Knoxville to visit Roy and Mildred and to see the Opry. After experiencing the beguilements of life in a trailer, the Neill Acuffs strongly urged Roy and Mildred to seek living quarters more suitable to the success Roy was beginning to receive. Accordingly, they sold the trailer and bought a home on Hillsboro Road in southwest Nashville.

The property's adjacent ten acres made it possible for the Acuffs to indulge in such country pursuits as raising chickens and peaches. Late frosts, though, kept the peaches from ever cropping up at their table or the stores. Ironically, just after they sold this house, the peach harvest was bountiful and the new owners needed trucks to haul it to market.

Roy's pet project at this time was raising Tennessee walking horses. "My idea is to breed walking horses with a lot of color. They may not all be white but I believe they'll all be flashy looking anyway." Soon he had one stallion, Pearl Harbor, and three mares. However, Pearl Harbor seemed to be impotent and he died from a corrective operation. Sadly, it was found that the operation had not been necessary because one of the mares was in foal. All but one of the original mares was sold before the Acuffs moved into their second house.

Roy and Mildred made a mistake with their first house: they put their name on the mailbox. Roy's attempts to get to WSM each morning were sometimes delayed by the gathering of families on the front lawn. A Florida couple actually moved in with the Acuffs and were there a week before Mildred was able to persuade them to leave. As they left, other fans pulled up and started unloading suitcases.

Aside from these encroachings on their privacy, the Acuffs felt some pressure opposite from admiration. Their southwest Nashville home was in the center of the city's high-society neighborhood—the so-called leaders of fashion and manners. Although most of the Nashville community had come to accept the Opry and the country music industry as a vital part of the city's economy, in the mid-1940s there was a very strong anti-Opry feeling among Nashville's social elite. Acknowledging that snobbery does not make good neighbors, in 1945 the Acuffs bought a rambling log house at 3614 Brush Hill Road, which was in a secluded spot in northeast Nashville.

The house didn't actually have a view of the Cumberland River, but their four acres extended to it. The Acuffs love to live near water, and since 1945 they have never lived very far from either a lake or river. Roy owned a small speedboat at this time, the *Precious Jewel.*

This house contained four bedrooms, two baths, living room, dining room, kitchen, breakfast nook, basement, storeroom, and game room. During the postwar phone shortage, Roy would call Ford Fush, who lived nearby, to the phone with a fox horn. He also used the horn when coon hunting, one of his favorite sports. Around 1948, a weekly radio program called "Supper with Roy Acuff" originated (with considerable hilarity) from the game room.

In 1951 the family moved to 1500 Winding Way, which was a little farther from the river but actually just around the corner. This home, which Mildred designed, was a one-story red brick ranch-style house whose 'interior was completely paneled, including the bathrooms, with knotty pine. The game room contained a pool table that was used by Roy, who was "just fair," and by Roy Neill. Subsequently the Acuff household has always contained a pool table.

In 1956 the Acuffs again felt the urge to move and were attracted to a development that was being constructed on a section of the proposed shore line of Old Hickory Lake at Hendersonville, 22 miles northeast of Nashville. This home closely resembled the one on Winding Way and, like it, was designed by Mildred. Its interior was paneled with many different woods.

When they moved into the house it was in a wooded valley, but that changed as more houses were built. The Acuffs built a boathouse and Shot's *Blind Barthimaeus* was launched as the water filled the lake. Later the Acuffs also had a 22-foot Correct Craft with a 215 horsepower inboard motor. Boating on the lake with the band and neighbors became a common pastime. Don Pierce, president of Starday Records, was their immediate neighbor to the right and Frank Clement for a time occupied the home to the left.

The Acuffs lived in Hendersonville 12 years. Roy and Mildred especially enjoyed the beautiful, serene view of their spacious back lawn and a finger of Old Hickory Lake in a distance. This lake is huge, and along its extensive shore live many of the country music greats.

Until the Exhibit was moved to Nashville early in 1965, the Acuffs were very happy living by the lake. Roy then found himself making almost daily trips into town to keep track of this project and to meet his fans. After awhile these daily 44 mile round trips over Gallatin Pike, which becomes exceedingly crowded near the city, began to bother Roy—he was feeling almost like an exile.

So in 1967 they bought a house on Moss Rose Drive only a few blocks from Brush Hill Road and Winding Way, and, unlike the other two houses, is located right on the river. An old house—built in the 1930s—it needed extensive remodeling, including the addition of an entire wing and a garage.

Meanwhile, the Acuffs sought a buyer for their lakeside home. Gladys Flatt, wife of Lester Flatt, happened to be in the market for a home on Old Hickory Lake. After looking at the Acuff residence, she returned home and told her husband, "I found the home I wanted, and you'll never guess whose it was." Lester accompanied his wife to look at the house and the transaction was sealed. Roy told him, "Let me know at once if I can help you in any way."

Lester replied, after glancing around the big yard, "I figure the lawn needs mowing about Tuesday." Roy declined, having already sold the little tractor used specifically for that huge job and on which he used to take rides into Hendersonville. "That's out," said Roy, "but I'll throw in the motorboat as a gift to you both from Mildred and me."

Roy and Mildred moved into their newly remodeled house in the fall of 1968. The previous owner had mentioned earlier that she thought their view of the Cumberland River might soon be enhanced by some sort of a park which was being planned for the other side. The Acuffs thought that a park would be nice, and thought no more about it. A year later when Bud Wendell, then manager of the Opry, came to the house to express his sympathies to Roy about his mother's death, the two walked into the backyard and looked out over the river. Wendell then informed Roy the land that WSM had purchased for Opryland could be seen clearly from Roy's backyard. Wendell had known this before Roy had purchased the house, but the secrecy was so tight that he had to wait before telling Roy. Roy enjoyed watching the park's construction and today he can clearly see the Opry House and the skyrides and hear the train whistle, and vaguely make out some of the music from the shows. Roy believes some form of destiny guided the purchase of this house.

Mildred has been responsible for running the five homes in which the Acuffs have lived since 1943. None of them would be considered mansions, but all have been large enough to make the job of upkeep a substantial one. By the time they moved into the Hillsboro Road house, Roy and Mildred felt they were sufficiently affluent to afford domestic help, and so they hired a black lady to work two half-days a week. In January 1944, when Roy Neill was six months old, they hired the lady's daughter, Nellie. The Acuff household has been

Nellie's job ever since. In recent years her husband, Theodore Byers, has done some of the heavier work for the Acuffs on Saturdays. Nellie has been a big part of the Acuff family—"a real sweetheart."

Because Nellie has never lived in, Mildred does much of the housework. She rises before seven each morning and attends to the light housework, as well as frequently doing such heavier tasks as polishing floors and washing windows.

If one is lucky enough to be invited to the Acuff home they'll find a superb hostess, for Mildred becomes completely absorbed in making each guest as comfortable and at home as possible. Her sincere, kindly concern for the wishes and feelings of others is heartwarming. And when a guest thanks Mildred for her attention and hospitality, she's been known to say, "Please don't thank *me*, I didn't do anything."

The Acuffs have had all shapes and sizes of dogs, with such names as Chief, Pup Acuff, Tommie, and Brownie. In 1948 Roy paid $3 for a macaw named Old Sarge. The man who owned it lived in Chicago and Roy sent Nellie and Theodore to Evansville, Indiana, to meet him half way and obtain the bird. No one knows how old the macaw is; its current residence is Shot Jackson's Sho-Bud shop. Another feathered friend was a mynah bird. Roy made tapes of what he wanted it to say, and these were played over and over. But the bird didn't pick up one word; instead, in an imitation of Mildred's voice, it said "hello" whenever the phone rang, and imitated the washer and squeak of the storm door.

"Roy is easy to please with food," says Mildred. "He, unlike most men, even likes vegetables." Roy also has a sweet tooth, for ice cream cones and candy. He praises Mildred's cooking—but takes the credit (with a grin): "I taught Mildred to cook. I . . . and my mother and her mother."

As important as Mildred's domestic responsibilities are, they are not as vital as her other activities. Her greatest contribution to Roy's success has been taking care of his business affairs. Actually, she initiated and directed the investments that parlayed his early earnings into a fortune. Besides her leading part in Acuff-Rose she has played similar roles in other ventures. Mildred acted as road manager only in the very beginning; however, she retained band payroll responsibilities, and fills out the complicated tax returns. When she was in the hospital after Roy Neill's birth, Roy brought the tax papers to her. She told him to take them to the tax office where help could be obtained, only to hear Roy say, "I don't know where it is." Not surprising, therefore, is Roy's answer when once asked about a financial matter: "I don't have much more idea about how we stand than that duck out there on the lake."

Being so well off now, why not hire a lot of servants and secretaries? "Well," Mildred explained, "we had to work back when we weren't going so good and we were happy. We still like the same things we liked back then. I don't see any use of changing just because you might make a little money." And when asked about what she considers is the most rewarding aspect of Roy's success, in which she has had so great a part, her answer was, "Being able to help people who needed and deserved help."

In her spare minutes at home she'll be working in the garden and keeping up her huge collection of scrapbooks about Roy. And when Roy played extended dates, Mildred took time off and accompanied him. During his extended Nevada engagement at Harrah's, for example, she enjoyed the penthouse and had fun playing blackjack. Occasionally, when the troupe toured Florida, the families were invited to join the Acuffs for a day's fishing. Mildred has never liked freshwater fishing, because she detested handling the bait, but deep-sea fishing is exciting and her favorite. Her biggest catch was a 17½-pound grouper.

After 35 years of married life Mildred went on what she considers to be her first real vacation. In February 1972 she and Roy spent two days in Rio de Janeiro and then went to South Africa, where they made extensive tours of several countries, visiting the game reserves and parks. Their homeward route was via Paris.

Subsequently, Roy and Mildred have taken pleasure trips almost annually. During the early part of summer in 1973 they toured northern Europe and went to Russia. In Moscow, Roy yodelled and sang as he walked along the streets. When he entered Red Square he stopped, looked at the vast expanse in front of him, and said, "Just like Maynardville. Oh, maybe this is a *little* bigger." (All in all, though, the Acuffs did not like the atmosphere in the Soviet Union.)

In the spring of 1974 Roy and Mildred went around the world. Via Anchorage, they went to Tokyo and then to Hong Kong, Thailand, Nepal, India, and Portugal. On the trip they were greatly shocked by the low standard of living and high inflation they encountered.

Mildred has had to contend with occasional bouts of ill health, a sometimes demanding husband, and the complexities of many business matters. Through all this, the brunette with the stunning personal appearance has stayed deliberately in the background and out of the limelight, quietly doing all the things that must be done to keep Roy Acuff and his career functioning smoothly and successfully. And Mildred has been praised as few wives ever have:

> Mimi has been the steadying influence in my life. She has looked after my interests like a mother. She is one of the truest and most honest persons I've ever known. I've always left all the business up to her and it's been in good hands. She's done a lot more for me than I can ever do for her.*

He is Following His Own Drum

Shortly after Roy and Mildred were settled in their first real house on Hillsboro Road, their only child, Roy Neill Acuff, was born. At eleven in the morning of July 25, 1943, Mildred, who thought she was still a very long time away from motherhood, took Roy to the train station for the start of a Texas tour. Upon returning home, she realized it was much later than she thought. She called Ford Rush and his wife who lived nearby, and they, living up to their names, rushed Mildred to the hospital where Roy Neill was born at five that afternoon. Rush also sent a message that intercepted Roy at Memphis, and he returned for a day or so, later rejoining the tour.

Roy's excitement and pride in his son's birth were dampened because his father, who had passed away a few months previously, hadn't lived to see the newborn. The baby was named after his grandfather. Columnist Bert Vincent was named godfather.

As Roy Neill was growing up, he saw even less of his father than did most youngsters because Roy was frequently on tour. Much of Roy Neill's upbringing was by Mildred and especially by Nellie. Despite the weeks of the tours, father and son had occasional good times together. Roy has always taken great delight that Roy Neill has favored him in personal appearance.

Soon after his son was born, Roy said in jest, "If that boy even looks like he's going to play a fiddle or sing, I'll take my belt and

---

*Elmer Hinton, "Along Came This Feller in a Red Roadster . . .," *Nashville Tennessean Magazine,* April 13, 1958, p. 26. This article provided other information for this chapter. Another useful article was by Dixie Dean: "The Woman Behind the Man," *Music City News,* December, 1965, pp. 17-18.

burn him up." This joking was never a threat, of course, but something was in the blood. It began when the Acuffs obtained a disc recorder after the war, and Roy played "A&R man" as he directed his youngster during two widely separate home recordings, on November 12, 1947, and March 6, 1952. Roy Neill gave renditions of "Stay a Little Longer," "The Old Chisholm Trail," "Old Dan Tucker," "Tennessee Central No. 9." and his favorite, "Jingle Bells." The young artist would stop frequently in the middle of a song and say, "Now play the record." But his request was granted only when, repeating after his dad, he signed off with, "This is Roy Neill Acuff. I hope you've enjoyed my little program. I'll be back on the mike again before long. Good night." These probably were the only recording sessions that concluded with the A&R man telling the star, "Good, now you can go play."

Roy Neill attended a public elementary school during the first and second grades. The next four years were spent in uniform, boarding at Castle Heights Military School in Lebanon, Tennessee, where the youngster was homesick and generally miserable. Roy Neill then attended two Nashville junior high schools, one private and one public, and his education was completed with four years at the Hendersonville High School, where he graduated in 1962. Although his parents wanted him to go to college, like his dad he never had any desire to attend college. At this time he planned to enter the navy after high school.

During Roy Neill's later high school years, education became more interesting to him when he met an extremely attractive blonde who attended the same high school. The handsome young couple were married in 1961, but the marrage failed within a few years. Their child Roy Neill Acuff, Jr., was born—handsome, blond, lively, and intelligent. He captivated everyone, including, above all, his granddad. Immediately after his grandson's birth Roy introduced himself by trying to sing to him. The results were not spectacular: "The child won't listen, " Roy commented. "Remember, I no longer croon or sing softly. I guess he prefers lullabies, or could be that he is a rock and roll fan. Well, anyway, I just can't seem to get through to that little feller yet." In subsequent years Roy succeeded in getting through to his grandson, who spent much time with his paternal grandparents. In fact, Roy saw more of young Neill in one summer than he saw of Roy Neill in ten years.

Roy Neill worked as a guide at Dunbar Cave during and after

high school. In 1963 he helped run the Gatlinburg Exhibit, where he met Bob Collins, who played a fine blues guitar. Collins's skill impressed Roy Neill so much that he became seriously interested in music and learned to play the guitar under his friend's tutelage. Roy Neill then began to learn to sing.

In 1964 Roy Neill was working in the shipping department of Acuff-Rose, processing the 2,500 weekly pieces of mail. At this time, Roy was asked if his son was musical. Not knowing of Roy Neill's new interest, he answered: "No, Roy Neill is not musically inclined. I wish he were, but he is turned more like his mother in that he is seemingly more interested in business and things of that nature than in music."

In 1965 Don Gant, a young fellow employee at Acuff-Rose who worked with artists and composers, was in the mail room and heard Roy Neill singing. When Don asked him if he would like to record, Roy Neill said "sure." Gant then made a private demonstration tape with Roy Neill and took it to Wesley Rose. Wesley liked what he heard and gave Roy Neill a contract. When Roy Neill informed his dad of the developments, the startled Roy said, "Record? Why, I didn't even know you could sing!"

Roy Neill proceeded to prove that he could indeed sing. His initial session—the first official recordings that were made in the new Columbia studio—was recorded on September 30, 1965, with Gant as A&R man. One of the recordings was a completely modern styling of the "Wabash Cannonball." Another, "Baby Just Said Goodbye," was much more typical of Roy Neill's emerging style.

These two songs were released as a single, with the professional name of Roy Acuff, Jr." Roy Neill didn't like Wesley's idea of making him a junior, but didn't say much, and with time has come to dislike the idea even more. While admitting that the name has helped his career, he feels that the junior has hurt it much more—an audience expects a Roy Acuff performance, and Roy Neill is not a Roy Acuff performer.*

When Wesley heard the results of the session, he said:

> The credit goes to Roy Junior and Don Gant. The "Wabash Cannonball" is the very first and probably the very last Acuff Senior song that Roy Neill will ever do. He doesn't sound like anybody but himself; he has

*Much of the information for this chapter was gained in talks with Roy Neill. Wesley Rose was also helpful about Roy Neill's recordings.

his own individual style. When I first heard him sing I knew he had a commercial sound.

We plan to make him a major artist. The first step is to get a hit record and the rest will come, like personal appearances. His voice has an upbeat bouncy quality, typical of modern-day music. His father's style is less lively. I didn't know he could sing, anymore than his father did, but he did just fine.

Less than a month after his first session Roy Acuff, Jr., made his first public appearance. It was on the Grand Ole Opry of October 23, 1965, during the annual disc jockey convention. His proud father introduced him:

> I've had many unusual and rare privileges since I've been at the Grand Ole Opry in my 27 years. And tonight I guess I'm a little more nervous than possibly I was 27 years ago, when I first walked on the stage of the Grand Ole Opry in a different building from what we are in tonight.
>
> Now the fellow that I'm going to introduce, the young boy, I know him *actually* better than I have known any other artist that I have ever introduced; but I've got very little that I can say in the entertainment field about him.
>
> I would like for you to know that this young fellow is making his very first appearance anywhere. He never sung on street corners, he never worked in the beer gardens, he has never been in front of an audience before, and he is going to be a very nervous young boy. I can tell you that.
>
> But I hope that he can get over to you what he did on the Hickory label when he and one of the boys out at Acuff-Rose got up their little session and went out and recorded it on their own. Without me, without the help of any of the older folks. They did it as a young artist, and we are very proud. I know that his mother is sitting in the audience tonight and she is just as nervous as Papa is. So if you will, I'd like for you to make him welcome, and he'll certainly do his very best for you.
>
> And I hope that through the years that he can take the place of his daddy right here on the stage, when he gets a little bit older and gets more in the groove of Grand Ole Opry. Will you make our son welcome? Roy Junior. Come on in here, Roy Acuff Junior.

Roy Neill sang "Baby Just Said Goodbye," while his dad bowed his head but beamed with pride, occasionally encouraging his son with comments like "Yea." This rendition was followed by considerable applause and so Roy Neill sang an encore of "Wabash Cannonball."

Roy Neill has continued to work at Acuff-Rose, moving from department to department to learn the operations of the company. Currently he feels more inclined to the publishing side, rather than the recording side, of Acuff-Rose. But he is continuing with his recording career. And, to paraphrase his dad, he is "getting more in the groove of Grand Ole Opry." Roy Neill has recorded several of his own compositions, such as "Back Down to Atlanta" and "Street Singer."

Roy Neill occasionally has worked fairs and even toured USO-NCO clubs in Germany. A few of these performances have been with his dad. He accompained the Acuff troupe on several spring Midwest tours and went with the gang on their Christmas 1967 Caribbean tour. During these excursions he has gained a greater respect for his father; but to know or really understand Roy has taken time, because the generation gap between Roy Neill and his dad has been very wide. Lately, however, the two are making substantial progress toward a warm father and son relationship. In the Decembers of 1973 and 1974, Roy Neill was one of several backup singers at two of his dad's sessions.

Despite some stage successes, Roy Neill does not enjoy the road: audiences make him nervous and he doesn't like the traveling and the rigors that life on the road usually entails. More than anything else, he desired a close family life.

This ambition was realized, but only for several years: shortly after his first marriage ended, Roy Neill met and married Aubrey Chastain. A boy, Alex Wolfgang Acuff (his granddad calls him Wolf) was born October 25, 1972. The infant weighed four pounds five ounces and soon graduated from his incubator. Roy Neill and Aubrey for a few years owned and operated an antique shop. Their other interests were interior decorating, Indian lore, animals, abstract art, philosophy, and the occult. However, despite a period of compatibility, this marriage, too, ended in divorce.

Roy Neill likes to record, and he has the ability, which is stimulating, to put over both popular and country songs. His recording sessions have produced intelligent and sensitive material. Today Roy Neill appears to be following the good advice in one of his favorite songs, "Follow Your Drum."

> Don't feel bad, Son. Don't feel blue, Son.
> If you ain't keepin' up with the feller up in front of you, Son.
> Don't let it grieve you. Don't let it peeve you.
> Don't get blue, Kid. You ain't stupid.
> You're just marching to the rhythm of a different drum, Son.
> Follow your drum. Follow your drum.
> Set your feet to the beat of your own drum, Son.

Be a man, Son. Understand, Son?
It'll all come if you just follow the rhythm of your own drum, Son.*

Sincerity, Showmanship, Success

"To hell with President Roosevelt, to hell with Babe Ruth, and to hell with Roy Acuff" was the way an enemy in World War II sassed the American who's who. It was fast company for a Smoky Mountain Boy but, without stretching things too much, it can be said that Roy Acuff deserved the company. He is quite likely one of the most enduring and successful of all the performers in country music. His formula? Let's see.

Roy began as a fiddler, but in time the pressures of putting on a network show made him hire fiddler Tommy Magness. However, since a fiddle was so much a part of old-time country music—and of himself—Roy had to devise a way to keep it in his act. The answer was to make it visible and part of the entertainment. Thinking back to his boyhood, and remembering that he could always draw an audience to him by balancing practically anything on his chin or nose, Roy began to balance the fiddle bow on the tip of his nose. He soon made this more spectacular by inserting the tip of the bow into a hole in the fiddle bridge and balancing both on his chin. Usually, Roy balances the bow alone on his nose, but sometimes on his chin or on his forehead, though the latter position is very difficult. The fiddle and bow combination is always balanced on his chin, usually between its tip and his lower lip.

Now that he no longer was playing breaks, Roy found himself with more idle moments on stage. However, inactivity makes him nervous, so in the late 1940s he revived the talent he had developed during his sunstroke recuperation—Yo-Yoing.

To this growing array of stage toys was added a ukelele, which Roy had learned easily to chord. In the early 1960s a small snare drum was added. Roy frequently plays it today with two brushes during breaks and at times brings the drum up to the microphone when he sings. Around the edges of this drum are hooks that dangle castanets and a tambourine.

Jimmie Riddle usually is responsible for seeing that the Yo-Yo and uke are in place on stage, and another band member takes care

---

*FOLLOW YOUR DRUM, John D. Loudermilk, ©1968, Acuff-Rose Publications, Inc. Used by permission of the publisher. All rights reserved.

of the drum and its related noisemakers. Roy plays with these toys never knowing what he will do before he does it. He hates to walk offstage while others are performing, but doesn't want to stand around as emcee. "I like to perform. When I'm out there I have to do something. I don't kill time on stage."

Roy's primary contribution to the act is his singing. Mimicking his sister Sue made him sing from the pit of his stomach—but it didn't do much for the technical quality of his voice. However, though lacking in artistic perfection, Roy's penetrating tenor raised in his mournful mountain style is truly unique. It's authentic. It provides Roy with an instant communication with his audience. "I'm a seller and not a singer," says Roy. "I'm strictly a seller. There's something about me. I'm able to reach the people. I don't claim to be a musician; but I like to think I'm an entertainer."

Most of his songs have been the old songs, the folk songs. The other songs have usually followed traditional style patterns. Thus Roy Acuff and His Smoky Mountain Boys are one of the few country music troupes that guarantees audiences indigenous mountain-style performances.

The Acuff act has changed very little through the years, yet the gang has kept it alive and fresh and highly entertaining. The boys are excellent entertainers, of course, but the basis for the longevity of the act has been Roy's showmanship. He once said, "To be successful in show business, an artist must bring to his audience something unique, something that will make his performance enjoyable and well remembered."*

On the stage he maintains rigid self-discipline, but his stage presence is graceful and is regarded as a masterful crowd-pleaser ranking as a drawing card with that of the theatrical greats.** "More than a singer, I'm a showman," says Roy. "When I hit a stage I go on there with one purpose only in mind—to entertain. If I get ahold of an audience, which I try to do real quick, I won't turn them loose as long as I'm on stage. Perhaps that is why I have lasted so long."***

Roy Acuff has parlayed fiddling and singing into a fabulous career by being more than a showman. By itself, showmanship is but visual effectiveness and wears thin quickly, as does a fad. What has

---

*Country Crossroads tape.

**Bill C. Malone, *Country Music U. S. A. a Fifty-Year History* (Austin: University of Texas Press, 1968), p. 202.

***Country Crossroads tape.

sustained Roy's ability? The answer lies in sincerity, and in an uncompromising honesty founded upon strong religious beliefs.

During his political campaign, when Roy Acuff spoke of the Ten Commandments and the golden rule he was not mouthing words, he was talking about his way of life. He has remained a devout Christian, although he attends church only rarely.* He is sincere in his belief that all religions and churches are good and that every scripture has some teaching. Of the Good Book he says, "It is hard for me to understand. I just try to believe." While not a student of the Bible, he does read it at home of an evening. During the campaign, when a speechwriter gave him the lines, "I'm still the same Roy Acuff you have known for a long time. I don't claim to be a new Moses to lead you out of the bulrushes," Roy changed the last part to "I don't claim to be a new Moses found in the bulrushes." Performances, especially political rallies, frequently include prayers, and Roy is insistent that his troupe always stand reverently while within hearing distance even though they might be offstage and preparing to leave for their next engagement. Several times Roy has been urged by fans to enter the ministry.

Roy's application of the golden rule has extended to down-and-out musicians and worthy newcomers. Unlike many entertainers he has never let success go to his head. He firmly believes, and acts accordingly, that he owes his success to his fans. Acuff fans are always treated with as much respect and courtesy as the mechanics and timing of the situation will allow.

Roy Acuff is honest to a fault. Some people have said that Roy Acuff doesn't know how to be tactful. While this isn't quite true, it is a fact that he always speaks his mind clearly, openly, and completely, and he admires others who do likewise. Beating around the bush isn't for him and lying is abhorred. At the dedication of the new Acuff-Rose building, he expressed his honesty in this way:

> The only way I know to do anything is to tell the truth about things. I'm an Abraham Lincoln type person. If I tell the truth standing in front of you, I won't lie in bed tonight wondering what I said and worry that if asked to repeat it tomorrow morning I won't be able to. Because if tomorrow you should ask me to repeat it, I know I can since it is the truth. I like to live that type of life: being truthful in what I say.

---

*Once he went with Frank Clement, and when the tray came around, Clement had no money. "Roy, do you have a five?" Roy only had two tens, and so they each put one in. Clement never paid him back, but said later, "Roy, that's the best $20 you ever spent!"

Honesty and considerate treatment for his associates and fans is the core of Roy Acuff's individuality. He is not just a showman, but a sincere showman. It is the sincerity of proud artist-to-listener communication that instantly moves his audiences. He sings with a shouting zeal and great emotion and projects himself into his songs so intensely that tears roll down his cheeks when the song is a sad one. Everything Roy Acuff does is authentic because he is.

Art Satherley once said that the first quality he looked for in a country singer was the ability to give a sincere rendition of a song.* Sincerity is the quality that made the name of Roy Acuff and country music synonymous. And it has enabled him, more than any other man, to elevate genuine country music to its present high national and international status. He once said, "Everything I am has growed up with me. It's the way we kind of people are."

In these days of high record sales and worship of mass media idols, brighter stars may shine here and there for a short time in the skies over country music, but not one is burning with a more enduring light than that of Roy Acuff.

---

*Maurice Zolotow, "Hillbilly Boom," *Saturday Evening Post,* February 12, 1944, p. 36.

Appendix A

Roy's Overseas Tours
1. November 13-27, 1949 (sponsored by Dept. of the Air Force).
Newfoundland, Germany, Austria, England, Azores, Bermuda

In 1949 a poll was taken of U.S. servicemen stationed overseas to determine what entertainment they'd like best. Their answer was the Grand Ole Opry. Based on the number of stars, this first tour was one of Roy's largest tours. A few of the notables were Red Foley, Hank Williams, Minnie Pearl, Jimmy Dickens, Grant Turner, and Rod Brasfield. The billing was "Grand Ole Opry" and marked the first time that Opry people entertained overseas. The tour began in New-foundland and then went to Germany and Austria, where most of the performing was done. To a person the troupe was aghast at the devastation of the war-torn towns they saw. On their return, they played at bases in England, the Azores, and Bermuda. This is the only one of Roy's tours having other superstars of country music.

Another member of this large contingent was Thelma Acuff, the Acuff's adopted daughter. Thelma entertained as a tap dancer. (A few years later she married Cully Gossett. They and their daughter and two sons live in Clarksville, Tennessee.)

2. March 19-28, 1950 (sponsored by Air Force Special Services).
Alaska

In Alaska the troupe performed at Anchorage, Fairbanks, Nome, the Aleutian Islands, Colbay Island, and Kodiak.

Note: Jimmie Riddle kept meticulous records of the dates and itineraries of all 21 tours. His documentation has been extremely valuable.—The author.

3. March 16-April 11, 1951 (sponsored by the Loyal Order of the Moose).
Azores, Germany, Austria, England, Iceland, Newfoundland

Some of the places visited were Loges in the Azores; Heidelberg, Bonn, and Frankfurt in Germany; Vienna, Austria; and Burtonwood, England. They also visited Scotland but didn't perform there.

During their stay in Germany, a tour of the salt mines was scheduled. As the leader Roy nonchalantly herded his flock, dressed in coveralls and caps, aboard the primitive little mine train, which was ridden by straddling the seats. Then he jumped on a seat. Soon, however, he began to sweat as he realized that the train was going deep underground. It took a great amount of will power for him to keep his claustrophobia under control on this excursion. Immediately upon his return to Tennessee he made a point of touring his own Dunbar Cave, something he had been unable to do before.

4. September 20-October 20, 1953 (sponsored by the USO).
Japan, Okinawa, Korea, Wake Island

A Grand Ole Opry group, including Ernest Tubb and Hank Snow, had toured Korea in the spring of 1953 during the actual fighting of the Korean War. In early July, when plans were underway for the Acuff troupe to go there, the truce was signed on July 27, 1953. Instead of cancelling the tour, Roy declared that as long as the troops were still there they were entitled to the show. Because of medical reasons, Robert Lunn and Dotty Swann stayed behind and their places were taken by Moon Mullican and Jerry Johnson.

When in Tokyo the troupe heard, with pleasure, the sounds of their own music over jukeboxes as they walked along the streets. During their stay, Roy and the rather stout Moon Mullican decided to tour the city in a rickshaw. Mullican took one look at the frail little driver and made him jump in with Roy, then Moon pulled the two-wheeled vehicle around the city.

It was on this tour that Jimmie Riddle added the title "correspondent" and sent back reports to the *Pickin' and Singin' News*. The troupe's first show in Korea was on September 28, and they played to 3,000 men. Then they were taken by trucks to visit the resting fighting men at the front lines who were sitting out the truce. On the second day of the Korean tour, September 29, they played to over 8,000 men. At night Roy and His Smoky Mountain Boys and Girl, Jerry Johnson, slept in sleeping bags inside tents. Oral Rhodes recalled that they were flown from base to base in small planes that carried only one passenger and the pilot, while their baggage and instruments traveled the rough terrain in trucks. The pilots would buzz low on the trips and describe the places over which they were flying. Odie remembers Seoul, Chuchon, Mason, Munsan, and Pusan.

All in all the troupe reported that the tour was a success, and that they were gratified by going on it.

5. December 4, 1954-January 6, 1955 (sponsored by the USO). Alaska

This was the first of many Christmases that Roy and his boys would spend away from home. It was a white one. Again, Jimmie Riddle was the correspondent.

The troupe left Nashville on November 28 and entertained military personnel in the Northwest for a week before arriving in Alaska. It was on December 1 that Roy received a phone call from Mildred telling the news of Fred Rose's death. All he could do was phone sympathy to Mrs. Rose.

On December 4 they were processed at Tacoma, Washington, and issued arctic clothing, then flown to Anchorage, which is called the "Banana Belt" because of its relative warmth. On the morning of the fifth they received a briefing, which included warnings against frostbite and information about survival in the arctic. Then they were driven into Anchorage where they bought a few necessities, such as long underwear. The prices were astounding, with eggs selling for $1.25 a dozen.

The sun rose about 9:00 A.M. and never was very high in the sky. At noon it was like 4:00 P.M. When they crossed the Artic Circle on December 15 the sun didn't rise at all. For this trip they received certificates making each a member of the Royal Order of Polar Bears and a prince of the Royal Arctic Realm.

By the nineteenth they were in Nome, from which they visited remote radar sites where maybe 20 lonely boys would be billeted in one building for the entire winter.

They were flown from site to site to present their hour and a half shows, and even though the planes had heaters, the temperature usually stayed well below freezing. During the flight from Barter Island to Fairbanks, at an altitude of 12,000 feet, the temperature inside the plane was below zero.

On December 21 they arrived in Fairbanks, one of the coldest towns in Alaska. Even though Fairbanks is less than 300 miles north of Anchorage, it is inland and on the other side of the Alaskan Range.

On their first day in Fairbanks they took it easy. Curly, Howdy, and Jimmie decided they needed haircuts—people were beginning to yell "Mush!" at them. During this day of leisure, a rare occurrence on their military tours, Roy and Os stayed in their room. Roy commented that he didn't mind Oswald just loafing around, but wished he wouldn't look out the window every hour and remark, "Sure looks like we're going to have a white Christmas!"

During their stay in Fairbanks, from December 21 to 30, they were transported to nearby sites in buses whose heaters were almost as bad as those on the airplanes. One day the temperature reached 43 below.

Christmas Day found them in a bus for the 50-mile ride to Murphy Dome, which was located on top of a mountain. On the way they saw tracks of moose, deer, and rabbit. Between their two shows they were treated to a Christmas dinner of shrimp cocktail, turkey, and ham, with all the trimmings. During a show they literally did "lay one of 'em in the aisle," when a boy sitting in the back of the small auditorium got so carried away he fell backward off a four-foot platform. He wasn't hurt, but the place was in an uproar for several minutes.

December 26, another day off. A scheduled snowshoe rabbit hunt had been called off because of the intense cold, and in the afternoon so were the dog sled races, with the temperature 46 below. The panting of the dogs could frostbite their lungs in temperature below minus 20 degrees. Howdy said, "If it's too cold for the dogs up here, it's too cold for me!"

But it was to get colder. On December 27 they were supposed to fly south to Anchorage, but a thick ice fog had set in and the temperature had fallen to 54 below. Jim reported that next day the planes were frozen solid, and any aircraft that came in from Anchorage had to leave in a hurry before it froze. The troupe was beginning to feel that "If the weather doesn't break soon, everything else will."

They were trapped in Fairbanks one more day. Finally, on December 30, they were able to fly to the warmth of Anchorage, a minus five below.

On the last day of 1954 the gang played three shows and on January 1 the servicemen of Anchorage were treated to two big shows.

At one was Robert (Bobby) Blake. (He played Little Beaver in Red Ryder pictures when he was growing up.) On January 2 they took a side trip to Kodiak and left Anchorage and headed for home on January 6.

Shortly after arriving in Nashville, Roy was presented an award "for services rendered above and beyond the call of duty."

6. October 13-December 21, 1958 (sponsored by the USO).
Germany, Italy, France

This tour started on October 14 with their arrival in Frankfurt, where they stayed through the twentieth. After touring other places in Germany, they went to Italy on November 7 and performed there until the twelfth, when they returned to Germany and remained until December 10. The following day they went to France, where they played at Verdun and Paris. The troupe returned to New York on December 21.

This was an especially grueling schedule and their troubles were compounded on two occasions. Once in Germany their bus broke down and they had to walk two and one-half miles through the snow to their next performance. On a side street of a little town near Rome, a rowdy attempted to mug Roy from behind. Roy shook himself free and landed a solid punch before the man fled.

7. February 21-April 25, 1959 (private tour).
Hawaii, Australia

Roy's first private overseas tour was the brainchild of two promoters, Oscar Davis and Frankie Moore, who talked Roy into signing a percentage deal rather than a straight payment contract, which is the usual way Roy is paid for personal appearances.

Besides Roy and the regular members of his band, the troupe consisted of Robert Lunn, Teddy and Doyle Wilburn, and Cornelia Ellis (who subsequently became the second wife of Alabama governor and presidential candidate George Wallace).

The troupe left Los Angeles on February 21 and spent the remainder of the month performing in Hawaii. Many of these shows were for military personnel.

They arrived in Sydney on March 3 and their performance, the first Opry show ever presented in Australia, opened in Sydney Stadium on March 5 and they had a crowd of 10,000—all the tickets had been bought by Fleming Food Stores and were given to customers who bought a certain amount of groceries. On Friday, March 6,

1,000 attended the first show and 3,500 the second. On March 7 the first two shows drew 4,500 and the last 5,000. One Australian in attendance was John Edwards, the famous hillbilly music collector (he died in an auto wreck in 1960). John was especially impressed by Jimmie Riddle's piano playing.

These attendances were good, but not good enough to meet expenses. The show itself was a topflight good old country music performance to which the talents of local Australians frequently were added. However, despite Roy's efforts at educating the audiences, the music apparently was too different and they failed to appreciate it. On March 8, the troupe's last day in Sydney, a newspaper published a review by Alexander Macdonald: "Night at the Grand Ole Opry or Is there a Doctor in the Stadium?"

> First there was Mr. Roy Acuff—a clear cut case of strangulation of the tonsils—who delivered an address in broken Choctaw, which moved even the hardened stadium fans to implore him to desist. Then came Bashful Brother Oswald of the split larynx; and Pap and his Jugband—a martyr to arthritis, who screeched with agony at every hop. It was more than I could bear.

Rather than a booking for the bigger cities of Melbourne and Brisbane, where bigger crowds would have been, the schedule called for Adelaide. During the first performance, Roy tried to educate the Aussies on the fine points of quality country music, but finally concluded it was hopeless. Although reports that objects were thrown and the group booed off the stage were false, the reception was so poor that after the single Adelaide performance Roy cancelled the rest of the personal appearances.

The gang considered returning to the United States but decided to try to recoup the staggering losses. On March 15 they returned to Sydney and spent the next five weeks—until April 25—making a series of 39 black and white 30-minute TV films entitled, *Roy Acuff Open House.* On these shows Roy sang many songs that he has rarely sung before or since, such as "Four Leaf Clover," "Highways Are Happy Ways," "Leaf of Love," "When You Wore a Tulip," and "I Get the Blues When It Rains." (Later he got the blues at home when he discovered that high royalties would have to be paid on many of the songs since they were neither in the public domain nor the property of Acuff-Rose. Injury was added to insult when this series of films turned out to be so costly.) Upon returning home ten copies of each of the 39 films were made at Memphis, and they were distributed by Acuff-Rose to subscribing TV stations from coast to coast. A few years later Roy turned over most of the copies of these films to the Armed Forces Radio and Television Service. They were played a great deal in Vietnam and Thailand.

8. December 13, 1959-January 13, 1960 (sponsored by the USO). British West Indies, Panama Canal Zone, Puerto Rico, Cuba

This tour actually opened in the United States with shows at an air force base in South Carolina. Then they went to Bermuda, December 16 through 20. On the twenty-first the troupe was back in South Carolina.

From the twenty-second until the end of December the troupe performed in the Canal Zone. They worked very hard, and were treated to sightseeing tours of Panama City and of the Miraflores locks and control tower of the canal. Christmas Day was completely free. Besides entertaining American servicemen, the gang also played in a hospital to Panamanians who enjoyed the show even though they didn't understand a word of English.

From the Canal Zone they flew to Puerto Rico and toured for four days. From January fifth through eighth they island-hopped, visiting Turks Island, San Salvador, Eleuthera, and Antigua, and on the tenth the troupe was back in Puerto Rico. On January 11 they were airlifted to Guantanamo Naval Base in Cuba, where they played for boys who hadn't been off the base for the 18 months since the Castro regime began.

Os remembers one hot day when he was lying on his hotel bed in a happier than sober condition. Shot Jackson used an exterior ledge to crawl from his room to get under Os's window. In a somber voice he commanded, "Os, this is the Lord talking. Os, get up and walk." Howdy, Os's roommate, caught on right away, but it took Os quite awhile. "I was really scared. It sounded like another voice inside the room."

9. October 2-December 17, 1960 (sponsored by the USO). Germany, Italy, France

The troupe arrived in Frankfurt on October 5 after two days in the Azores with engine trouble. They toured Germany for almost two weeks. On an off day, Jimmie visited the Hohner factory at Trossingen and paid $72 for 25 chromatic harmonicas. From October 17 to 24 they played in many Italian cities, visiting the Leaning Tower on the twenty-first. They returned to Germany on October 24 and remained until November 28. On November 16 Howdy and Jimmie visited the Soviet Zone. The last country in which they performed was France, which they visited from late November until December 16. On that day they left France and came home via Scotland, Newfoundland, and New York.

10. December 12, 1961-January 10, 1962 (sponsored by the USO).
Spain, Morocco

This tour was one of the first times the gang saw grinding poverty, and people living as they did in Bibical times. Their common realization was: "We don't know how well off we are!"

11. October 20-December 12, 1962 (sponsored by the USO).
Sicily, Italy, Crete, Turkey, Lebanon, Saudi Arabia
Ethiopia, Jordan, Cyprus, Greece, Libya

In Catania, Italy, Jimmie and Benny Martin were in their hotel room and heard loud noises outside. Jim was sure World War III was starting, because the Cuban missile crisis was then in progress. The airport was seven miles away and Jim figured the noises were coming from a distance of seven miles, which unfortunately agreed with his thinking that the airport was the only nearby strategic target. While all this was passing through his mind, he was fighting to open the window shades. Finally the attempt was successful and the "war" noises turned out to be the fireworks of the town's annual fiesta.

In the bay of Naples the troupe performed on the *USS Shenandoah*. It was when they arrived in Turkey that Roy received the telegram informing him of his election to the Country Music Hall of Fame.

Roy, Jim, and Benny Martin took a side trip to Lebanon and Jordan, and a tour of the Holy Land. Roy especially enjoyed seeing the Bible lands he had learned so much about from his father.

12. May 30-June 17, 1964 (private tour).
Japan

Although the group performed at many military clubs, the primary purpose of this tour was to bring country music directly to the Japanese people. During their performances they had an interpreter, and the audiences' further understanding was aided by a beautifully printed program written almost entirely in Japanese. The troupe kept carefully to the programmed order of songs because a description and some verses to each were given in the program.

While they were in Tokyo the big earthquake of 1964 occurred. Roy was the only one of the gang who didn't feel it because he was in a cab. Shot, looking at the hotel pool, thought it turned sideways. Jimmie and Howdy were eating and the chandelier in the middle of the ceiling ended up on the wall along with their food. June Stearns was putting on her makeup and became perhaps the only person in Japan wearing lipstick and eye shadow on the back of her head.

Roy performed on the Tokyo Grand Ole Opry and said of the event, "They sing my songs just like me and don't even know what they're saying. One of them calls himself 'The Smoky . . . . . .' something, I can't remember what."*

13. December 21, 1964-January 3, 1965 (sponsored by the USO).
Germany

The troupe brought enjoyment and Christmas cheer to the boys in 19 performances from December 22 through January 1. December 27 was a day off.

One performance was seen by a lady violinist who was appalled when she saw Roy balancing his fiddle bow on his nose. After the show she confided that she admired his musical talent but wondered how he could risk a part of his musical instrument, explaining that she paid $500 for each bow. Roy replied that he spent about 1 percent of that on his bow.

14. June 14-21, 1965 (sponsored by the USO).
Dominican Republic

Roy and his troupe were the first United States entertainers to visit this revolt-torn country. And the fiercest outbreak of fighting since the American troops had arrived in the country the previous April broke out as they arrived. When it was suggested that Roy cancel the shows until the area became less dangerous he said, "We don't like to change our schedule."

The tour opened in Santo Domingo and Roy's usual comment— "Maybe some of you aren't familiar with our kind of music, but we'll try to play something you like"—wasn't needed because the audience applauded and hollered its acceptance. Much of this approval was directed at curvaceous Joyce Moore, who stole the show.

On military tours Roy always takes along girls whose looks aren't

---

*Roy was thinking of Robert Tainaka and his Smoky Rangers. Robert is one of Japan's most ardent Acuff fans.

exactly what a country boy would meet in the south 40. However Bashful Brother Oswald from the south 40 usually steals the
show.

In the middle of another show a soldier tried a little show steal-
ing of his own. He walked up to Roy as he was talking and handed
him a can of beer. Roy proceeded to pour the beer over the boy's
head.

En route to one of their performances they were advised to
lie down on the seats of their bus because of sniper fire. During
the performance they heard machine guns between songs, and
some members of the group actually saw someone shot in the street.
Roy came home saying, "Those men are really on the front!"

15. December 6, 1965-January 3, 1966 (sponsored by the USO).
South Vietnam, Philippines, Okinawa, Japan, Korea

The first leg of this exhausting tour was December 8 to 14 in
Vietnam, where they played two performances each day. Roy had
been looking forward to this tour many months and had been especially concerned that his injuries from the wreck might make him
miss it. In giving his reasons for making the trip he said:

> Even though I have long since been out of politics for good, I'm still
> interested in 'em and in what's going on. That's why I wanted to make this
> trip. I figured it would give me a chance to gain some knowledge and at
> the same time we could bring the boys some downhome music.

In Saigon he was fascinated by the traffic. "Good Lord!" he said
on one street corner, "How do they keep from getting killed?"

It is customary to give awards for crossing such geographical
places as the Artic Circle, equator, and international date line. So the
group added duplicates on this trip when they became, for at least
the fourth time, members of the Order of the Golden Dragon for
crossing the international date line.

From December 14 to 18 they performed in the Philippines, with
only one free morning. For the next few days they had no free time
while playing Okinawa. In fact an extra show had to be added on the
final day because of the tremendous audiences.

On December 23 they left for Japan and spent Christmas in
Tokyo. Korea was the next stop, beginning December 27. The troops
in Korea experienced quite a change of pace in their entertainment
when Roy's show appeared—Helen Hayes had been presenting Shake-
spearian readings the previous week.

The gang was given January 2 off to rest for their return trip. They were issued arctic clothing since their return to Nashville was via Anchorage, Alaska. Just after midnight on the morning of January 4 the troupe arrived home safely, having had no sleep for 36 hours. Roy slept for 14 hours.

In a few days an avalanche of mail began to pour in from the armed forces in Vietnam requesting records, tapes, live talent—anything country. However, other tours couldn't follow Roy's at that time because the Defense Department had laid down a security ban. But soon WSM received a request to tape a special Grand Ole Opry TV show to be shown in Vietnam. With only a two-day notice many Opry stars gathered on January 14, 1966, at the WSM studios for a hurry-up taping. The show had been scheduled for one half-hour but was doubled. Roy was the master of ceremonies and also performed.

Shortly thereafter a plane flying over Vietnam transmitted by videotape the first television program seen in Vietnam. It was shown over the AFRS station in Saigon. The first hour of the show was a Hollywood variety spectacular, starring Bob Hope. The next hour was a Nashville country music spectacular, starring Roy Acuff.

16. March 15-April 5, 1967 (Sponsored by the USO).
South Vietnam, Thailand (Siam)

The Vietnamese part of this exhausting tour came first and lasted until March 30. As before, the troupe played to appreciative fighting men, sometimes from little bamboo stages.

When they arrived in Thailand the group was particularly tickled by the following message posted in their hotel rooms:

Your cooperation is *reguested* on the following points:

1. Lady guests are permitted to visit your rooms, however it is *reguested* that they enter and leave the hotel by rear entrances.

2. Should you desire to entertain your lady guests in the hotel bar or restaurant, please insure that she is *presently* dressed.

Thank you,
The Management

Jimmie reported their trip home this way: "We left Bangkok at 4:40 A.M., April 5th, and arrived at Travis Field, San Francisco at 6:00 A.M., April 5th—fast flying." Here was a feat that could only be performed by members of the Order of the Golden Dragon.

17. December 19, 1967-January 3, 1968 (sponsored by the USO).
Canal Zone, Puerto Rico, Cuba, Bahama Islands

Shortly before Christmas in the Canal Zone they kept out of a record rain, two inches in one hour. Their performance in Cuba was at the Guantanamo base.

18. August 17-September 3, 1969 (sponsored by the USO).
South Vietnam

During all of their Vietnam tours the troupe had heard gunfire at a distance; but on this trip the intensity and volume were especially noticeable. Hour after hour, almost the only sound they could hear was that of gigantic artillery weapons.

19. December 18, 1969-January 3, 1970 (sponsored by the USO).
Guam, Philippines, Japan, Hawaii

This trip was unique in that Roy left the band at home, for a much appreciated vacation, and took Mildred, who had not accompanied him overseas since the first tour of 1949. The Acuffs concentrated on shaking the hands of wounded servicemen in hospitals.

20. November 10-early December, 1970 (sponsored by the USO).
South Vietnam, Thailand

Mildred went along as manager. Jimmie did not go because of his "Hee Haw" commitments.

21. June 16-July 5, 1971 (private tour)
Germany

The troupe, which didn't include Jimmie, was based in Wiesbaden and played mostly at military clubs. The crowds were good, but the logistics of travel, food, and lodgings were not handled expeditiously and the troupe was not happy.

Appendix B

The author is particularly in debt to the following record companies for their assistance:

Columbia
Hickory
Decca
United Artists

Availability of Roy Acuff's Recordings

Almost a third of Mr. Acuff's released Columbia titles have been reissued on 6 LPs.

Harmony Label

HL 7082 - HS 11289	Great Speckled Bird and Other Favorites
HL 7294	That Glory Bound Train
HL 7342	The Great Roy Acuff
HL 7376 - HS 11334	Waiting for My Call to Glory
HS 11403	Night Train to Memphis

Columbia Label:

CS 1034	Roy Acuff's Greatest Hits

("Jesus Died for Me" and "Cheating" are on anthology albums HL 7265 and HS 11296)

In the following tables Xs marked with an asterisk indicate the Columbia titles that are on these albums and therefore are probably still available.

251

Virtually all of Mr. Acuff's released titles on Capitol, Decca, MGM, Hickory, and United Artists should still be available on 33 rpm albums or 45 rpm singles.

List of titles recorded by Roy Acuff for commercial recording companies. Columbia (and subsidiaries); Capitol (title of one unreleased master isn't known); Decca; MGM; Hickory; United Artists. Titles are in alphabetical order. "A," "An," or "The" are ignored if they are the first words of a title.

Titles can sometimes be tricky for various reasons. Some labels might give a song one title and some another, (Example: Columbia— "I Heard a Silver Trumpet"; Hickory—"Goodbye My Love"). With other songs the record labels are consistent; but the songs are popularly known by other titles, or even introduced by different titles on the air by Mr. Acuff. Examples of some tricky titles follow. In each case the title used in this list is given first.

Before I Met You	That Was Before I Met You
Beneath that Lonely Mound of Clay	Lonely Mound of Clay
If Brother Jack Were Here	Mother Was a Lady
I Heard a Silver Trumpet	Goodbye My Love
I'm Movin' On	Movin' On
Little Moses	Meeting in the Air
Lord, Build Me a Cabin	Build Me a Cabin
My Pal of Yesterday	Old Pal of Yesterday
That Glory Bound Train	Glory Bound Train
This World is Not My Home	I Can't Feel at Home in This World Anymore
Where the Soul Never Dies	Canaan's Land

Titles	Col[1]	Cap	Dec	MGM	Hic	UA	Comments
Advice to Joe	X						
All Night Long	X						
All the World Is Lonely Now	X*				X		One Hickory is unreleased
Along the China Coast			X				
Answer to Sparkling Blue Eyes	X						
Are You Thinking of Me Darling	X						
As Long As I Live	X				X		
Automobile of Life					XX		
Back in the Country					X		
Baldknob Arkansas	X						
Beautiful Brown Eyes	X				X		One is from a live show
Beaver Creek Dam					XX		One is unreleased
Before I Met You							
Be Honest with Me	X*						
Beneath that Lonely Mound of Clay	X	X			X		
Birmingham Jail					X		Fiddle instrumental by Magness
Black Mountain Rag	X						Unreleased
Black Smoke					X		
Blue Eyed Darling	X*						
Blue Eyes Crying in the Rain	XX				XX		One Columbia is unreleased / One Hickory is unreleased
Blue Ridge Sweetheart	X						
Blues in My Mind	X						
Bonnie Blue Eyes	XX				X		One is unreleased
Branded Wherever I Go	X				X		
Broken Heart	X						

[1]"Col" in this discography includes various labels which were subsidiaries of the old American Record Company, as well as the Columbia label. See p. 29.

Titles	Col	Cap	Dec	MGM	Hic	UA	Comments
Brother Take Warning	X*						
Budded Roses					X		Fiddle instrumental by Magness
Bully of the Town	X*						
Candy Kisses					X		Unreleased
Carry Me Back to the Mountains	X				X		
Charmin' Betsy	X						
Cheating	X*						
Cold Cold Heart							
Columbus Stockade Blues	X				X		Unreleased
Come and Knock	X				X		
Come Back Little Darling	X				X		
Come Back Little Pal	X	X					
Coming from the Ball	X				X		Both are unreleased
Coney Island Baby	X						Unreleased
Conscience Set Me Free					X		
Corrine, Corrina					X		Unreleased
Country Home Folk					X		
Crazy Worried Mind			X				Fiddle instrumental by Magness
Dance Around Molly	X						
Day They Laid Mary Away	X				X		
Devil's Train	X*						Cataloged as by the "Bang Boys"
Doin' It the Old Fashioned Way	X						
Don't Be Angry	X						
Don't Hang Your Dirty Linen on My Line		X					
Don't Judge Your Neighbor							
Don't Know Why					X		
Don't Let Me Cross Over					X		
Don't Make Me Go to Bed and I'll Be Good	X				X		

Titles	Col	Cap	Dec	MGM	Hic	UA	Comments
Don't Say Good-Bye		X					
Don't Tell Mama					X		
Don't Wait 'Till Judgement Day	X						Unreleased
Don't Worry 'Bout the Mule					X		
Doug MacArthur	X						
Down in Union County	X						Unreleased
Do You Wonder Why	X				X		
Drifting Too Far from the Shore	X						
Each Season Changes You					X		
Easy Rockin' Chair	X				X		
End of the World					X		
Eyes Are Watching You	X						
Family Who Prays					XX		
Farther Along	X*						
Filipino Baby					X		
Fireball Mail	X*	X			X		
Fly Birdie Fly	X						
Foggy River							
Freight Train Blues	XX*				X		One Columbia is a Hatcher vocal
Gathering Flowers from the Hillside					X		Unreleased
Give My Love to Nell					X		
Glory Is Coming					X		
Golden Treasure	X				XX		One Hickory is unreleased
Gone Gone Gone	X				X		
Gonna Have a Big Time Tonight	X						
Gonna Raise a Ruckus Tonight	X						
Goodbye Brownie	X						Vocal is Red Jones
Goodbye Mr. Brown	X		X				Duet with Kitty Wells

Titles	Col	Cap	Dec	MGM	Hic	UA	Comments
Gray Eagle	X*						Fiddle instrumental by Magness
Great Judgement Morning	X*	X					
Great Shining Light	X*						
Great Speckled Bird	X*	X			X		
Great Speckled Bird No. 2	X*						
Great Titanic		X			X		
Haven of Dreams	X						
Heartaches and Flowers	X						
Heartbreak Avenue	X				X		Unreleased
Heart that Was Broken for Me	X						
Hey Good Lookin'					X		Unreleased
Hi Hattin' Blues	X						
Hillbilly Fever					X		From a live show
Hold to God's Unchanging Hand				X	X		Hickory is unreleased
Honky Tonk Mammas	X			X			
How Beautiful Heaven Must Be				X	X		
Hundred and Forty Four Thousand							
I Called and Nobody Answered	X						
I Can't Find a Train					X		
I Can't Help It					X		
I Closed My Heart's Door		X					
I Couldn't Believe It Was True					X		
Ida Red	X						
I Didn't Want You to Know	X						
I Don't Care If You Don't Love Me					X		Unreleased
If Brother Jack Were Here					X		
If I Could Hear My Mother Pray Again	X*						
I Gambled and Lost	X						Unreleased

Titles	Col	Cap	Dec	MGM	Hic	UA	Comments
I Had a Dream	X						
I Heard a Silver Trumpet	X				X		
I Know We Are Saying Goodbye	X						
I Like Mountain Music			X				
I'll Always Care	X						
I'll Be Alone	X				X		Unreleased
I'll Fly Away	X						
I'll Forgive You But I Can't Forget	X						
I'll Go On Alone					X		
I'll Reap My Harvest in Heaven	X*						
I Love You Because	X				X		
I'm Building a Home		X			X		
I'm Movin' On					X		
I'm Planting a Rose		X			X		
I'm So Lonesome I Could Cry	X*				X		
In the Shadow of the Smokies	X*						
I Saw the Light	X*				XX	X	One Hickory is from a live show
Is It Love or Is It Lies		X					
I Talk to Myself About You	X						
I Think I'll Go Home and Cry	X						
It's All Right Now	X				X		
It's Hard to Love			X				
It's So Hard to Smile	X						
It's Just About Time	X						
It's Too Late Now to Worry Anymore	X*				X		
It Won't Be Long	X*		X				
I Wanta Be Loved							Unreleased
I Wish I Had Kissed You Goodbye	XX						Both are unreleased

Titles	Col	Cap	Dec	MGM	Hic	UA	Comments
Jambalaya	X*				X		
Jealous Heart	X				X		
Jesus Died for Me				X	X		
Jole Blon	X				X		
Just a Friend	X*						
Just Inside the Pearly Gates	X*						
Just to Ease My Worried Mind							
Kawliga					X		
Last Letter					X		
Legend of the Dogwood Tree				X			Listed on the label as "Were You There When they Crucified My Lord?" but is actually this recitation
Let Me Be the First to Say I'm Sorry	X						
Letter Edged in Black					X		
Life's Railway to Heaven					X		
Life to Go					X		
Little Mary					X		
Little Moses		X					
Little Rosewood Casket					X		
Live and Let Live	X						Unreleased
Living on the Mountain Baby Mine	X						
Lonesome Indian	X						Fiddle instrumental by Magness
Lonesome Joe		X					
Lonesome Old River Blues	X*						
Lonesome Valley	X						
Longest Train	X						Unreleased
Lord, Build Me a Cabin				X	X		

Titles	Col	Cap	Dec	MGM	Hic	UA	Comments
Lost Highway					X		
Lost John He's Gone	X*				X		
Low and Lonely	X				X		
Lying Woman Blues							
Making Believe					X		
Mansion on the Hill					X		
Midnight Train	X				X		
Mommy Please Stay Home with Me					X		
Money Won't Buy This Soul of Mine	X						Unreleased
Mother Hold Me Tight			X				Duet with Kitty Wells
Mother Prays Loud in Her Sleep					X		Unreleased
Mother's Prayers Guide Me	X						
Mountain Guitar					X		
Mule Skinner Blues	X*						
My Gal Sal	X						Vocal is Red Jones
My Mountain Home Sweet Home	X						
My Pal of Yesterday					X		
My Tears Don't Show	X*				X		
Nearest Thing to Heaven					X		
Nero Played His Fiddle					X		
New Greenback Dollar	X						
Night Spots		X					
Night Train to Memphis	X*	X			X		
Nobody's Darling but Mine					X		
No Letter in the Mail	X				XX		Unreleased
No One Will Ever Know	X				X		One Hickory is unreleased
Not a Word from Home	X				X		Hickory is unreleased
Oh Those Tombs		X					

Titles	Col	Cap	Dec	MGM	Hic	UA	Comments
Old Age Pension Check	X						
Old Fashioned Love	X				X		Vocal is Red Jones
Old Three Room Shack	XX						One is unreleased
Old Time Sunshine Song					X		
Once More					X		
One I Love Is Gone					X		
One Old Shirt	X						
Oh Lonesome Me					X		
Pale Horse and His Rider	X*				X		
Pan American					X		
Pins and Needles	X*	X			X	X	Unreleased
Plant Some Flowers by My Grave			X				
Plastic Heart	X				X		
Please Daddy Forgive		X					
Please Don't Talk About Me When I'm Gone	X						Unreleased
Pliney Jane	X						
Po' Folks	X						
Polk County Breakdown	X*						Fiddle instrumental by Magness
Precious Jewel	X*	X			X	X	
Precious Memories					X		
Pretty Little Widow	X*						Fiddle instrumental by Magness
Prodigal Son	X						
Put My Little Shoes Away					X		
Radio Station SAVED	X				X		Columbia is unreleased
Railroad Boomer	X						Unreleased
Red Lips	X						Vocal is Red Jones
Red River Valley					X		
Rising Sun	X				X		

Titles	Col	Cap	Dec	MGM	Hic	UA	Comments
River of Crystal		X			X		
Roll on Buddy	X				X		Unreleased—Rachel and Oswald
Roof Top Lullaby		X					
Rushing Around							
Sad Memories	X						Vocal is Red Jones
Sailing Along	X				X		
Satisfied Mind					X		
Searchin' for Happiness					X		
Send Me the Pillow You Dream On							
Shake My Mother's Hand for Me				X			
She Isn't Guaranteed	X						
She No Longer Belongs to Me	X				X		Unreleased
She's My Curly Headed Baby							
Short Changed in Love	X						
Shout Oh Lulu	X						
Shut Up in the Mines					X		
Sing a Country Song					X		
Singing My Way to Glory	X						Vocal is Red Jones
Sinner's Death	X*						
Six More Days		X			X		
Sixteen Chickens and a Tambourine		X			X		
Small Country Towns					X		
Smoky Mountain Memories							
Smoky Mountain Moon	X						
Smoky Mountain Rag	XX						One is an old instrumental; one is a Magness fiddle tune
So Many Times					X		
Somebody Touched Me					X		

Titles	Col	Cap	Dec	MGM	Hic	UA	Comments
Songbirds Are Singing in Heaven	X*						Unreleased
Southbound Train	X						Vocal is Dynamite Hatcher
Steamboat Whistle Blues	X						
Steel Guitar Blues	X						Old instrumental
Steel Guitar Chimes	X						
Stuck Up Blues	X						
Streamlined Cannonball	X				X		
Streamline Heart Breaker		X					
Sunshine Special		X			X		Hickory is from a live show
Swamp Lilly		X					
Sweep Around Your Own Back Door		X					
Sweeter Than the Flowers	X*				X		
Take Me Home Country Roads					X		
Take My Hand Precious Lord				X	X		
Take These Chains from My Heart					X		
Tell Me Now or Tell Me Never	X						
Tell Mother I'll Be There	X*						
Ten Little Numbers	X*						
Tennessee Central No. 9	X				X		
Tennessee Waltz	X*						
Thank God	X*			X	X		
Thanks for Not Telling Me					X		
That Beautiful Picture	X						
That Glory Bound Train	X*				XX		One Hickory is unreleased
That's Country					X		
That Silver Haired Daddy					X		
That's What Makes the Jukebox Play		X					
There'll Be No Teardrops Tonight					X		

Titles	Col	Cap	Dec	MGM	Hic	UA	Comments
There's a Big Rock in the Road	X						
They Can Only Fill One Grave	X						
They'll Never Take Her Love from Me					X		
Thief Upon the Tree		X					
Things That Might Have Been	X*				X		
This World Can't Stand Long	X*				X		
This World Is Not My Home				X			
Thy Burdens Are Greater Than Mine	X						
Tied Down		X					
'Till No Longer You Cared					X		
Time Will Make You Pay					X		
Today My Love Came Back to Me					X		
Tomorrow Never Comes					X		
Touch the Morning					X		
Traveling the Highway Home					X		
Trouble Trouble	X						
Turn Your Radio On					X		
Two Little Orphans					X		
Uncle Pen					X		
Unclouded Day				X			
Unloved and Unclaimed	X				XX		One Hickory is unreleased
Vagabond's Dream	X						
Wabash Blues	X						Old instrumental
Wabash Cannonball	XX*	X			XX		One Columbia is a Hatcher vocal; one Hickory is from a live show
Wait for the Light to Shine	X*				X		
Waiting for My Call to Glory	X*						
Walk a Mile in Your Neighbor's Shoes					X		

Titles	Col	Cap	Dec	MGM	Hic	UA	Comments
Walkin' in My Sleep	X						
Waltz of Broken Vows	X						Vocal is by La Croy Sisters
Waltz of the Wind	X*X				X		One Columbia vocal is by the La Croy Sisters
Weary Lonesome Blues	X						
Weary River	X						
We Live in Two Different Worlds	X						Unreleased—Rachel and Oswald
We Planted Roses on Our Darling's Grave	X						
Were You There When They Crucified My Lord	X*				X		Unreleased
What a Friend We Have in Jesus					X		For the MGM release see "Legend of the Dogwood Tree"
What Do You Think About Me		X					Unreleased
What Good Will It Do	X						
What Will I Do		X					
What Would You Do with Gabriel's Trumpet	X						
When I Lay My Burden Down	X				X		
When Lulu's Gone	X						Cataloged as by the "Bang Boys"
When My Money Run Out	X						
When They Take That Last Look at Me	X						
Where Could I Go but to the Lord				X			
Where the Soul Never Dies				X			
Whoa Mule		X					
Whole Month of Sundays					X		
Why Don't You Love Me					X		
Willie Roy the Crippled Boy					X		
Will the Circle Be Unbroken	X					X	UA is with Maybelle Carter and others
Wonder Is All I Do	XX						One is unreleased

Titles	Col	Cap	Dec	MGM	Hic	UA	Comments
Worried Mind	X*						
Would You Care	X				X		
Wreck of the Old 97					X		
Wreck on the Highway	X*	X			XXX	X	One Hickory is unreleased / One Hickory is from a live show
Write Me Sweetheart	X				X		Vocal is Red Jones
Yes Sir, That's My Baby	X						
You Are My Love	X						
You'll Reap These Tears	X						
Your Address Unknown	X						
Your Cheatin' Heart	X				X		
You're a Heavenly Thing	X*						Unreleased
You're My Darling	X						
You're the Only Star	X						
You've Gotta See Mama Every Night							
You Win Again					X		
Zeb Turney's Gal					X		
	201	36	8	12	177 −6 / 171	5	

Col: 174 released, 27 unreleased

Cap: All 36 released (There probably was additional one not released.)

Dec: 6 released, 2 unreleased

MGM: All 12 released

Hic: Of the 177, 19 are unreleased

UA: All 5 released

Comments: In the total of 433 masters, the six titles from live shows were not counted because they were not done in a studio and were never assigned master numbers. The one unknown Capitol unreleased master isn't counted in either the title total or master total.

Total of 341 different titles. This 341 includes: live show album, La Croy Sisters, all different vocalists such as Red Jones, instrumentals—everything but the one unknown Capitol.

Bibliography

A. PERSONAL CONTACTS

The heart of this biography has been the information gained during my four extensive visits to Nashville, Tennessee.

These trips were planned to fall during times when the troupe was not on long tours. However, if they did play an out-of-town date I was usually included. Besides Tennessee, these excursions have been to places in Kentucky, Indiana, Georgia, and even as far away as Sunset Park in Pennsylvania.

I was also included in many special Nashville activities. Two examples are the official opening of the new Acuff-Rose building on July 10, 1967, and the recording session of July 24, 1967.

Each of these trips has included visits with Roy and Mildred in their home.

Every courtesy was shown to me at all times, and these privileges offered rare and wonderful opportunities to not only have a wonderful time but to gather much information.

1964: Monday, July 6 to Tuesday, July 21.
1967: Wednesday, July 5 to Wednesday, July 26.
1970: Monday, July 6 to Monday, August 3.
1973: Monday, July 16 to Wednesday, August 8.

In addition to these four extended trips, I have also had personal contacts with the troupe on the following occasions:

Cleveland, Ohio. Wednesday, February 9, 1955.
Nashville, Tennessee. Saturday, February 19, 1955.
Columbus, Ohio. Sunday, February 19, 1956.

San Diego, California. Saturday, May 14, 1960.
San Diego, California. Saturday, January 21, 1961.
San Diego, California. Saturday, September 30, 1961.
West Covina, California. Friday-Saturday, March 3-4, 1967.
Long Beach, California. Wednesday, March 26, 1969.
San Diego, California. Saturday, March 29, 1969. (On this occasion the troupe was entertained by my mother and me in our home.)
Anaheim, California. Sunday, March 30, 1969.
Buena Park, California. Friday, November 19, 1971.
Buena Park, California. Saturday, January 6, 1973.

A. 1. ACUFF FAMILY

Acuff, Briscoe. Roy Acuff's older brother. Clarksville, Tennessee. Tuesday, July 28, 1970.
Acuff, Claude. Roy Acuff's younger brother. Chapel Hill, Tennessee. Sunday, July 12, 1970.
Acuff, Mr. and Mrs. Roy Claxton.
Acuff, Roy Neill. Roy Acuff's son. Nashville, Tennessee. Brief contacts in 1964 and 1967. More extensive contacts on Monday, July 27, 1970, and Monday, July 23, 1973.
Allen, Mrs. Robert L. Sue Acuff, Roy Acuff's younger sister. Clarksville, Tennessee. Sunday-Monday, July 19-20, 1964.
Phillips, Mrs. Hartsell D. Juanita Acuff, Roy Acuff's older sister. Clarksville, Tennessee. Sunday-Monday, July 19-20, 1964.

A. 2. ACUFF BAND

Some of these musicians have been good company and very helpful on many occasions, particularly Jimmie Riddle, Pete Kirby, and Howdy Forrester. Where contacts have been limited, dates are given.

Collins, Charlie.
Forrester, Mr. and Mrs. Howard.
Green, Joe. March 1969.
Jackson, Harold.
Jackson, Tommy. Monday, July 24, 1967.
Johnson, Jerry. Saturday, July 11, 1964.
Kirby, Pete.
Martin, Benny. Thursday, July 16, 1970.
Martin, Gene. 1964 and 1973.
McNeely, Larry. 1967 and March 1969.

Nelson, Doyle. 1967.

Nelson, Jay. 1967.

Phelps, Jackie. September 1961, 1967, 1970.

Riddle, Mr. and Mrs. Jimmie.

Stearns, June. 1964.

Summey, Clell. Saturday, July 8, 1967.

Wheeler, Onie. 1967.

Wilson, Lonnie. Saturday, July 15, 1967.

Zinkan, Joe. Tuesday, July 18, 1967.

A. 3. OTHERS

The identifications are those which are felt will be most informative. Usually these contacts are identified by the position they held at the time of the interview.

Buck, Louis. WSM announcer of the Royal Crown Cola show and later employed by WSM in other capacities. Nashville, Tennessee. Monday, July 10, 1967, and Friday, July 17, 1970.

Cooper, Bob. WSM executive. Nashville, Tennessee. Tuesday, July 7, 1964, and Tuesday, July 18, 1967.

Crook, Herman. Old-time Opry member. Nashville, Tennessee. Saturday, July 18, 1964.

Devine, Ott. Opry manager. Nashville, Tennessee. Tuesday, July 25, 1967.

Dopyera, John. He, along with his brothers, developed the Dobro guitar. Escondido, California. Saturday, March 23, 1968, and Thursday, April 11, 1968.

Dunkleberger. A. C. Editor of the *Nashville Banner* and author of *King of Country Music: the Life Story of Roy Acuff*. Nashville, Tennessee. Tuesday, July 14, 1964; Wednesday, July 19, 1967; and Friday, July 21, 1967.

Emery, Ralph. WSM announcer. Nashville, Tennessee. Monday, July 13, 1964.

Forrester, Clyde. Brother of Howdy Forrester. Nashville, Tennessee. Saturday, July 11, 1970.

Gable, Dorothy. Employed at the Hall of Fame. Nashville, Tennessee. Tuesday, July 18, 1967, and Saturday, July 18, 1970.

Hanserd, Tom. WSM announcer. Nashville, Tennessee. Tuesday, July 18, 1967, and Friday, July 21, 1967.

Huddleston, John. Very old and dear Acuff family friend. Maynard-ville, Tennessee. Thursday, July 9, 1964.

Hutcherson, Bert. Old-time Opry member. Nashville, Tennessee. Just about every Friday and Saturday night during all four Nashville trips.

Kilpatrick, "D". Former record company executive and former Opry manager. Nashville, Tennessee. Wednesday, July 19, 1967; Friday, July 20, 1973; and Friday, July 27, 1973.

Lucus, Joe. Acuff-Rose executive. Nashville, Tennessee. Wednesday, July 8, 1970.

Lunn, Robert. Tennessee State Museum employee and former Opry performer. Nashville, Tennessee. Saturday, July 11, 1964.

Moore, Vaughn. Very old and dear Acuff family friend. Maynard-ville, Tennessee. Thursday, July 9, 1964.

Pelletieri, Mr. and Mrs. Vito. He was Opry stage manager emeritus. She was an accomplished musician. Nashville, Tennessee. Monday, July 10, 1967.

Ritter, Tex. The country music great. Nashville, Tennessee. Saturday, July 21, 1973.

Rose, Wesley. President of Acuff-Rose. Nashville, Tennessee. Wednesday, July 19, 1967; Wednesday, July 8, 1970; Friday, July 10, 1970; and Monday, July 23, 1973.

Stamper, Mr. and Mrs. Powell. He was a National Life executive for many years. She held many executive positions with the Opry for many years. Nashville, Tennessee. Goodlettsville, Tennessee. This gracious couple entertained me often during all four Tennessee visits, both in the city of Nashville and on their farm at Good-lettsville.

Thomas, Jean. Acuff-Rose employee. Nashville, Tennessee. Monday, July 23, 1973, and Sunday, August 5, 1973.

Turner, Grant. WSM announcer—"The Voice of the Grand Ole Opry." Nashville, Tennessee. Mr. Turner and I have talked on many occasions during my four Nashville visits, but especially at breakfast on Friday, July 17, 1964, and at lunch on Wednesday, July 15, 1970.

Wells, Kitty. "Queen of Country Music." Sunset Park, Pennsylvania. Sunday, July 29, 1973.

Willis, Guy. Opry performer. Nashville, Tennessee. Monday, July 17, 1967.

B. PERIODICALS

A few magazine articles have been exclusively about Roy Acuff. Many more mention him in connection with the Opry or country music in general. Others don't even mention him but contain valuable material. Many articles have been consulted; the ones that were the most helpful are listed here.

Coleman, Emily (ed). "Country Music is Big Business, and Nashville Is Its Detroit," *Newsweek,* August 11, 1952, cover and pp. 82-85.

Davidson, Bill. "Thar's Gold in Them Thar Hillbilly Tunes," *Colliers,* July 28, 1951, pp. 34-35, 42, 44-45.

Deen, Dixie, "The Woman Behind the Man," *Music City News,* December, 1965, pp. 17-18.

Goldstein, Steve. "Opryland to Politics to Yo-Yos . . . An Interview with Roy Acuff," *Country Music,* October, 1972, pp. 32-39.

Green, Ben. "Dunbar Cave Always Reflects Roy Acuff's Love for People," *Country and Western Jamboree,* August, 1957, cover and pp. 8-9, 34.

Greenway, John. "Country-Western: the Music of America," *American West,* November, 1968, pp. 32-41.

Hartwell, Dickson. "Caruso of Mountain Music," *Colliers,* March 5, 1949, pp. 26, 39, 42.

Holman, Ross L. "King of Mountain Music," *Coronet,* September, 1948, pp. 44-48.

Moore, Thurston (ed.). "The King of Country Music," *Hoedown,* July 1966, cover and pp. 8-14.

Powel, Bob. "Bob Powel Interviews Roy Acuff," *Country Music People,* June, 1970, pp. 36-37; July, 1970, pp. 32-33.

Riddle, Jimmie. Roy Acuff and his troupe were frequently mentioned in *Pickin' and Singin' News.* However, the most useful articles were Jimmie Riddle's reports of the Korea tour which appeared in some issues of October 1953; and his reports of the Alaska tour which appeared in December 1954 and January 1955.

Schlappi, Elizabeth. "Bashful Brother Oswald," *The Dobro Nut,* Beverly King (ed.), March-April, 1975, cover and pp. 5-6, 10-11.

Smith, Bonnie. "Brother Oswald: That Good Ole Country Music," *Bluegrass Unlimited,* April 1975, cover and pp. 18-24.

Whaley, Cecil (ed.). "King of Country Music," *KFDI Country,* December, 1967, cover and pp. 4-8.

Whisenhunt, Elton. "The Engagement Roy Acuff Never Played," *Billboard- The World of Country Music,* October, 1965, pp. 64-65.

Zhito, Lee (ed.). "A Handshake and a Promise," *Billboard,* February 3, 1968, 25-page center section celebrating the twenty-fifth anniversary of Acuff-Rose.

Zolotow, Maurice. "Hillbilly Boom," *Saturday Evening Post,* February 12, 1944, pp. 22-23, 36, 38.

C. BOOKS AND BOOKLETS

A few books and booklets deal with Roy Acuff extensively; many more mention him. The ones most helpful are listed here.

Dunkleberger, A. C. *King of Country Music the Life Story of Roy Acuff.* Nashville: Williams Printing Co., 1971.

Hay, George D. *A Story of the Grand Ole Opry.* Nashville: Radio Station WSM, 1945.

Hurst, Jack. *Nashville's Grand Ole Opry.* New York: Harry N. Abrams, Inc., 1975.

Lord, Bobby. *Hit the Glory Road.* Nashville: Broadman Press, 1969.

Malone, Bill C. *Country Music U.S.A. a Fifty-Year History.* Austin: University of Texas Press, 1968.

McDaniel, William R. *Grand Ole Opry.* New York: Greenberg, 1952.

Schlappi, Elizabeth. "Roy Acuff," pp. 179-201, *Stars of Country Music—Uncle Dave Macon to Johnny Rodriguez,* Bill C. Malone and Judith McCulloh (eds.). Urbana: University of Illinois Press, 1975.

Schlappi, Elizabeth. "Roy Acuff—A Smoky Mountain Boy," pp. H48-62, Pictorial History of Country Music Section of *Country Music Who's Who—1972.* New York: Record World Publications, 1971.

Shelton, Robert, and Goldblatt, Burt. *Country Music Story.* New York: Bobbs-Merrill Company, Inc., 1966.

Tassin, Myron, and Henderson, Jerry. *Fifty Years at the Grand Ole Opry.* Gretna, Louisiana: Pelican Publishing Company, 1975.

Williams, Roger M. *Sing a Sad Song the Life of Hank Williams,* New York: Doubleday and Company, Inc., 1970.

WSM. *WSM Official Grand Ole Opry History-Picture Book.* Nashville: WSM, Inc., Volume 1, 1957; Volume 2, 1961; Volume 3, 1966; Volume 4, 1969; Volume 5, 1972.

D. TAPE RECORDINGS

My collection includes hundreds of tapes dealing with Roy Acuff. A few of the major ones are listed here.

Acuff, Roy. A brief talk to servicemen at the end of a Korea tour. January 1, 1966.

———— Short speech outlining the history of Acuff-Rose, at the dedication of the company's new building. Monday, July 10, 1967.

———— and Cherry, Hugh. Sixty-minute interview. Recorded on March 4, 1967, in Los Angeles, California. Played over radio station KGBS on March 12, 1967.

———— and Loflin, Bob. Interview at the dedication of the new Acuff-Rose building. Monday, July 10, 1967.

———— ————. Series of interviews recorded in the spring of 1972 for the Southern Baptist radio show, Country Crossroads. Played at various times over the Southern Baptist Network. (Tape courtesy of the Country Music Foundation.)

———— and Schlappi, Elizabeth. During my 1973 visit to Nashville, Roy and I agreed that the next draft of this biography would be the final draft. So he consented to sit down with me at home and turn on a tape recorder. We talked for two hours and 20 minutes, clearing up the last remaining biographical questions. Friday, August 3, 1973.

———— and Stone, David. Thirty-minute interview, later broken into five parts. Roy and his old friend, a former WSM executive, obviously enjoyed talking informally. Recorded on February 15, 1962, in Minneapolis-St. Paul, Minnesota. Played over radio station KSTP on February 19-23, 1962.

E. NEWSPAPERS

Roy Acuff has been mentioned in countless newspapers. These have feature articles.

Green, Ben A. "Dunbar Deacon—Roy Acuff," *Nashville Banner,* September 8, 1956, pp. 1-2.

Hinton, Elmer. "Along Came This Feller in a Red Roadster . . .," *Nashville Tennessean Magazine,* April 13, 1958, pp. 14-15, 26.

Hurst, Jack. "Roy Acuff: Still the King!" *Nashville Tennessean,* October 21, 1965, pp. B 11, 13.

_____"And Still the King!" *Nashville Tennessean Souvenir Edition Magazine,* October 15, 1972, cover and pp. 6-8.

O'Donnell, Red. "Shot Shoots Off Note—He Has To," *Nashville Banner,* July 23, 1965, pp. 1-2.

F. RECORD ALBUM JACKET NOTES

Most record album jackets contain information about the artists or songs. A few of these album jacket notes were of use; two were of particular value.

Green, Archie. *Babies in the Mill,* Testament Records T 3301. Information about "Wreck on the Highway."

Rinzler, Ralph, and Rinzler, Richard. *Old-Time Music at Clarence Ashley's,* Folkways Records FA 2355. Information about the medicine show.

G. TELEPHONE CONVERSATIONS

Of my many phone conversations concerning Roy Acuff's life, these are the most significant.

Acuff, Roy. The subject was the presidential Yo-Yo lesson he had "administered" the previous day. Sunday, March 17, 1974.

Hinton, Elmer. *Nashville Tennessean* feature writer. The subject was Roy Acuff's 1944 gubernatorial nomination. Monday, July 20, 1970.

Huddleston, Mrs. John. She is a very old and dear Acuff family friend. The subject was Roy Acuff's early life. Saturday, August 4, 1973.

O'Donnell, Red. *Nashville Banner* feature writer. The subject was general, although emphasis was on Roy Acuff's political career. Wednesday, July 19, 1967, and Tuesday, July 25, 1967.

H. CORRESPONDENTS

In my 20-plus years of collecting Roy Acuff memorabilia, I have corresponded with over 1,000 people. Generally, the subject of this correspondence has been more discographical than biographical, five very helpful people are listed here.

Deneumoustier, Lou. Cheswold, Delaware.
Earle, Eugene. Culver City, California.
Hearne, Will Roy. Los Angeles, California.
Wadin, Eric. Manitoba, Canada.
Wardlow, Gayle. Meridian, Mississippi.

I. SCRAPBOOKS

From the time she and Roy were married on December 25, 1936, Mildred Acuff has kept scrapbooks pertaining to the career of her husband. The collection now numbers well over a dozen. The early books are pretty worn and the pages are loose; but they contain extremely valuable information, such as: letters, telegrams, contracts, scripts, photos, tour itineraries, and many newspaper clippings.

I was given the privilege of looking through and taking notes from these scrapbooks on Wednesday, July 12, 1967, and Thursday, July 13, 1967, and again on Wednesday, July 22, 1970. Articles pertaining to Roy Acuff's political career comprised the single largest category of information; however, the scrapbooks supplied information on a multitude of subjects.

For memorabilia, on Thursday, July 23, 1970, I was permitted a rummage through the Acuff attic. This was a lot of fun and very informative.

J. UNPUBLISHED MATERIALS

Hay, George D. A 93-page typed manuscript telling the story of the Grand Ole Opry more informally than Hay's published account.

Stamper, Powell. Political speeches for Roy Acuff's gubernatorial campaign.

K. DISCOGRAPHY

The discography in this book is streamlined, its information condensed. The information in the Appendix is more up to date, but not as detailed as that in the 1966 discography listed below, which is in traditional style, i. e., recording sessions, masters, dates, etc.

Schlappi, Elizabeth. *Roy Acuff and his Smoky Mountain Boys—Discography*. Denton, Maryland: Baker Publishing Company, 1966. Copyrighted by Disc Collector Publications, Cheswold, Delaware.

L. SONGBOOKS AND OTHER ACUFF BOOKLETS

While some biographical information was obtained from the sources listed below, the reason for this category is that the reader will know these items exist. They are listed informally, to be more informative.

1. SONGBOOKS

Folio of Original Songs—Featured over WSM Grand Ole Opry. This is a 6" by 4¼" picture postcard fold-out type of folio. It contains a short biography by Jack Harris, director of publicity, WSM; 14 songs and four pictures. This is the earliest Acuff song folio and it played a big part in his initial success. It was published in 1941.

Roy Acuff's WSM Grand Ole Opry Song Favorites. This booklet measures 8½" by 5¼" and contains 48 pages. Roy Acuff signed the following dedication: "This book is sincerely dedicated to you, and our many other friends and listeners, whose graciousness has made our every success possible." It contains: a short biography by Albert E. Gibson, promotion manager, WSM; signatures of the Smoky Mountain Boys and Girls; over 50 songs; a middle section of ten pages with pictures. It was published in 1941 or 1942. This book was printed several times, and different copies vary as to arrangement.

Roy Acuff Songbook—Grand Ole Opry Edition—50 Songs. This book measures 11" by 7½" and part of it was copyrighted by Acuff-Rose Publications around 1944. Besides the 50 songs, it contains many pictures, with color pictures on both the front and back.

Roy Acuff and His Smoky Mountain Songs. This is a regular 9" by 12" songbook. It was copyrighted by Acuff-Rose Publications in 1943, with a foreword by Fred Rose. It has 20 songs and several pictures. The *Special WSM Edition* is identical but only measures 8" by 6".

Roy Acuff—Song Folio 102. This is a regular 9" by 12" songbook. It was printed by Acuff-Rose Publications around 1945, with a short biography by Fred Rose. It has 20 songs and several pictures.

Roy Acuff—Nashville, Tennessee. These are 6½" by 4½" picture postcard fold-out type of folios. They were put out over a period of around 15 years in various colors and editions to publicize Dunbar Cave and later the Hobby Exhibit. They each contain eight songs and ten pictures, with titles and subjects changing from time to time.

Songs of the Soil—All Star Hillbilly Folio—Featuring Six Select Stars.

This is a regular 9" by 12" songbook. It was copyrighted by Western Music Publishing Company in 1942 and then the copyright was assigned to Gordon Music Company in 1944. The stars are: Gene Autry, Roy Rogers, Roy Acuff, Tex Ritter, Jimmie Davis, and Zeke Manners. It contains a short biography of each star. Two pages are devoted to Acuff pictures, but none of the 14 songs are particularly connected with Roy Acuff.

The Hillbilly Hit Kit—15 Big Song Hits Featured by 5 Great Artists. This is a regular 9" by 12" songbook. It was copyrighted by Western Music Publishing Company in 1945. The stars are: Gene Autry, Ernest Tubb, Roy Acuff, Tex Ritter, and Zeke Clements. Two pages are devoted to Acuff pictures, and possibly one of the 16 songs could be said to be connected with Roy Acuff.

Songs for Home Folks. This is a regular 9" by 12" songbook. It was copyrighted by Acuff-Rose Publications in 1956. It features Roy Acuff, Kitty Wells, and Johnny and Jack. It contains 20 songs and quite a few pictures and a letter by George D. Hay. The contents of the book are very closely connected with the Acuff/Wells/Johnny and Jack tour of 1955-56.

2. OTHER ACUFF BOOKLETS

Roy Acuff's Simplified Popular Guitar Albums. The original was followed by *No. 2* and *No. 3*. These 9" by 12" booklets were copyrighted by Acuff-Rose Publications and printed by Chas. H. Hansen Music Company in 1951, 1952, and 1953. Roy Acuff is on the cover of each album; otherwise he is not mentioned in the books, which are instruction books on how to learn to play the guitar.

Souvenir Picture Albums. Many varieties and types have been made through the years to be sold at performances. These albums frequently measure 8½" by 11" and contain pictures and sometimes biographies of Roy Acuff and the Smoky Mountain Boys. Two of them are:

The Smoky Mountain Boys—Picture Album. Blue cover with a cabin, contains five large pictures featuring the Smoky Mountain Boys and Rachel.

Roy Acuff—Souvenir Album—Direct from the WSM Grand Ole Opry. Green cover. Four pages with small pictures and lots of printed information.

Fan Club Journals. Through the years there have been several Roy

Acuff Fan Clubs. Two are:
  Glasscock, Mrs. Gussie. *Smokey Mountain Melody.* 1949.
  Glenn, Willis, *Dunbar Digest.* Mid-1950s.

Index

Acting: as a child, 6; in high school, 11; in burlesque, 14; in medicine show, 21; in movies, 173-81; showmanship, 235, 236, 238

Acuff, Alex Wolfgang, 234

Acuff, Arthur, 4

Acuff, Briscoe, 5, 6, 12, 13, 17, 18, 31, 168, 221

Acuff, Charles, 9, 19

Acuff, Claude (Spot) 5, 6, 10, 22, 24, 38, 52, 140, 168, 218

Acuff, Corum, 3, 4, 7, 183, 204

Acuff, Evart, 92

Acuff, Frank, 5

Acuff Gladys, 168

Acuff, Herbert, 4, 18

Acuff, Ida Carr, 4, 5, 6, 8, 9, 16, 19, 20, 31, 38, 167-168, 185, 224, 227

Acuff, Juanita (Mrs. Hartsell D. Phillips), 5, 13, 32, 43, 153, 168

Acuff, Judd, 4

Acuff, Mildred Douglas: first meeting with Roy, 16, 19, 20; marriage of, 30-31, 37, 38, 40; life in trailer park, 41-42, 43, 46, 51, 52, 68, 74, 87, 98, 104, 114; and automobile wreck, 144-46; business advice of, 141, 149, 228-29; and Acuff-Rose, 149, 150, 152, 154, 157, 161, 170, 179; opinions of Roy's candidacies, 184, 204, 208, 209, 217-18, 220; domestic duties of, 224-28; Roy's

debt to, 230; and son, 230, 233; and overseas tours, 250

Acuff, Neill, 4, 5, 6, 7, 9, 10, 13, 15, 16, 18, 19, 20, 28, 31, 38, 91, 167, 183, 204, 207, 220, 221, 224, 230

Acuff, Roger, 168

Acuff, Roy Claxton: ancestry of, 3-4; childhood of, 4-10; in high school, 10-13; after high school, 13-17; sunstroke of, 17-18; sunstroke recuperation of, 18-20; in medicine show, 20-21; in Knoxville band, 22-25; first recording sessions of, 25-30; marriage of, 30-31; getting on the Opry, 32-43; old band quits, 39-40; forms new band, 40-41; life of in trailer park, 41-42; first songbook of, 42-43; in Prince Albert show, 44-45; articles about, 46; TV shows appeared on, 46; reading poems on the Opry, 46-48; typical Opry show of, 48-50; and Opry tent shows, 50-51; leaving the Opry, 51-53; returning to the Opry, 53-54; attitude of toward the Opry, 54, 58, 59, 60; attitude of toward the old-time bands, 55-57; helping the other Opry members, 57-58; opening the new Opry House, 60-63; helping others in country music, 63-64; opinions of about music, 64-67; relationship of with

fans, 67-70; and band members, 71-91, 93-95, 96-102; fiddles and fiddling, 91-93, 95-96; relationship of with band, 102-5; Acuff Sound, 106-14; recording an album, 114-19; greatest songs of, 119-24; and song writing, 124-25; traveling in U.S., 126-35; traveling abroad, 135-38, 239-50; and crowds, 138-39; income and managers of, 139-41; and automobile wreck, 141-48; Acuff-Rose, 149-62, 164; Roy and Hank Williams, 162-64; at Dunbar Cave, 164-69; collections of, 169-71; and other business ventures, 171-72; in movies, 173-81; near campaign of 1944, 182-87; and gubernatorial campaign of 1948, 188-204; subsequent political activities and beliefs of, 205-14; and Dizzy Dean, 215-17; election to the Country Music Hall of Fame, 217-18; personality and health of, 218-24; and wife, 224-30; and son, 230-35; reasons for success of, 235-38; and discography, 251-65
Acuff, Roy Neill, 111, 113, 114, 218, 226, 228, 230-35
Acuff, Roy Neill, Jr., 231
Acuff, Shirley, 168
Acuff, Sue (Mrs. Robert Allen), 5, 13, 19, 168-69, 236
Acuff, Thelma, 239
Acuff, Theobald, 3
Acuff, Timothy, 4
Acuff-Rose Artists' Corporation, 95
Acuff-Rose Far East, 158
Acuff-Rose International, 158
Acuff-Rose Publishing Co., 43, 69, 96n, 104, 110, 123, 140,149-64, 228, 232, 233, 244-45
Acuff Sound, 82, 91, 106-14, 193
Addams, Vee & Abbott, Inc., 153
Adkins, Ray, 81
"Advice to Joe," 212
"After the Fire is Gone," 113
Albertson, Frank, 180
Allen, Bob, 168, 169
Allen, Rex, 90
Allen, Robert L., 168
Amati, 92

American Federation of Musicians, 196, 213n
American Record Company, 26, 29, 30
American Society of Composers, Authors, and Publishers (ASCAP), 149, 150, 153, 154
Anderson, Bill, 61, 90
Appendicitis, 176
Arnold, Eddy, 140, 205
Artists' Service Bureau (WSM), 33, 50n, 53
Ashley, Tom (Clarence), 21
Astor Hotel Roof, 133
Atkins, Hobart, 15
"At the Grand Ole Opry Tonight," 45, 46
"Automobile of Life," 30
Automobile wreck, 97, 98, 141-48, 248
Autrey, Gene, 151, 175, 215

"Baby Just Said Goodbye, 232, 233
"Back Down to Atlanta," 234
"Back in the Country," 113
Baez, Joan, 64
Bailes Brothers, 98
Bailey, Ed, 216
Baker, Howard, Jr., 61, 208
Baker, Howard, Sr., 190
Balancing fiddle and other objects, 6, 8, 84, 121, 147, 148, 205, 216, 235, 247
"Baldknob Arkansas," 78
Baltimore Park, 139
Bang Boys, The, 28
"Be Honest with Me," 151
Beatles, The, 66
Beeler, Earl, 6
"Beneath that Lonely Mound of Clay," 124
Benny, Jack, 213n
"Beverly Hillbillies," 178
"Billy Boy," 179
Blackface makeup, 21, 24, 40
Black Shirts, The, 25
Blake, Bobby (Little Beaver), 243
Blanchard, Lowell, 23
Blind Barthimaeus, 103, 226
Blish, Edward, 142-44
Bluegrass, 65

"Blue Ridge Sweetheart," 30
Bobcats, 11, 12, 13
Bond, Johnny, 90
Boone, Pat, 139
Bowes, Margie, 97
Bradley, Donald, 144
Bradley, Owen, 115
"Branded Wherever I Go," 124
Brasfield, Rod, 239
Broadcast Music Incorporated (BMI), 150, 154, 156, 207
Brock, William, 61
Brown, Bud, 159, 160
Browning, Gordon, 133, 188, 191, 192, 194, 200, 202, 204
Brunswick label, 150
Bryant, Anita, 90
Buck, Frank, 73
Buck, Louie, 169
Buerger's Disease, 177, 221-22
Burlesque, 14
Butler, Carl, 117
Byers, Nellie, 119, 227-28, 230
Byers, Theodore, 228
BYPU, 9

"C" Club, 11
Calaway, William R., 27, 29, 30
Campaign issues of 1948: TVA, 195; roads, 195; tourists and parks, 195; states' rights. 196; poll tax, 196; labor, 196; sales tax, 196, schools and education, 196-97; taxes, 197; benefits and old age pensions, 197; tax on churches, 197; veteran's bonus, 198; bipartisan cabinet, 198; voting, 198; Davidson County Machine Coldmere Club, 199; Roy's qualifications, 200-203
Campbell, Archie, 23, 25, 63
"Candy Kisses," 116
Capitol label: 100, 109, 110; discography, 251-65
Carlisle, Bill, 23
Carlisle, Cliff, 81
Carr, A. W., 4, 5, 7
"Carry Me Back to the Mountains," 49
Carson-Newman College, 4, 13, 32
Carter, A. P., 120n
Carter, Mother Maybelle, 112, 145, 147

Carter, Roy, 25n
Cash, Johnny, 209
Cash, W. J., 26
Cassady, Andrew Lafayette (Fate), 91
Caswell Park (Knoxville), 17
Central High School, 10-13, 14, 16, 17
Century of Progress (exposition), 73
Charles, Nick, 12
Charles, Ray, 66
"Charlie over the River," 21
"Charmin' Betsy," 28
Charts, songs on, 110, 112, 113
Chastain, Aubrey, 234
Cheshire, Harry (Pappy), 180
"Chiquita Banana," 100
Christian, Bill, 75
Christian beliefs, 5, 8-9, 13, 18, 194, 237, 246
Clarkston Hotel, 38, 40, 41
Clarksville (Tenn.), 165-67, 193, 239
Classical Routine, 99, 100, 101-102, 205
Claustrophobia, 223, 240
Claxton, P. P., 5
Clement, Frank, 57, 66, 128, 207, 208, 226
Clements, Zeke, 212
Cleveland, George, 180
Cline, Patsy, 57, 127
Collections (Roy's), 169-71, 219, 223-24
Collins, Bob, 232
Collins, Charlie, 95, 96n, 99-100, 102, 104, 115, 210
Columbia label: 26, 29, 30, 53, 86, 108, 109, 122; discography, 251-65
"Columbia Stockade Blues," 78
"Coming from the Ball," 78
Communists, 191, 208, 212-13
"Complaints About Napkins," 47
Conqueror label, 29
Cooper, Bob, 58, 64
Cooper, George, 213
Cooper, Prentice, 182
Cooper, Wilma Lee, 97
Copas, Cowboy, 94, 127
Copeland, John, 14, 19
Cotton, Carolina, 180
Cottonseed Clark, 47
Country Music Association, 207, 217
Country Music Foundation, 207, 220n

Country Music Hall of Fame, 10, 170, 217-18, 220n, 246
"Cowards over Pearl Harbor," 211
Cowboy Canteen, 174, 178
Cox, Alma, 25
Cramer, Floyd, 114
Crazy Tennesseans, 23, 24, 27, 36, 40, 73, 82
Crook, Herman, 34
Crook Brothers, The, 34, 55, 56
Crooning, 23, 33, 37, 39, 107, 231
Crosby, Bing, 33, 108
Crowds, 20, 109, 114, 138-39, 219
Crump, Ed, 182, 184, 185, 188, 191
Crustine Ranch Boys, 86
Cummings, Eddie, 59
"Czardas," 102

Davis, Oscar, 140, 243
Davis, Sammy, Jr., 210
Dawson, Bart, 154
Day, Sonny, 87, 98, 101, 178, 191
Dean, Dizzy, 145, 147, 166, 215-17
Dean, Jimmy, 90
"Dear John," 219
Decca label: 75, 87, 88, 110; discography, 251-65
"Deed I Do," 150
Delmore Brothers, 35, 36, 37
Dewey, Thomas E., 190
Dickens, Jimmy, 57, 239
Dillon, Sarah, 25n
"Dill Pickle Rag," 86
"Dinah Shore Show," 46
Dixieliners, The, 33
Dixie Tabernacle, 34
Dixon, Dorsey, 122-23
Dixon, Howard, 122
Dobro guitar, 22, 23, 27, 28, 29, 34, 40, 50, 73, 79-82, 83, 91, 98, 100, 107, 108, 109, 110, 111, 114, 115, 117, 118
"Doin' It the Old Fashioned Way," 28
"Don't Hang Your Dirty Linen on My Line," 109
"Don't Let Me Cross Over," 117, 118, 119
"Don't Make Me Go to Bed," 151
Dopyera, John, 80, 81
Dopyera Brothers, 80
Douglas, Louis, 31

Douglas, Nell, 31
Douglas, Nell Sharp, 31
"Doug McArthur," 212
"Down in Union County," 49, 175
"Do You Wonder Why," 124
Dunbar Cave, 98, 103, 165-69, 171, 188, 215, 231, 240
Duncan, Charlie, 14
Dunkelberger, A. C., 208
Dunn, Winfield, 61

Easterday, Jess, 22, 23, 24, 27, 29, 30, 34, 37, 39, 40, 41, 82-83, 100, 129; and movies, 174-75, 177-78, 191
Easterday, Wilma Jean, 83
"Easy Rockin' Chair," 169, 178
Edwards, John, 244
Eeephin, 88
Eisenhower, Dwight, 208
Eliviry, 175
Ellington, Duke, 213n
Ellis, Cornelia (Wallace), 243
ESP, 223-24
Esty, William, 44
Ethridge, Floyd, 93
Everly Brothers, 160
"Eyes Are Watching You," 41

"Falling Star," 110
Fan Fair, 75, 96
Fans, 67-70, 171, 215, 219, 221, 222, 225, 226, 237, 238
"Farther Along," 57
Fiddle and fiddling: as a child, 8, 9; while recuperating from sunstroke, 18-20; in medicine show, 20-21; in Knoxville, 22-25; on early recordings, 27, 29, 30; when first on the Opry, 33, 34, 38; fiddles and fiddling, 65, 91-93, 95-96; in the Acuff Sound, 108, 117; Uncle Jimmie's fiddle, 170-71; as a 1948 campaign issue, 200; keeping it in the act, 235
Fiddlin' John Carson, 18
"Filipino Baby," 116-18
"Fireball Mail," 75, 107, 153, 177
Fist fighting, 13, 15, 16, 129, 174, 243
Flame, The (Minneapolis), 134
Flatt, Gladys, 227

Flatt, Lester, 227
"Flatt and Scruggs Show," 75
"Foggy River," 116, 119
Foley, Red, 45, 53, 90, 133, 239
"Follow Your Drum," 234-35
Foree, Mel, 155, 159
"For the First Time—Roy Acuff Sings
    Hank Williams," 164
Forrester, Billie (Sally Ann), 94
Forrester, Bobby, 94
Forrester, Clayton, 93
Forrester, Clyde, 93
Forrester, Howdy, 50, 66, 92, 93-95,
    102, 104, 111, 113, 115, 116, 129,
    160, 210, 216, 242, 246, 247
Forrester, Joe, 93
Forrester, Uncle Bob, 93
Forster, Fred, 152, 153, 154, 155
Fountain City Missionary Baptist
    Church, 13, 206
Four Guys, 90
"Four Leaf Clover," 244
Fowler, Wally, 64
Fox, Jimmy, 99, 110, 141-43
"Fox Chase," 87, 88
Francis, Connie, 90
Frank, Joe L., 32, 33, 34, 39, 140,
    165
Frawley, William, 180
Fred Rose Music, 156
"Fred Rose's Song Shop," 151
"Freight Train Blues," 28, 107, 180
"Friday Night Frolic," 167
Fruit Jar Drinkers, The, 34, 55, 58
Fulton, Ralph, 210

Gant, Don, 232
Gatlinburg (Tenn.), 49, 169-70, 232
Gayoso Hotel (Memphis), 41, 86
Gehrig, Lou, 17, 60
Georgia Slim, 94
Gibson, Don, 161
Gid Tanner and the Skillet Lickers, 18
"Girl I Love, The," 78
Glasscock, Gussie, 68
"Glen Campbell Show," 99
Glenn, Willis, 68
"Glory Bound Train," 178
"God Bless America," 63
Gold Record (Columbia), 29, 109,
    170, 200n

Gold Record (United Artists), 113
Goldwater, Barry, 208
"Gonna Raise a Ruckus Tonight," 28
"Goodbye Brownie," 30
"Good Bye My Love—I Heard a Silver
    Trumpet," 211
"Good Deal Lucile," 157
Goodman's (Harold) Tennessee Valley
    Boys, 94
Gossett, Cully, 239
Grammy nomination, 113
Grand Ole Opry (movie), 42, 61, 173,
    175-77
Grand Ole Opry: getting on the show,
    32-43; network, 44-45, 182; typical
    Acuff Opry show, 46-50; Opry tent
    shows, 50-51; leaving the Opry, 51-
    53; returning to the Opry, 53-54;
    Roy and the Opry, 54-60; opening
    the new Opry House, 60-63; Opry
    outside Nashville, 133-35, 239,
    244, 249; Roy Neill on the Opry,
    233
"Grand Ole Opry," (TV show), 46
Great Smoky Mountains, 7, 9, 36, 71,
    83, 169
Great Speckled Bird (airplane), 26,
    127
"Great Speckled Bird," 25-26, 27, 28,
    33, 34, 35, 37, 38, 49, 92, 112,
    119, 123, 136, 147, 175, 176
"Great Speckled Bird No. 2," 29
Green, Joe, 95, 148
Gresham, Hassie, 11
Guarnerius, 92
Gubernatorial campaign of 1948, 188-
    205
Gully Jumpers, The, 34, 55, 56

Hadacol Caravan, 131
"Hail to the Chief," 62
Hamilton, Ollie, 50, 52, 140, 169
Hankins, Esco, 124
"Happy Birthday," 62
Harman, Buddy, 115
Harmony label, 251
Harrah's Headliner Room (Reno), 135,
    229
Harris, Perry, 77
Hatcher, Sam "Dynamite," 24, 27, 28,
    73, 120, 211

Hauer, 20, 21, 22
Hay, George D. (The Solemn Old Judge"), 32, 34, 54, 55, 57, 59, 60, 63, 175
Hayes, Helen, 248
Heart attack, 222
Heathcock, Joe, 180
Hebb, Bobby, 100
"Hee Haw," 88, 99, 104, 250
Hendersonville (Tenn.), 168, 226, 227, 231
Henry Horton State Park, 168
Hickory label: 110, 111, 157-58, 160, 233; discography, 251-65
"Highways Are Happy Ways," 244
"Hills of Roane County," 121
Hi Neighbor, 174, 177
Hinton, Elmer, 182-83
Hollywood Canteen, 178
Home in San Antone, (movie) 174, 179-80, 204
"Home in San Antone," 153, 180
"Home on the Range," 176
Homes, 4-5, 10, 16, 30, 31, 38, 41-42, 43, 224-28
"Honest and Truly," 150
Honorary awards, 205
Hope, Bob, 62, 135, 210, 249
Horton, Johnny, 90
"Hot Canary," 101
Huddleston, John, 6, 7, 8, 10
Huddleston, Lilly, 7
Hull, Cordell, 201
Humphrey, Hubert, 206
Huskey, Junior, 101
Hutcherson, Bert, 56

"I Can't Stop Loving You," 156
"I'd Die for the Red, White and Blue," 211
"I Didn't Hear Anybody Pray," 122
"I Didn't Know God Made Honky Tonk Angels," 26
"I Get the Blues When It Rains," 244
"I Know We Are Saying Goodbye," 177
"I'll Reap My Harvest in Heaven," 153, 159
"I'm Thinking Tonight of My Blue Eyes," 25, 26
"I'm Walking," 100

Income, 24, 25, 30, 31, 35, 38, 40, 41, 42, 43, 139-41, 149, 152-53, 164
"It's All Right Now," 168

"Jackie Gleason Show," 46
Jackson, Andy, 157, 201
Jackson, Shot, 26, 50, 98-99, 103, 109, 119; and automobile wreck, 141-48, 216, 226, 228, 245, 247
Jackson, Tommy, 93, 115, 118
James, Jesse, 166
James, Joni, 90
Jamup and Honey, 50
Jenkins, Floyd, 154
Jennings, Waylon, 135
"Jimmy Dean Show," 46
"Jingle Bells," 231
John Edwards Memorial Foundation, 160
Johnny and Jack, 23, 81, 98, 109, 131-32, 139
"Johnny Cash Show," 46, 64
Johnson, Jerry, 97, 240
Johnson, John E., 92
John Wayne Theater (Knott's Berry Farm), 106
Jones, Eva Thompson, 171
Jones, Grandpa, 58
Jones, Red, 18, 22, 23, 24, 27, 28, 29, 30, 33, 34, 37, 38, 39, 40, 107
Jug Band, The, 100
"Just a Friend," 78
"Just to Ease My Worried Mind," 124

"Kansas City Blues," 86
"Kate Smith Show," 46, 133
Kaydets, 17
Kefauver, Estes, 191, 192, 200
Kentucky Slim (Little Darling), 25
Kilpatrick, "D." 55, 134, 160
King, Martin Luther, 58
King, Pee Wee, 23, 32, 39, 41, 56
"King and Queen of Country Music," 110, 131-32
King of Country Music, 46, 216-17, 224
Kingsport (Tenn.), 148, 192-93
Kirby, Billy, 73
Kirby, Linda, 73
Kirby, Lola, 73
Kirby, Pete (Beecher Ray), 25, 26, 40,

41, 42, 43, 48, 50, 59, 60, 71-82,
84, 93, 96, 97, 98, 99, 100, 101,
102, 103, 104, 107, 109, 110, 111,
112, 113, 114, 115, 117, 118, 119,
121, 122, 128, 131, 133, 139; and
automobile wreck, 141-44, 162,
166; and movies, 174-79, 191, 206,
210, 216, 223; on overseas tours,
242, 245, 248
Knoxville Smokies, 17
Korea, 240-41, 248
"Kraft Music Hall," 46
Kramer, Russel, 182
Kriesler, Fritz, 183
KRLD, 94

La Croy Sisters, 97
Landau, Marty, 52
Landmark Hotel (Las Vegas), 135
Lane, Allen, 180
Last Picture Show, The, 180
"Lay My Old Guitar Away," 68
"Leaf of Love," 244
LeBlanc, Senator Dudley, 131
Lightnin' Chance, 115, 117
Lincoln, Abraham, 46, 237
Lind, Jenny, 166
"Little Willie Green," 21
Locklin, Hank, 114
"Lonesome Joe," 109
Lonzo and Oscar, 39n
"Lost Highway," 107
"Louisiana Hayride," 97, 98
Louisville & Nashville Railroad and
Baseball Team, 14, 17, 120, 123
Louvin Brothers, 114,
"Lovesick Blues," 163
"Low and Lonely," 153, 177
Loyal Order of the Moose, 206, 240,
Lucus, Joe, 151, 159
Lulubelle and Scotty, 180
Lunn, Robert, 32, 51, 100, 240, 243
Lunsford, Jimmy, 95
Lynn, Loretta, 113

MacArthur, Douglas, 212
McCluskey, Bob, 160
McConnell, Jim, 95
McCord, Jim, 188
McEuen, Bill, 111, 112
McFaddin School, 42

McGee, Kirk, 33, 34, 37, 51, 55, 59,
75
McGee, Sam, 33, 34, 37, 51, 55, 59,
73, 74
McMillan, Edith Gordon, 92
McNeely, Larry, 99, 115, 117
Macon, Doris, 175
Macon, Uncle Dave, 34, 37, 50, 51,
57, 78, 127, 175
Magness, Tommy, 93, 95, 129; and
movies, 174, 178-79, 191, 235
Managers and Agents, 54, 90, 140
Market Hall (Knoxville), 23
Martin, Benny, 93, 95, 99, 141, 246
Martin, Carl R., 18
Martin, Gene, 99, 209
Martin, Jimmy, 112
Marx, Harpo, 131
Mathis, Dutch, 12
Matty and Jim, 24
May, Dean, 159
Maynardville (Tenn.), 3, 4-10, 11, 64,
223, 229
Medicine show, 20-21, 22, 107
Melotone label, 29
Mercury label, 94
MGM label, 110, 157; discography,
251-65
"Mid-Day Merry Go Round," 23
"Mike Douglas Show," 46
Milene Music, 154, 156
Miller, Cleo, 144, 146, 221
Miller Clinic, 144, 222
Milo Twins, The, 180
Milstein, Nathan, 66
Mind of the South, The, 26
Mint, Las Vegas, 134
Mocoton Tonic, 20-21
Monroe, Bill, 51, 57, 65, 93, 94
Montgomery, Melba, 97
Moore, Frankie, 140, 243
Moore, Joyce, 247
Moore, Vaughn, 6, 7, 8
"Mountain Dew," 79
Movies, 42, 45, 61, 81, 82, 87, 173-81,
188, 204, 219, 221
"Moving On," 117, 118
Mullican, Moon, 240
Murray, Robert, 188
"Music from the Land," 46
"My Gal Sal," 29

"My Mountain Home Sweet Home," 28, 124
"My Untrue Cowgirl," 86
"My Wild Irish Rose," 62

Nashville Sound, 65, 117, 157
Nashville Symphony Orchestra, 205
National Life and Accident Insurance Company, 43, 54, 60, 127, 141, 154, 156, 184, 190
Nelson Brothers, 99, 110
Nervous breakdown, nervousness, 18, 23, 33, 34, 96, 181, 218, 222, 223, 233, 235
New Deal, 191, 193, 211-12
Newman, Jimmie C., 110
New York Yankees, 17
Nicknames, 215-16, 219
Night Train to Memphis (movie), 45, 81, 174, 178-79
"Night Train to Memphis," 122, 135, 178, 189
Nitty Gritty Dirt Bank, 66, 111-12
Nixon, Pat: opening the new Opry House, 61-62
Nixon, Richard: opening the new Opry House, 60-63; Roy's support of, 208-10; gives POW dinner, 210-11
"Nobody's Business," 78
"No One Will Ever Know," 178
Norman, Bill, 22, 25
Norris Dam, 14
"Not a Word from Home," 124, 178
Nunn, Earl, 212

O' Day, Molly, 156
O' Delle, Doye, 180
Okeh label, 29
Oklahoma Wranglers," 157
"Old Age Pension Check," 211
"Old Chisholm Trail," 231
"Old Dan Tucker," 179, 231
"Old Fashioned Love," 29
Old Harp Singing Style, The, 21, 72, 107
"Old Hen Cackle," 33
"Old Three Room Shack, An," 5, 9, 10, 29, 30
"Old Time Barn Dance," 93
"Old Time Sunshine Song," 113

O' My Darling Clementine, 174, 177-78, 221
"Once More," 110
"One Take Ache," 108, 112, 116, 122
Opening of the new Opry House, 60-63
Opryland, 49, 60, 67, 104, 171, 222, 227
Opry Tent Shows, 45, 50-51, 75, 130
Orange Bowl, 139
Oswald. *See* Kirby, Pete
Oswald, Lee Harvey, 76
"Our Prayer," 211
Ousley family, 7
Overseas tours, 135-38, 214, 217, 234, 239-50

Palace Theater, 132
"Pap." *See* Wilson, Lonnie; Zinkan, Joe
Parker, Colonel Tom, 140, 172
Parsons, Louella, 176
Parthenon, 219
"Pass the Biscuits, Mirandie," 177
Pastore, John O., 207
Pearl Harbor (horse), 77, 225
Pearl, Minnie, 57, 58, 131, 145, 239
Peebles, Hap, 148
Pellettieri, Vito, 37, 150, 164, 219
Perfect label, 29
Peters, Sarah, 11
Pets, 42, 228
Phelps, Jackie, 95, 99, 101, 109, 115, 117, 118
Phillips, Foreman, 52, 139
Phillips, Hartsell D., 168
Picardini, Salvatore, 92
Pickin' and Singin' News, 57, 240
Pierce, Don, 226
"Pins and Needles," 112, 150, 153
Pleasure trips, 209, 229
"Porter Wagoner Show," 75
Possum Hunters, The, 34, 55
POW dinner, 209-11
Precious Jewel (boat), 225
"Precious Jewel," 68, 107, 112, 121-22, 123, 124
Presley, Elvis, 65
Price, Ray, 127
Prince Albert Show, 45, 48, 51, 53, 54, 56, 92, 179

Pritchett, John A., 188
Public service organizations and charity work, 205-7
Public service programs, 136, 205-206
Pyle, Ernie, 136

QRS Company, 150

"Rabbit in the Log," 79
Rachel. *See* Veach, Rachel
"Radio's Famous Hawaiian Duo," 24
"Raggin' the Rails," 86
Rand, Sally, 73
Ray, Johnny, 90
Record World, 113
"Red Hot Mama," 150
"Red Lips," 29
Red Network, 44
Reece, Carroll, 191, 193, 195, 200, 204
Reeves, Jim, 90
Rehearsals, 49-50, 106, 115
Renfro Valley Hoedown, 96
Reynolds, R. J., Tobacco Co., 44, 59
Rhodes, Oral (Curly), 84-85, 87, 100, 101, 174, 240, 242
Riddle, Almeda, 89
Riddle, Jimmie: 8, 50, 51, 52, 75, 76, 77, 85-91, 96, 98, 99, 100, 101, 102, 104, 106, 114, 115, 118, 119, 121, 127, 128, 129, 130, 139; and automobile wreck, 141-43; and movies, 174, 177-79, 191, 195, 210, 235; on overseas tours, 239n, 240, 241, 242, 244, 245, 246, 247
Riddle, Steve, 89, 90
Riddle, Susie Gusler, 89, 90
Ritter, Mrs. Tex, 61, 62
Ritter, Tex, 60, 148, 178, 180
"River of Crystal," 109
Rivoli Hall (Chicago), 134
Robbins, Marty, 208
Rock and roll, 65, 110, 117
Rodgers, Jimmie, 81, 107, 217
"Roll on Buddy," 75, 78
Rooney, Mickey, 131
Roosevelt, Franklin, 136, 191, 211, 235
Rose, Fred, 65, 109, 110, 123; Acuff-Rose, 150-64, 211, 217, 241
Rose, Lester, 160

Rose, Lorene, 154, 241
Rose, Wesley, 59, 60, 111, 114, 115, 116; Acuff-Rose, 154-63, 232-33
Rosenburg's Trailer Park, 41, 224
Roy Acuff Cannonball Kitchens, 172
Roy Acuff Collection, 220n
Roy Acuff Flour, 172
Roy Acuff Food Systems, Inc., 172
Roy Acuff Hobby Exhibits, 49, 78, 119, 146, 170-71, 220, 226, 232
"Roy Acuff, Jr.," 232-33
Roy Acuff Music Hall, 171, 220, 222
Roy Acuff Open House (TV films), 244
Roy Acuff's Folio of Original Songs Featured over WSM Grand Ole Opry, 42-43, 149, 150
"Roy Acuff Sings Famous Opry Favorites," 114-19
"Roy Acuff Songbook Show," 43, 48
Roy Acuff Square Dance Hat, 171
Roy Acuff's Smoky Mountain Sausage, 172
"Roy Acuff Story, The" (comic strip), 172
Roy Acuff Tent Theatre, 52, 87
"Royal Crown Cola Show," 48, 53
"Run, Nigger, Run" 85
Rush, Ford, 50, 52, 140,169, 226, 230
Ruth, Babe, 17, 60, 136, 235
Ryan, Irene, 177-78
Ryman Auditorium, 34, 49, 59, 60, 67, 77, 99, 182, 200

"Sad Memories," 11
"Sailing Along," 29
Sarie and Sally, 34
Sarrett, Imogene (Tiny), 25, 37, 39, 40, 73
Satherley, Art, 30, 86, 108, 109, 124, 158, 238
"Satisfied Mind," 118
Scruggs, Earl, 112
"Searching for a Soldier's Grave," 211
Seeger, Pete, 64
"Send Me the Pillow," 118
Sequoyah, 11, 12
Shawn, Emmett, 12
"She's My Curly Headed Baby," 75
Sho-Bud Guitar Company, 98, 99, 119, 228

"Shot Gun Boogie," 100
Shot Jackson Ferry, 103
Showboat (Las Vegas), 134
Showmanship, 235, 236, 238
Shreve, Richard, 92
Shriners, 206
Sincerity, 235, 237, 238
"Singing My Way to Glory," 27
Singing (pre-Grand Ole Opry): as a child, 8-9; in high school, 11; in church, 13; while recuperating from sunstroke, 19; in medicine show, 21; in Knoxville, 23, 25; on early records, 25-30
Sing Neighbor Sing, 82, 87, 174, 178
"Sing Neighbor Sing," 178
"Sixteen Chickens and a Tambourine," 100
"Smilin' Joseph." *See* Zinkan, Joe
Smith, Arthur, 33, 92, 93
Smith, Guy, 190, 193
Smith, Hal, 93, 97
Smith, Lonnie, 92
Smith, Rev. Guy, 25
Smith, Ross, 17
Smithdeal, Hack, 190
"Smoke on the Water," 177, 212
Smoky Mountain Boys: the band gets its name, 36; old band quits, 39-40; new band is formed, 40-43; Jug Band, 100; Classical Routine, 101-102; relationship of with Roy, 102-105; producing the Acuff Sound, 106-14; recording a session, 114-19; adventures of, on the road, 127-41; and automobile wreck, 141-44; in the movies, 174-79; on the campaign trail, 191; on overseas tours, 239-50. (Note: Individual band members are listed under their names.)
Smoky Mountain Melody, 174, 179, 188
"Smoky Mountain Moon," 179
Snow, Hank, 240
Soldier Key (Fla.), 17
Songwriting (Roy), 28, 29, 30, 42, 45, 121, 123, 124-25, 152-53, 211-12
"Southern Moon," 79
Sports: as participant, 6, 11, 12, 14, 15, 16, 17; as spectator, 13, 19, 216-17
Stamper, Powell, 113, 190, 195
Stamper, Trudy, 82, 113, 190
"Stay a Little Longer," 63, 231
"Steamboat Whistle Blues," 28
Stearns, June, 97-98; and automobile wreck, 141-47, 247
"Steel Guitar Chimes," 29
Sterling Records, 157
Stevens, George, 20, 22
Stewart, Jimmy, 209
Stone, David, 33, 34, 35, 36, 39, 50n, 57, 73, 74
Stone, Harry, 36, 52, 53, 54, 150, 151, 164, 183, 184
Stoneman, Pop, 58
Stout, Allen, 23
Strawbridge, Allen, 191
"Streamlined Cannonball," 124
"Street Singer," 234
"Stuck Up Blues," 177
"Sugar in the Gourd," 96
Summey, Clell (Cousin Jody), 22, 23, 24, 25, 27, 28, 29, 30, 34, 37, 39, 40, 81
"Sunshine Special," 109
Sunstroke, 17-20, 235
"Supper with Roy Acuff," 226
Surely Is a Train," 78
Swain, Dotty, 240
Swift Jewel Cowboys, 86

Taft Hotel (New York), 134
Tainaka, Robert, 247n
"Take an Old Cold Tater and Wait," 57
Taylor, Bob and Alf, 188
Teardrops of Nature, 206
"Tears on My Pillow," 151
"Ten Little Numbers," 109, 168
"Tennessee Central No. 9," 147, 179, 231
Tennessee Citizens for Nixon-Agnew Committee, 208
Tennessee Crackerjacks, 22, 40
Tennessee Ramblers, The, 180
Tennessee walking horses, 77, 225
"Tennessee Waltz," 156
Terry, Al, 157
"Thank God," 158, 179

"That Beautiful Picture," 30
"That's My Weakness Now," 85
"They Cut Down the Old Pine Tree,"
    100
"Thief upon the Tree, The," 109
"Thirty Days," 100
"This Proud Land—the South," 46
Thomas, Jean, 159
Thompson, Hank, 127
Thompson's Garage, 22
Thornburgh, Sam, 15
Three Rolling Stones, 22, 24
"Three Trees," 87
"Thy Burdens Are Greater than
    Mine," 58
Tindell, Jake, 21, 24, 40, 41, 73
Titanic, 9
Tomlinson, Homer A., 25n
"Tomorrow Never Comes," 117-19
"Tomorrow Show," 46, 64
Travis, Merle, 112
Truman, Harry, 191, 194, 212, 213n
Tubb, Ernest, 53, 117, 118, 178, 240
Tucker, Sophie, 150
"Turkey Buzzard," 33, 96
Turner, Grant, 169, 239
"Tweedle-O-Twill," 151
Twitty, Conway, 113

"Uncle Eeeph's Got the Coon," 100
Uncle Jimmie Thompson, 170-71
"Uncle Noah's Ark," 100
"Uncle Pen," 118, 119
Uncle Rube Turnipseed and the Pea
    Ridge Ramblers, 86
United Artists label, 112, 113;
    discography, 251-65
USS Shenandoah, 246

Vagabonds, The, 94, 151
Vague, Vera (Barbara Jo Allen), 177
V-Discs (AFRS), 108
Veach, Rachel, 40, 41, 73-76, 79, 93,
    96, 121; and movies, 174-78, 191
Venice Pier, 139
Veterans' recruiting and informational
    programs, 136
Vietnam, 95, 126, 137, 144, 146, 147,
    168, 209, 245, 248-49, 250
Vincent, Bert, 230
Vocalion label, 29

Voice (Roy's), 19, 21, 37, 49, 107,
    108, 115, 117, 236, 238

Wabash Cannonball (train), 120
"Wabash Cannonball," 28, 49, 61, 99,
    112, 119-21, 123, 136, 175, 189,
    210, 216, 217, 232, 233
Waikuiki, Rudy, 73
"Wait for the Light to Shine," 58, 178
Wakely, Jimmy, 180
Walden, Pinkie, 12, 15
Walker, Charlie, 114
Walker, Frank, 157
Wallace, George, 208, 243
"Waltz of Broken Vows," 97
"Waltz of the Winds," 97
Washington, George, 201
Watergate, 63, 209
Watson, Bill, 75
Watson, Doc, 112
Wayne, John, 180, 210
Weakley, Harold, 59
"Weary Lonesome Blues," 75, 78
Weaver, William, 61
Weaver Brothers, 175
Webb, June, 97, 103
"Wedding Bells," 115
Wells, Kitty, 23, 98, 109, 110, 131-32,
    139
Wembley Pool (London), 114
Wendell, Bud, 227
WFDF, 72
"What Do You Think About Me," 109
Wheeler, Onie, 88, 99, 121, 141-43
"Wheeling Jamboree," 97
"When I Lay My Burden Down," 78
When Lulu's Gone, 28
"When You Wore a Tulip," 244
Whiteman, Paul, 150
Wilburn Brothers, 57, 145, 243
"Wilburn Brothers Show," 75, 96
"Wildwood Eeeph," 88
Wilkerson, George, 34, 58
Williams Audrey, 156, 162, 163
Williams, "Big Boy," 179, 180
Williams, Hank, 104, 114, 115, 131,
    133, 156-57, 159, 162-64
Williams, Mildred, 96
Williams, Velma, 76, 96-97; and
    movies, 174, 177-78
"William Tell Overture," 88, 102

"William the Conqueror," 8
Willis Brothers, 157
Willis, Bob, 56, 139
"Will the Circle Be Unbroken"
   (album), 113
"Will the Circle Be Unbroken," 112
Wilson, Bob, 15
Wilson, Dixie, 43
Wilson, Don, 180
Wilson, Gail, 83
Wilson, Lonnie (Pap), 22, 40, 41, 43,
   73, 74, 83-84, 85, 87, 99, 101, 102;
   and movies, 174-75, 177-79, 191
WMC, 86
WNOX, 23, 25
"Wreck of the Old 97," 28n
"Wreck on the Highway," 112,
   122-24, 142, 145
Wright, Bob, 22, 25
"Write Me Sweetheart," 124
WROL, 23, 25, 27
WSM, 31, 33, 35, 36, 38, 44, 45, 53,
   54, 64, 82, 104n, 127, 134, 141,
   150, 151, 156, 157, 167, 169, 171,
   177, 183, 184, 185, 206, 216, 225,
   227, 249

"Yakety Eeeph," 88
Yarborough, Wayne, 92
"Yes, Sir," 100
"Yes, Sir, That's My Baby," 28
"Yesterday's Roses," 151
York, Sergeant Alvin, 177
"You Are My Sunshine," 61
"You Ca De—You Ca Da," 179
"You Don't Have to Be from the
   Country," 216
"You're the Only Star," 28
Yo-Yo, 19, 48, 49, 61-63, 78, 147,
   172, 235

Zinkan, Joe (Pap), 84, 85, 100, 101,
   102, 129; and movies, 174, 178-79;
   191